THE SMALL WORLDS OF CHILDHOOD

The Small Worlds of Childhood

PHILOSOPHY, POETICS, AND THE
QUEER TEMPORALITIES OF EARLY LIFE

Lauren Shizuko Stone

FORDHAM UNIVERSITY PRESS   NEW YORK 2025

Copyright © 2025 Fordham University Press

This book is freely available in an open access edition thanks to the CU Boulder Open Monograph Fund, with the generous support of the University of Colorado Boulder Libraries.

This title is licensed under the Creative Commons Attribution-NonCommercial 4.0 International License (CC BY-NC). Read the license at https://creativecommons.org/licenses/by-nc/4.0/legalcode.

DOI: https://doi.org/10.5422/TOME/2280

Fordham University Press has no responsibility for the persistence or accuracy of URLs for external or third-party Internet websites referred to in this publication and does not guarantee that any content on such websites is, or will remain, accurate or appropriate.

Fordham University Press also publishes its books in a variety of electronic formats. Some content that appears in print may not be available in electronic books.

Visit us online at www.fordhampress.com.

Library of Congress Cataloging-in-Publication Data available online at https://catalog.loc.gov.

Printed in the United States of America
27 26 25   5 4 3 2 1
First edition

*For Frances Yukino,
whose heart is connected to mine*

Contents

Introduction: Small Worlds, Local Theories 1
"A joyful, shining festive thing," 4 · Childhood's
Long History as the Not-Yet of Adulthood, 10 · Reading
for Childhood's Good Surprises, 14 · Queer Experiments
in Childhood Storytelling, 16

1 **Adalbert Stifter's Topographical Worlds of Childhood** 23
Children's Forts, Not Grown-Up Arbors, 23 · *Indian Summer*:
Childhood's Time Is Out of Order, 28 · "Tourmaline"
and Childhood's "Bad Timing," 38 · "Limestone" and the
Cartographic View of Childhood, 45 · Stifter's Revolving
Worlds of Childhood, 55

2 **Rainer Maria Rilke's Lifeworlds of Childhood** 57
The View from Childhood, 57 · "Seeing more; *not more
than seeing*": What Children See in "Pierre Dumont,"
63 · Playing Dead: Childhood Reflection, 71 · Toy Souls:
What Children Apprehend, 75 · The Fantastic World
of Childhood in the "Notes" and the *Notebooks*, 79 ·
"Wise incomprehension . . .": On the Model of
Being-Child, 92

3 Walter Benjamin's Small Worlds of Childhood   95
   Children's Play and Reflections of the World, 95 ·
   Leibniz's *Monadology* and Childhood Intuition in
   Benjamin's Early Essays, 102 · Technologies of Representation
   in "Portraits of Children" and "Enlargements," 107 ·
   "Multum in Parvo": Aphorism, Miniaturization,
   and the Project of *Berlin Childhood around 1900*, 115 ·
   Small Worlds of Childhood: Memoir and Fragment, 121 ·
   Childhood as Metaphysical Paradigm, 132

   **Coda: Sigmund Freud, Childhood, and the
   Return of Futurity   139**

   ACKNOWLEDGMENTS   147

   NOTES   149

   WORKS CITED   203

   INDEX   217

THE SMALL WORLDS OF CHILDHOOD

Introduction
Small Worlds, Local Theories

> Doesn't reading queer mean learning, among other things, that
> mistakes can be good rather than bad surprises?
> —JOSEPH LITVAK VIA EVE KOSOFSKY SEDGWICK[1]

One of Austrian realist writer Adalbert Stifter's most popular stories was a Christmas tale "Bergkristall" ("Rock Crystal"), published in 1852 as part of a collection of stories subtitled, "a gift for a special occasion," marking the book's imagined role in the holiday celebration.[2] The story begins with a narrator unfolding a classic mountain village holiday scene—a "set piece," as Martin Swales calls it—that moves from the church calendar to village activities in the crisp nighttime air, before eventually settling into a homey interior scene of children on Christmas Eve.[3] Much like our contemporary conventions for the holiday in the United States, Stifter's opening depiction of gift-giving involves two tales: one of the parents, who orchestrate the appearance of gifts and trimmings, and one of the children, who encounter and delight in the appearance of these new objects. Stifter's two views of Christmas, we might say, appear like a parallax—two observational standpoints, though oriented toward the same matter, that appear differently. He deploys his poetic realist technique in a way that emphasizes this difference as the temporality of experience: While parents enjoy the children's activities in a nostalgic way, the experience of childhood by children themselves is profoundly bound up with the present time of enjoyment:

> Lights are lit, usually a great many of them, often little candles poised
> on the handsome green boughs of fir or spruce tree in the middle of

the room. The children are not allowed to come until the sign is given that the Holy Child has been there, and has left behind the presents he brought with him. Then the door is opened and the little ones are let inside, and in the marvelous glimmering splendor they see, hanging from the tree or arrayed on the table, things that far surpass all the visions of their imagination, things which they dare not touch and which at last, once they have received them, they carry about in their little arms all evening, and take to bed with them.[4]

Although the tale's plot will take a threatening turn, as the narrative follows its two child-protagonists Sanna and Konrad through a blizzard on their way back from grandmother's house, the opening vision of the holiday nonetheless invites the reader to tarry in the cozy microcosm of the home, where the cold winter is only softly perceptible through the windows:[5] "When the next day comes, Christmas Day, it seems so festive to them when they stand in the warm parlor attired in their finest clothes . . . when there's a festive midday meal, better than on any other day of the year, and . . . [s]cattered throughout the parlor, on a little chair or on the bench or on the windowsill, lie the presents of the evening before, magical but already more familiar."[6] With an eye to the ordinary details, the narrator sets the "festival of the home" in parallel with the Holy Child in a curious way. In the nineteenth century, the Austrian and southern German figure of the Christ Child (*Christkind*) was the traditional *unseen* bringer of gifts, often imagined as an angelic childlike figure,[7] but in "Rock Crystal" Stifter instead describes the figure as something belonging to the children's *visible* world: namely, "a joyful, shining festive thing" ("ein heiteres glänzendes feierliches Ding").[8] This brief narrative sequence recasts the story of Christmas as the familiar narrative of the transfiguration of the gifted object into ordinary experience: from the eruptive delight in *finally* getting to open a present, to the seamless absorption of that treasured surprise into the background of the child's quotidian world.

By contrast, the grown-ups, having already orchestrated the Christmas tree and gifts, are called to make their annual wintery trek to midnight mass; tasked with carrying out the business of religious tradition, they are mere spectators of the child's experience of Christmas.[9] For them, the figure of the Holy Child, the "joyful, shining festive thing," appears neither as a messiah nor as the material splendor of gifts, but as a fleeting phenomenon of aging: "the glimpse of times gone by, flitting on bright shimmering wings across the bleak, sad, emptied night sky."[10] Christmas in adulthood is not an experience of the immediacy of the present festivities, but rather like "a long echo" of one's own childhood that "reaches so far into old age."[11] Whereas the child perceives the splendorous world of "things" as something that "surpass[es] the imagination," the adult can only approach this world in a specular fashion: The grown-up encounter with the "joyful, shining festive thing" is indirect; it is the "reflected splendor" ("Abglanz") of their own childhood, a belated enjoyment that only arrives in "watch[ing] as the children celebrate and rejoice in [theirs]."[12]

In short, Stifter's characterization of the very spirit of Christmas—a classic childhood notion—repeats a bifurcation in the temporality of experience, in which children are tethered through their visual perception to the here and now while adults are left only with retrospection and mediation. This difference has two important consequences that extend well beyond the representation of grown-up nostalgia in ways that exemplify the central thesis of this book. First, the author's literary attention to ordinary experience in childhood (especially in the description of seeing), shifts the effect of its representation from an aesthetics of longing (as is the case with the parents) to, as I argue in this book, a fundamentally philosophical endeavor. To paraphrase the philosopher Hans Blumenberg, the work of transforming the cognition of phenomena into literary representation is "the oldest problem in philosophy."[13] Second, the scene of childhood, in its insistence on ordinary experience, resists normative temporal regimes that emphasize the child's future as its telos (e.g., growing up, becoming a wife, a mother, a citizen, etc.). And as this introduction will show, this resistance—which is also a resistance to heteronormative regimes of (social) reproduction—can in fact be productively approached through the lens of contemporary queer theory. By naming and prizing forms of life that exist outside of heteronormative time, this body of scholarship gives us language to reevaluate the temporal schema at work across a range of representations of bourgeois childhood, transforming the way we think of German and Austrian realist and modernist literary histories of ordinary childhood experience and revealing a queer counter-history. I call these counter-historical narratives "small worlds." We find them not just in Stifter's stories, but across scenes of nineteenth-century childhood in experimental prose by Rainer Maria Rilke and Walter Benjamin. These small worlds appear even in unexpected places that—as we see with Stifter's "Rock Crystal"—were often read, precisely with an eye to the future, for example, as didactic "improving literature."[14]

Before turning to such small worlds in these three canonical authors, the book unfolds the consequences of the bifurcated forms of experience that I have outlined in the opening of Stifter's illustrative Christmas story. In depicting how children perceive and cognize the world, and especially how they name the things that they encounter, the tale's conclusion also makes an exemplary philosophical-poetic argument—about the relationship between ordinary language and conceptual thinking. Disconnected from the grown-ups'

Romantic longing for their own unrecoverable past and unburdened by the expectations that they come of age, the child here lingers in their own time of ordinary worldly experience. By attending to the temporality of seeing and naming, Stifter's story reimagines the philosophical value of childhood and, in this way, also makes a queer critique of the normative expectation that the literature of childhood will be oriented toward the future.

"A joyful, shining festive thing"

Returning now to the ending of Stifter's story, its philosophical-poetic quality and the queerness of its temporality (as well its resistance to familiar Romantic tropes) will come into view. Here, Stifter emphatically repeats the bifurcation of Christmas narratives, but this time it is the wintery natural world that appears as either one of perception (childhood) or retrospective meaning (adulthood). After their harrowing night in the mountains, just before their rescue, the children experience the world as moment of optical delight. "[They] sat where they were with open eyes gazing out into the stars".[15]

> In the sky before them a pale light blossomed amid the stars, and traced a faint arc between them. It had a green glimmer that drifted gently downward. But the arc grew brighter and brighter, until the stars receded before it and faded. It sent a light to other regions of the sky, spilling glimmergreen gentle and alive among the stars. Then sheaves of variegated light rose like a crown's prongs from the apex of the arc and blazed. The light spilled brightly through the neighboring regions of the sky, it sent out soft showers and passed through long spaces in gentle tremors.[16]

The narrator's voice then momentarily interrupts the description of what the children witnessed, wondering aloud with a grown-up scientific curiosity whether "the unprecedented snowfall" somehow produced some unusual static electrical event, before continuing: "Bit by bit, it grew fainter and fainter, the sheaves fading first, until gradually and imperceptibly it lessened. . . . Neither child said a word to the other, they sat on and on gazing wide-eyed into the sky."[17]

As elsewhere in Stifter's oeuvre, this passage deftly represents the temporality of perception of the gradual appearance and disappearance of the northern lights.[18] Crucially, though, the deployment of his realist technique here is reserved *only* for the wide-eyed children. The adult narrator's interpolation, by contrast, is concerned not with the present experience, but with the difficulty in assessing its local historical meaning ("unprecedented") and its natural historical meaning ("some other cause in unfathomable nature"). This tale not only emphasizes once again the notion that the child's world consists in the moment of perception; it also reiterates a distinction between this perception and that of the grown-ups. When Sanna, one of the two children, reports their sighting of the northern lights as having "s[een] the Holy Child," her mother, who does not understand that the child is referring to an optical phenomenon and not to a mythical bringer of gifts, reassures her that there are presents waiting at home (thus also retrospectively encouraging the reader to reinterpret the entire set of events as a Christmas message).[19] Sanna's calling the geomagnetic light show "the Holy Child" repeats the two-world structure of Christmas: The child's present-time experience, what we might think of as an immersion in sheer worldliness, starkly contrasts with the grown-up impulse toward mediation, in which objects of perception require retrospective investment in various forms of historical and social valuation.

This moment of the child's (mis-)naming and the parent's (mis-)understanding draws our attention to a second, overlapping domain of philosophical representation of childhood cognition: the relationship between experience and meaning. Sanna, we recall, belongs to a Christmas world in which children are told that gifts (which parents have secretly arranged) are brought by the "Holy Child," a figure who certainly sounds like something belonging to perception, something quite see-able: "a joyful, *shining festive thing.*" The children had heard of but never seen the Holy Child, and, until just this point, had also not yet seen an aurora borealis. As Stanley Cavell has argued, there is a certain inextricability of a given world of experience with the possibility of naming objects, that is, that knowing "what a thing is called" involves already "having a concept."[20] In Cavell's view, childhood experience is particularly exemplary, in that what already belongs to a child's world provides, as it were, both the possibilities and the limits of any given word's ability to have meaning.[21] Taking Sanna's perspective then: She has a concept of a visibly shining festive thing that appears (though unseen) at Christmastime, and after seeing the shimmering spectacle on Christmas Eve, she logically reports having seen the "Holy Child." In this way, she rightly names the event. By contrast, in the world of adulthood, lodged as it is in nostalgia and disconnected from experience, the mother does not understand the phrase "Holy Child" to mean something literally seen glimmering festively on Christmas Eve. The concept(s) available to the mother for this phrase are the gift-bringer (e.g., herself or another adult in the house) and, perhaps, the sense of the fleeting specter of one's own memories.[22] Therefore, given the differences between what the grown-up and childhood worlds each contain, the only possible outcome to Sanna's utterance can be infelicitous: The mother misunderstands.

For Cavell, the question of "what a thing is called" expands the field of possible objects beyond those cited in what he calls "traditional epistemology," (that is beyond "generic objects," e.g., tables, chairs, and horses); it also invites us to consider the more difficult instances in which our ability to "name," to "call" (or "point to"), objects feels compromised because our conceptual grasp is weak ("in doubt," "unpossessed," or "repressed").[23] Here, I suggest, we can see Stifter deploying his child protagonists in such a way that the relationship between concept and language becomes visible. The fact that the narrator does not describe what the children encounter by their scientific names, but instead, to borrow Elisabeth Strowick's phrase, "stages visual perception," thus making the problem of conceptual graspability—the sheer scale of the geophysical and meteorological events that the children experience—legible. The child (and the reader) tarry with and get lost in the perceptual details in the snowflakes, ice, darkness, and cracks, showing us where naming is unstable or infelicitous, suggesting that sometimes it is not possible to properly say what a thing is called.

Stifter's grown-up world of Christmas may recall for us English Romantic poetics of early life, such as Wordsworth's nostalgia or Walter Pater's Romantic aesthetics, in whose texts childhood only gains its meaning belatedly as objects in a grown-up's dreams and memories, and where representation must always grapple with the problem of forgetting and loss in its retrospection.[24] But as I have suggested here, Stifter's story insists instead that the world of childhood appear through the representation of ordinary experience—it is *childhood* that now becomes prosaic. This runs against the conventions of the English Romanctic view of childhood lost to an unrecoverable past, in part, because we don't see the children in "Rock Crystal" grow up; moreover, adulthood in this tale is marked by the impoverished shimmer of the *memories* of Christmases past. Stifter's literary-realist attention to detail represents the children's Christmases by locating the story within a rich now-time of experience. This is the warmth of the parlor, the sight of the candle-lit tree, and all the festival's trimmings—bounty that belong to the ordinary home. But it is also the sensation of silence in the white-out blizzard, and the clear night sky followed by the slow dawning of warm daylight. Indeed, the children experience *this* festival (and *this* geomagnetic storm) not because the child has no other past to remember, but because, as Stifter implies, they live in a vivid material present: For the young merrymaker, "an eternity has passed" since the last Christmas joy, which "lies far away in a fog-gray region."[25] Crucially, such an emphasis on the present is what makes the intersection of the poetic representation of experience and the philosophical entanglement of language and concepts visible.

Stifter's child characters are exemplary of those featured in this book—not only because they encounter the world in their own present time, but because this commitment to ordinary experience enables philosophical-poetic inquiries in areas of epistemology, phenomenology, and metaphysics. In "Rock Crystal" childhood is thus untethered from the expectation that meaning culminates only retrospectively in adulthood. Likewise, each scene of childhood examined in the chapters of this book also overturns a set of expectations long since outlined in queer theory: that representations of childhood reliably and even ubiquitously represent social, political, and sexual reproductive futurity. In this small example of childhood in "Rock Crystal," we can see that by taking the child's worldly experience seriously, the child's representational labor shifts away from being the maternal and pedagogical product of sentimental domesticity which, as Dana Luciano argues, envisions the child subject as "bound at once for the progressive and cumulative temporality" whose eventual value comes to fruition as "national progress" and Christian redemption.[26] The tale's insistent elaboration of the experience of *being* a child detaches it from the anxiety of *becoming* an adult whose social, moral, or spiritual normativity is not guaranteed. This frees Stifter's characters from what Lauren Berlant calls the "supericonicity" of child figures as the "blueprint for the reproductive form that assures the family and the nation its future history."[27]

Perhaps the most influential formulation of this is Lee Edelman's argument that child-figures are not only ubiquitous—as political images, literary figures, rhetorical weapons—but also intimately bound up with our "fantasies" of normative futurity.[28] In Edelman's view, the figure of the Child derives its social and political world-structuring potency from its capacity to represent the latent normative expressions of heterosexual adulthood (being wife/husband, consumer, laborer, etc.) that reinforce the "fantasies of futurity" in which children provide the promise of individual transcendence over finitude and of posterity for our social reality.[29] In Edelman's account, the queer position is thus the agon of the Child: the "unregenerate," the radical negation of any such commitment to social and sexual reproductive futures.[30] Unlike the radical negativity of *No Future*'s central thesis, his formulation of the child figure of reproductive futurism feels like an uncontroversial truism of queer theory. Sara Ahmed has suggested, contesting his theory of negativity, that even in optimism there is a "logic of deferral," where suffering in the present gains its meaning by virtue of an imagined future—and for which children conventionally signify the fantasy future in which one's present unhappiness will find its point.[31] But as this brief excursus into Stifter's world of childhood Christmas has shown, when the story attends to the now-time of childhood perception and cognition, in all of its marvelousness and ordinariness, child-figures need not represent the promise that "the movement of life is always forward."[32] Against queer theory's expectations, Stifter's tale reminds us that sometimes childhood stories are not always so *straight*.

The Small Worlds of Childhood asks what happens when a child-figure resists its conventional service to futurity? By looking at narratives in which childhood isn't always or only about growing up and looking back, this book overturns expectations of what childhood's poetic and philosophical capacities might be. When childhood's philosophical investment in experience means that children get lodged in the *present* or, failing to move forward, force the tale to turn back and repeat, such child characters can be seen as *out of character*.[33] Just such a queer predicament occurs with surprising frequency and variability in depictions of childhood in the nineteenth century, ones that are rooted even in the straightest of bourgeois sensibilities. This book offers readings of German and Austrian realist and modernist prose that question the universality of queer theory's claims of childhood's heteronormative "supericonicity" and instead show us all manner of orders and temporalities also belong to childhood.[34]

In literary representations that range from Adalbert Stifter's (1805–1868) detail- and order-obsessed novellas to the poetic prose experiments of modernist writer Rainer Maria Rilke (1875–1926) and the philosophical-poetic prose of Walter Benjamin (1892–1940), children tarry in their own encounters with the ordinary world, unsettle assumptions about the directionality of childhood, and exploit narrative techniques such that even the *telling* of childhood stories ends up queer. Prose that turns away from "straight" stories of childhood can revel in the ways that conventional temporalities of family and kinship may be altered or upended. The realist and modernist literary techniques in these prose texts about childhood enable an exploration of philosophical questions related to cognition and perception because they attend to the ordinary experience of the present in ways that recall a narrated scene from the history of philosophy. Much like Descartes's gaze on melting wax or Husserl's attention to the things on his desk, child characters examined here are interested in the objects that make up their world, and as a result the stories themselves evince an experimental willingness to violate the norms of sequential, developmental, or progressive representation—some loudly, others quietly. In the chapters that follow, we will get to see how, as Ahmed says, "to make things queer is certainly to disturb the order of things. . . . The effects of such a disturbance are uneven, precisely given that the world is already organized around certain forms of living—certain times, spaces, and directions."[35] This book also reveals the novel effects of poetic representation that are made possible when childhood is released from the telos of adulthood, freed from what Kathryn Bond Stockton calls the "vertical movement" of "growing up."[36]

The Small Worlds of Childhood explores depictions of childhood in the second half of the nineteenth century that inadvertently decouple the figure of the child from the trajectory of growing *up*. The resistance to conventional conceptions of childhood as embodiments of futurity, it turns out, can be found even in the straightest of genres: the *Bildungsroman*, novellas and short stories, and autobiography. This "disturbance" in the direction of things appears, in part, because the scene of childhood is afforded increasing value of its own: Children move from the background to the foreground, or from the beginning of the story to the whole story, as both narrative and descriptive territory is provided for them and the worlds in which they live. This book investigates the results of just such a transvaluation of child-figures in grown-up literature and storytelling—that is, when childhood no longer only serves its future. I show that these stories of childhood are also epistemological and phenomenological ones: What do children know about the world, and what does it look like when adults—writers and theorists—imagine their ways of knowing? How would one go about representing the experience of things from a child's perspective? *The Small Worlds of Childhood* explores how narratives of children in the late nineteenth century and early twentieth century respond to precisely these questions. I show that select German and Austrian writers who were grappling with representations of everyday life not only turned again and again to the child protagonist in their ordinary surroundings, but that their poetic efforts provide novel strategies for depicting familiar philosophical terrain. Through their play, exploration, learning, and failure, as well as boredom and everyday habits, children in this period appear intimately entangled with their material surroundings. Largely unbothered by the demands of society, children's cognition is thus freely informed by their experience of the world of things.

The task of portraying what children see in their relationship to the everyday world to which they belong becomes an engagement with the links between forms of experience and representation of objects and the processes by which they produce judgments and knowledge. Modernism and realism, this book shows, each centered children as worthy philosophical subjects: that is, as prized objects for portrayal and even more so as sui generis thinking subjects. To meet the challenge of depicting the cognitive richness of childhood subjectivity, writers must turn to their toolboxes of poetic techniques—and here, I argue, it is both the poetic realist's attention to the material world and the modernist's experimentation that are needed. In the chapters that follow, I also show that when the entire fictional world is inflected with the temporality of childhood that exists for itself and on its own time, storytelling also becomes queer: Adults have trouble growing up; literary forms become more poetic, experimental, or fragmentary; ways of knowing the world are no longer tied to grand chronologies or sequences. In allowing stories of child-figures to become linked with philosophical inquiry, rather than vessels for the reproduction of adult social reality, the narrative forms and forms of kinship and knowledge represented therein are revealed to be queer in the sense of backward (Love), out of line (Ahmed), out of joint (Freeman).[37]

Although individual publication dates vary, the stories of childhood explored in *The Small Worlds of Childhood* take place between roughly the mid-nineteenth century until the turn of the century. These texts offer a glimpse into a relatively brief window of literary history, marked on either end by familiar poles: They portray scenes of childhood after the Enlightenment and Romantic periods' pedagogical visions and prior to the influence of Sigmund Freud's writings on childhood and sexuality in the early 1900s and feminist Ellen Key's landmark provocation that children should be regarded as full political subjects in *The Century of the Child*, published in 1900.[38] Whether short or long format, the prose of childhood examined here, I argue, takes a queer path: By embracing the radical present-time of the world in childhood, these texts sever the narratives of children from the aims of puberty, family, and capitalist (re-)production. Stifter's, Rilke's, and Benjamin's novels, short stories, and prose vignettes employ novel philosophical-poetic strategies to imbricate narration and description with the now-time of childhood cognition. In their lifelong occupations with depicting children as both subjects and objects of inquiry, these authors imagine an experience of the world unfettered by the distractions and demands of family and society or the belated effects of nostalgia and trauma, and thus children appear with their capacities to perceive and understand the material world in their immediate proximity, still undisturbed. A key corollary, however, is that this queer approach does not persist. My book's Coda situates Freud's use of literary techniques in his depictions of childhood as straightening, as it were, the child-figure, and thus returning it to all manner of productive and reproductive futurity. This book therefore argues for the necessity of recognizing these pre-Freudian texts on childhood as able to engage *literary* language in the service of a variety of *philosophical* attitudes: Their arsenal of poetic techniques can tell us something extraordinary about moments of ordinary experience and the manner with which humans, and especially children, cognize the world.

Childhood's Long History as the Not-Yet of Adulthood

It has been said that the European concept of childhood began to take shape following the Enlightenment and starting around 1800, and that with the development and solidification of bourgeois subjectivity and the growing valuation of the nuclear family, the modern categorical distinctions between child and adult appear.[39] This intellectual historical conceptualization began with Philippe Ariès, who first characterized this history as the gradual "discovery" of the "idea of childhood" in *Centuries of Childhood*, where shifts in visual, literary, and rhetorical representations of children reflect the movement from medieval portrayals of "small adults," where "childhood was a period of transition which passed quickly and which was just as quickly forgotten" to modern conceptions of family where "the child became an indispensable element of everyday life, and his parents worried about his education, his career, his future."[40] In Ariès's work, childhood goes from the barest of temporality (brief and forgotten) to recognizably modern childhood, which can be understood according to the chronobiopolitics of its own futurity.[41] Just as childhood gains in conceptual and developmental significance, the present-time of being-child increasingly gives way to being-for-the-future. Ariès is thus right when he suggests a throughline from Rousseau's articulation of the childhood's "irrationalism" to the modern attitudes he identifies. The work of childhood has long been seen as the project of becoming-adult; in the transformation from instinctual being to a reasoned citizen we see what Edelman considers to be the straight work of social reproduction: "To serve as the repository of variously sentimentalized cultural identifications, the Child has come to embody for us the telos of the social order and come to be seen as the one for whom that order is held in perpetual trust."[42] In this sense, social history offers contemporary readers a vision of the child that also makes legible our own contemporary expectations. Or as James Kincaid has observed,

> Ariès is doing the rarest kind of history, a history of the present, aiming at de-naturing "the child," exposing our own constructing apparatus, freeing us, at least a little, from the tyranny of our eccentric seeing. He points out, in other words, radical difference, a difference so great that it seems to take the form of the difference between something and nothing, between a modern child that is there and a medieval child that is not. The effect of such a project is not to substantiate our modern perception but to show that the child is the perceptual frame we have available to us for fitting in just about anything we choose—or nothing. What the child *is* matters less than what we *think* it is and just why we think that way.[43]

As Kincaid suggests that representations of children offer us "pure difference" and "negative inversions" of the condition of being adult (e.g., having erotic desires, knowledge, worldly experience, etc.), they thus also appear as pure neutrality and emptiness.[44] Despite this tendency in literature of the nineteenth century to empty out childhood's own content—and to replace it with one inextricably tied to becoming/being an adult—we will still find that this same century offers us its threshold cases and its exceptions. These narratives, in which childhood gets its own story, are the subject of this book: We will see both character studies and plotlines that neither free children from impulse, desire, and error, imagining them as empty innocence, nor cast them as merely irrational subjects, the not-yets of adulthood. Instead, we will see writers contemplating the possibilities of human experience in the messy entanglements with everyday worlds around them.

German studies scholars who focus on the periods in and around the nineteenth century have regarded childhood as both a retrospective phenomenon and as a developmental stage of life whose meaning appears in opposition to its telos, adulthood. Scholarship exploring modern depictions of childhood can be largely organized into two distinct yet sometimes overlapping fields of approach: Literary representations of childhood, following Ariès, reflect a contemporary *idea* of childhood and/or offer a window into the workings of memory (of one's childhood) and the challenges posed in representing one's past. In the former, scholarship often takes an epochal approach to describing the conceptual work that childhood offers. For example, the influence of Enlightenment discourses on literary representations of childhood show what Dieter Richter calls the "Chiffre des Noch-nicht-Menschen" (figure of the not-yet-human).[45] As Reiner Wild notes, such depictions accord little value to childhood subjectivity itself but rather treat children as merely the necessary starting point from which adults are made—as pure transitoriness that thus enables childhood to gain its meaning only as retrospection.[46] Romantic ideas of childhood appear variously as a utopian contrast to the "Zeitgeist" of the adult world (Jean Paul), as a paradise lost (Goethe, Brentano), and as both veiled totality and teleological figuration in Orientalist anthropological discourses that construct non-European peoples as "primitive" and fundamentally other (Herder).[47] These analyses characterize modern historical ideas of childhood as a stage of linear development that applies as much to the individual as to the nature of historical sequence on a global level.[48] The idea of childhood thus participates in what Julia Kristeva described as the gendered linearity of the temporality of both nation-state and of history—the masculine time of "progression," "prospective unfolding," and "arrival"—against the timeless or monumental time of woman and home.[49] And even though Romantic notions imagine childhood as an unrecoverable golden age (*Blütezeit*), forever lost to adulthood, it is a past that still consists only in its own future; with its botanical metaphors of seed and growth, the idea of childhood submits easily to the temporal regimes and routines of futurity.[50]

Even in the case of German Romantic fairy tales, whose readership included both adults and children, where the narratives engage in realist-like literary representations of childhood, the conceptual basis expressed by these texts shares the aforementioned framework:[51] Childhood appears as representative of a prior (and now lost) golden age of humanity, it reminds adults of their own origin, and it offers a medium for a very straight utopian imaginary.[52] If we take, for example, E. T. A. Hoffmann's familiar *Nußknacker und Mausekönig* (*Nutcracker and Mouse King*) from 1816, we find that despite the detailed descriptions of the festive family home, and the psychological realism afforded the protagonist Marie, the tale foregrounds a Romantic ennoblement of childhood fantasy, a world of wonder, that exceeds the finitude of ordinary reality.[53] Despite the rich description of confections and toys on Christmas Eve, the framing of the scene reinforces the normative temporality of belated fruition, as the narrative's readerly reception requires the engagement of nostalgia for one's own long lost childhood vision:[54] "I appeal to you, kind reader, or listener, whatever may be your name, Fritz, Theodor, Ernst, I beg you to vividly call to mind the last table that was so bountifully bedecked with brightly colored Christmas gifts. Then you too will probably be able to imagine the children as they stood there silently with eyes sparkling."[55] If the tale's opening imagines looking back from adulthood, the conclusion of the story suggests in no uncertain terms that the view from childhood is future-facing, as the children's adventure leads them seamlessly toward marriage when the playmates, Marie and the nutcracker (Godfather Drosselmeier's young nephew), enact their "happy ending" with the fantasy of a royal marriage.[56]

Scholarly commentaries that have attended to literary representations of childhood as descriptions of the workings of memory have often emphasized that nostalgic, belated, or psychoanalytic qualities, by aligning the poetics of recollection with the author's biography, aesthetics, or philosophical perspective.[57] In each case, these discourses of nineteenth-century childhood—whether or not they are seen as inflected with Proust's or Freud's poetics of memory—emphasize the process of recovery. In other words, what is at stake here is not so much childhood itself but rather the dual problems of representation: the act or experience of remembering and the content of the memories themselves (childhood). Literature, in these cases, is concerned primarily with childhood's future, with the adult who must recall it.[58] Poetic and philosophical autobiographies stand unmatched in this regard, uniting problematics of authorship, poetics, and the (un)reliability of childhood memories, in examples that range from the first book of Goethe's *Dichtung und Wahrheit* (*Poetry and Truth*) in 1811 to Theodor W. Adorno's description of his own youth at the turn of the century in *Kindheit in Amorbach* (*Childhood in Amorbach*) from 1966. Commentaries on these often poeticized and even fictionalized accounts of childhood implicate above all the writer's own grown-up aims. In Paul Fleming's phrasing, for example, Goethe's remembering and representing of his own childhood is the "view[] from the posterity"—and thus the assessment of childhood's "broken promise" is retrospective, underscoring that the child's full meaning only appears in the future.[59] Likewise, Adorno's childhood experience may well be one of a utopia; but, as Susan Gillespie has remarked, it remains translatable to adult thinking (i.e., to memory) "with a remainder," as his depiction of childhood's unmitigated happiness appears amid the writer's own oscillation toward his later historical experience of the world as no utopia.[60] Across this long century, the representation of one's childhood thus appears with its visible trail of breadcrumbs that leads directly to the stakes of adult writerly experience.

Reading for Childhood's Good Surprises

This book argues that there are some exceptions to this historically entrenched view of childhood as potentiality and futurity, stories that challenge the logic of progression. In a productive revision of the late-nineteenth-century ideology of childhood—namely, "that childhood was not only a separate stage in life, but the best of those stages"[61]—these authors have produced a literature of childhood in which there are no demands that children grow up. The tarrying in childhood in which Stifter, Rilke, and Benjamin engage, however, is not a fantasy world or an expansion of "Neverland" in which the world has no adults, but rather stories about the everyday world where ordinary childhood is permitted to take up space.[62] I accordingly read these narratives as engaged in a mode of worldly representation akin to what Joseph Litvak terms "the distinctive gayness of Proust's sophistication" characterizing his queer "second naïveté." By this, Litvak, liberally borrowing from Adorno's *Notes on Literature*, means that Proust's "striv[ing] for immediacy" stands in opposition to the heteronormative demand to "grow up" and to "clos[e] off various receptivities that make it possible to find the world *interesting*."[63] With Litvak, I see Adorno's characterization of Proust's fidelity in writing as instructive for us in the consideration of what literature on childhood makes visible: "[Proust] kept faith with the childhood potential for unimpaired experience and, with all the reflectiveness and awareness of an adult, perceived the world in as undeformed a manner as the day it was created."[64] Adorno's admiration for how Proust's prose "examines an internal and external reality" illuminates a key to representing children without the demand for verticality or futurity: the procedure of looking to the present-time of children's reality and their encounters with the quotidian—the "kid stuff" that makes up the world that they inhabit.[65]

In *The Small Worlds of Childhood*, I read childhood's queer temporalities of lingering, backward gazes, and achronicities by attending to the philosophical poetics in each text—where literature deploys the tools of poetic representation with a phenomenological sensibility, portraying the intersections of the "internal" (e.g., ways of knowing, forms of cognition, fantasy) and the "external" (the world of objects to be perceived, mapped, or imagined). Although some of my readings in *The Small Worlds of Childhood* proceed in ways that admittedly queer the text at hand—irreverently and against the grain—others yield queer results from the straightest of readings (while Ahmed has made Husserl a queer-theoretical hero of sorts, no one calls for Leibniz, Blumenberg, or Agamben when they are ready to see things queerly . . . although perhaps now they might). In this way, I share the "relaxed, unseparatist hypothesis of the much to be gained by refraining from *a priori* oppositions between queer texts (or authors) and non-queer ones" that Sedgwick identifies as forming a basis for reparative reading.[66] My approach to prose by Stifter, Rilke, and Benjamin therefore involves a comfort with contingency and errancy—one that is indebted to the "deroutinizing methodologies" that exemplify Sedgwick's proposal.[67]

In describing the overlaps and intersections of children's literature and queer theory, Kenneth B. Kidd has remarked that "queer theory works both inside and against existing philosophical and theoretical systems and is perhaps a minor literature in [e.g., Deleuze and Guattari's] sense, although that might be overstating its positionality. Whatever its own status in the academy or beyond, queer theory seeks out and celebrates minor energies and minor moments, sometimes in connection with the child."[68] *The Small Worlds of Childhood* takes up this "connection" and interprets with a queer minor energy, in that it embraces the language of adulthood (poetics and philosophy) but in the otherwise impossible service of representing a lingering in childhood experience.[69] The philosophical alliances that appear in my analyses of childhood storytelling cross forward and backward between the seventeenth and twentieth centuries—some evidently bear a close affinity while others might feel like a "stretch." However, as Sedgwick explains, this may well underlay the novelty or the "good surprise" that queer reading makes possible: "There may be resonant homologies between this queer way of risking historical 'anachronism,' on the one hand, and on the other hand that intimate anachronism by which a queer grown-up can sometimes keep drawing on the energies, incredulities, and discoveries of an earlier moment of passionate, incompetent reading and recognition."[70] In this way, this book's practice of reading perhaps also implicates both my own desire for self-recognition, like an (aging) queer child "reading for important news about herself," as well as queer theory's backward investments in the queer child that are so often regarded as growing the wrong way.[71] My readings here may also seem like they go the wrong way—starting from queer theory and working backward to the "straight theory" of philosophy, or worse, reading straight theory as if it were queer.[72] In keeping with Sedgwick's unseparatist and reparative approach, *The Small Worlds of Childhood* makes its claims through a series of (dis)continuous readings that can do no more than produce weak theories—e.g., the philosophical trajectory I claim about Benjamin will not hold or even be legible for either Rilke or Stifter, and likewise in each direction. I show that childhood's philosophical filiations are indeed restricted: Each one has its own "local theor[y] and nonce taxonom[y]"; each comprises but one of literature's small worlds.[73]

Queer Experiments in Childhood Storytelling

From Berlant to Edelman, queer theory has long provided us with a strong theory of childhood since *most* of the time representations of childhood are quite straight. But it also offers us a way of reading childhood, locally and against this grain. And although *The Small Worlds of Childhood* argues for "weak" theoretical approaches, the book can nonetheless be described broadly as unfolding at the intersection of three intellectual traditions: German-language literary history (nineteenth-century bourgeois realism through early twentieth-century modernist projects), European philosophical history with a strong a German accent (from Leibniz, through a long history of phenomenology, and into continental philosophy), and queer theories of childhood and temporalities (including those by Freeman, Edelman, Stockton, Sedgwick).[74] Although the chapters are organized by author, moving roughly in chronological order, the epochal shifts in technique from realism through modernism are not intended to appear as hard lines: Indeed, realism's investment in the details of ordinary reality turn out to be quite persistent. This book tracks what I have suggested by way of example in this introduction, that when writers resist staging childhood as the not-yet of adulthood, and instead engage in representing childhood as a philosophical description of the material world, things start to become queer. By contrast, familiar Romantic viewpoints become acutely legible either as a condition of being a grown up (Pater, Jean Paul, Goethe), in the recognition of an unrecoverable loss (Wordsworth, Goethe), or in one's lost capacity for fantasy that exceeds the real world (Hoffmann). Collectively, the chapters show authors experimenting with representations of childhood, anachronistically inviting us to read them with contemporary queer theory. The book concludes with a reading of Freud as a literary author, who, despite the importance of his psychoanalytic system *for* queer theory, appears now as a relatively "straight" writer of childhood. Like German Romantic writers, Freud represents the scene of childhood with a similar sense that childhood matters belatedly for the grown-up. And much like Hoffmann's story of Marie and her Nutcracker prince, even when the narrative of childhood includes something of the child's desire, the story always culminates in relation to adult sexuality.

In Chapter 1, "Adalbert Stifter's Topographical Worlds of Childhood," realist stories of children appear out of densely narrated passages filled with all the bourgeois trappings of domestic life—and what begins with variations of the would-be idyllic scene of family life quickly veers off into the strange. Whether in the home or in the garden, children in Stifter's fictional universe repeatedly present readers with an opportunity to think about one's gaze on the world of things, and about how we organize and represent experience and knowledge in visual and spatial registers—from the ordering capacity of the child's miniature dwellings (forts) to the immobilizing decor in the bourgeois child's home. In reading across a selection of short prose, novellas, and a novel, I show how Adalbert Stifter's nineteenth-century narratives of childhood depend on backward appeals to seventeenth-century forms of knowledge: a history of spatial forms of scientific representation (taxonomies, maps, herbaria) that Michel Foucault listed among the "classical epistemes" and Michel de Certeau later theorized as "place" ("lieu") and "space" ("espace"). Although children populate so many of Stifter's stories, they often appear as relatively secondary—sometimes they are (in) the background. In his three-part novel, *Indian Summer* (a *Bildungsroman* of a young scientist in the making), the protagonist's childhood is but a fraction of the total page count yet the spatial logic of child and knowledge echo through the text. In his collection of stories, *Motley Stones*, children do not belong to modern geological discourses, despite their mineral titles.[75] Childhood, like the classical forms of knowledge it evinces, appears and reappears outside of the "linear time of representation" and instead enjoys the "simultaneous space" of resemblances.[76]

Rather than being imagined as a teleological symbol, the figure of the child ends up entirely dislodged from normative temporalities of history, progress, or generation. In these stories, the result is a queer deformation of genealogies and the overturning of the idea that children turn into grown-ups. Stifter's texts repeatedly reflect a queer affinity within the sentimental aesthetics of the nineteenth-century family, and the antiquarian obsession with collecting, naming, and visually representing articulated in his texts reveals that the figures of childhood and the family are visible only when located outside of time or facing back in time. With their anachronistic commitment to ways of knowing the world that, as Foucault tells us, belong to centuries long past, Stifter's writings on childhood manifest neither stasis nor dynamism, but rather mirror their own "queer affect"—what Freeman describes as "the stubborn lingering of pastness (whether it appears as anachronistic style, as the reappearance of a bygone events in the symptom, or as arrested development)."[77] Indeed, knowledge in Stifter's storytelling appears more like "a 'revolution' in the old sense of the word, as a turning back."[78]

With Chapter 2, "Rainer Maria Rilke's Lifeworlds of Childhood," I turn to literature attending to depictions of children that, to quote Adorno slightly out of line, retain the "infinite possibilities of experience" and reflect a commitment to the present in "listening to reality with such precision."[79] Reading across Rilke's corpus, I show how he dilates the view from childhood in a way that allows child-figures to appear as figures of resistance against adult regimes—not in the sense of teenage rebellion but rather like critical reminders of the matter that composes our lifeworld and the very strangeness of its perception. In examining scenes from well-known prose texts, such as his essay on dolls and his novel *Die Aufzeichnungen des Malte Laurids Brigge* (*The Notebooks of Malte Laurids Brigge*) alongside stories from among Rilke's earliest prose, which has received less scholarly attention, I show that the phenomenological qualities others have identified in his lyrical work have an altogether different, even queering, effect on representations of childhood experience.

In contrast to the world of adults, the world of children is marked by their attention to the ordinary world of experience (their lifeworld). In telling stories of childhood, Rilke narrates children as attuned to the world—in the divine thimble, the impossibly giant sunflowers and tiny cottage doors, in the puzzling semblance that appears in the nothingness of the doll, and finally in the fantastic bivalence of domestic spaces. Children tell us something about the limits and missteps of grown-up attention. Rilke's philosophical-poetic project mirrors the work of phenomenologists such as Husserl and Blumenberg, for whom the task of philosophy is, in some ways, merely rendering the world into language, and for whom *seeing* and being able to adequately *describe* what one sees are the critical acts. In Rilke, the work of literary description becomes the privileged and productive mode of depicting the world. These texts about childhood also serve as disturbances to theory: much like Hans Blumenberg's characterization of the Thracian woman's laughter at the sight of the astronomer, Thales, tumbling into a well while stargazing, Rilke's child-characters offer readers a critical reminder of the lifeworld that undergirds reality.[80] Children appear like laughing bystanders: They disrupt the accepted wisdom of adulthood and are thus charged with returning readers to the world—to the "thicket of things"—right in front of them, even against the prevailing adult world of fragmented modern subjectivity.[81]

Resisting the industrialized temporalities that produce modern experience—the rhythms of labor and production, and public culture—children appear phenomenologically invested in their own present.[82] In contrast to what Dana

Luciano calls the "chronobiopolitics" of the nineteenth century, Rilke's child-figures also resist the "anterior" and eternal time of the home and the futurity of childhood as "investment." Instead, they dally in their own wayward time, the nonprogressive time of sensation.[83] Rilke's child-characters likewise cross boundaries of narration, their appearance indicating how a commitment to the present disturbs the easy forward gaze of adulthood; and their philosophical capacities produce queer effects: With Kathryn Bond Stockton, we might say that children in Rilke's corpus do not "grow up" but "grow sideways" where the lateral movement of perception and imagination make the "width" of their "experience or ideas . . . bringing 'adults' and 'children' into lateral contact."[84]

In Chapter 3, "Walter Benjamin's Small Worlds of Childhood"—the namesake of the present book—I offer a reevaluation of Benjamin's significant prose engagement with childhood, both in his autobiographical and theoretical writing. I show that Leibniz's monad repeats as a critical component of the philosophical paradigm that Benjamin's wide-ranging work on childhood produces, one that reaches well beyond his early explicit endeavors at theorizing conceptual thought as such. Benjamin seems to not only have been struck by the similarity between the structure of the monad as philosophical thought (as idea), but also by the necessity of spatial metaphors for representing philosophical concepts in general.[85] Leibniz's concepts of perceptual distinctness, universal expression, and the microcosm, as they appear in his *Monadology*, in my reading inform and shape Benjamin's writing on childhood to a significant degree. Indeed I argue that Benjamin, in his essays on and depictions of nineteenth-century bourgeois childhood, creates what amounts to an entire crypto-monadology.

By reading the deployment of certain metaphorical tendencies in Leibniz, I show how Benjamin is able to elevate the child subject out of the discourse of mere nostalgia or innocence, and into the pantheon of philosophers. Benjamin also makes visible a view of childhood experience as unfolding within what I identify as the queer temporality of Leibniz's monad, an expansive present that simultaneously expresses times prior to and after. Benjamin's scenes of children occur in the nonlinear plurality of monadological time. Childhood's microcosmic appearance refers its reader backward in time, like a palimpsest, while also being, as Leibniz says, "pregnant with the future."[86] With the queer temporality of the monad, Benjamin's utopian descriptions of childhood extend in all directions, recalling José Esteban Muñoz's description of an "ecstatic and horizontal temporality" that makes possible "a movement to a greater openness to the world."[87]

Leibniz's monad and the image of the child's small world—as a detail, a finitude which points to the infinite, a dialectic of visibility and invisibility, and the queer temporalities this entails—enable Benjamin to articulate the "philosophical experience of the world and its reality" or, as Gershom Scholem says, his "metaphysics."[88] This philosophy of childhood is only legible in the backward view of Leibniz, and by virtue of what Giorgio Agamben describes as a paradigm—a form of knowledge, that, like an ensemble, appears queerly (as I am claiming) at the "crossing of diachrony and synchrony"[89] The paradigmatic reading not only untethers the figure of the child from its individual task of "shor[ing] up" the fantasy futurity,[90] but also enables the early appearance of Leibniz in Benjamin's *The Origin of German Tragic Drama* to sit a-chronologically at ease alongside his later observations and vivid fragments on childhood. In the paradigm, the future adult reader is also demoted, as it were, no longer part of a "dichotomous logic" of origin and end. In other words, a paradigmatic reading also horizontally refigures each of Leibniz's theses in the *Monadology* as well as Benjamin's monadological childhood writings as *one among many* individual contributing phenomena. Childhood thereby finds the fullness of its expression in all directions.

The Small Worlds of Childhood concludes with a brief coda on the literary techniques Sigmund Freud employs in his writing on children, and his depictions of himself and his patients as children, in particular. By focusing on what I describe as tropes of vectors and directionality, I argue that Freud commits childhood to a linear temporality in line with what Elizabeth Freeman calls "chrononormativity." I read Freud's *narratives* of childhood as the undoing, as it were, of the philosophical poetics of childhood representation that I carefully trace in each of the preceding chapters. What becomes visible in Freud's poetics of childhood is the decided loss of philosophical subjectivity, as his depictions of child-figures are not animated by the idea that writing about childhood is an opportunity to examine ordinary experience as such. Instead, we find that his spatial and even geometrical language always straightens, to paraphrase Ahmed, in a linear fashion toward the eventual adult subject. By treating Freud as a prose writer, I show how he uses literary language to center the child as future-oriented and, in Edelman's sense, return the literature of childhood to the task of regulating adult reality. In returning the child-figure to its promise of the future, Freud's writing signals the end of the queer experiment in childhood storytelling.

This small book endeavors to show that there are in fact literary worlds in which we might read childhood queerly, where children, as characters, may be emancipated from the conventional burden of helping grown-ups envision their own fantasies of social, political, and reproductive futurity in being given more substance than the pure difference of adulthood's Other.[91] By letting child-figures extend laterally or horizontally in the world, rather than only growing up, Stifter, Rilke, and Benjamin permit them their epistemological, phenomenological, and metaphysical say on the world. Reading stories like these about childhood is still meaningful *for adults*: These scenes of childhood help us see what *literature* can show us about ordinary experience, what the world looks like beyond the chrononormative world of adulthood. This queer literature on childhood helps us see the world, in other words, in all its variety as strangeness, contingency, backwardness, and immediacy, as local theory and nonce taxonomy.

1
Adalbert Stifter's Topographical Worlds of Childhood

Children's Forts, Not Grown-Up Arbors

What does childhood look like and why should we think about it as a kind of world-making of its own? In this chapter we will see that answering this question concerns not only the extent to which childhood is something visually and even spatially apprehensible but also, equally important, that it also means asking what representing childhood tells us about writerly ways of knowing. The basic outline of the problem posed by European thinking about childhood after Rousseau—that any investigation of it necessarily comes belatedly—situates us on the outside looking in. To paraphrase Foucault, in representing children the writer reveals themself as the spectator whose gaze transforms that fleeting and occasionally chaotic time of childhood into a stable object.[1]

As a poetic realist author, Adalbert Stifter's writing makes childhood discursively visible, attempting to solve the epistemic problem through the articulation of patterns, identities, and differences. In his 1866 essay, "Die Gartenlaube" (The garden arbor),[2] Stifter ruminates on the familiar piece of garden architecture that was "one of the most charming and coziest things" of his own childhood.[3] The temporal gap of nostalgia that one might initially expect instead moves quickly to descriptive categories—observations of what children can be seen doing in comparison with how adults experience the garden space. Stifter situates himself alongside the "millions who share his feelings" for the small botanical arbor, elaborate gazebo, or a summer house, noting that these can be seen in nearly every garden, large or small, only to quickly turn from the grown-up affinity for the garden arbor to a similar kind of structure, what we might today call the child's fort:[4]

> Does not the child build a little house out of clay or little stones or sticks near their father's home, and delight in the exterior of such a tiny thing; indeed, do they not build a little house from playing cards on the table? . . . The children build themselves a little room from sheaves in the field or from willow branches and they perch inside and rejoice, or they tunnel into the haystack, or they crawl under a stone overhang or into the dovecote or even into the doghouse when they are empty, or under a board or any work equipment when it creates a kind of little roof. . . . It is the refuge from the open to the narrow and circumscribed.[5]

Departing immediately from the particulars of his own biographical childhood, Stifter's contribution to the journal instead offers the reader a host of vignettes of children at play in their imaginative, tiny dwellings in the field and in the garden. The child, Stifter suggests, delights in the creation of their *own* interior space, the distinguishing feature of which is its separation from the parental home and, of course, its proportionally smaller scale. This image of a distinct and dedicated room—a little chamber, a small room, a little house, or the space under a little roof[6]—repeats as a hallmark of Stifter's many depictions of childhood. The re-creation of the enclosed space of everyday domestic life doubles as the sequestration of childhood in his own literary representations. This aesthetics of enclosure, however, operates as more than a romantic reminder of the idyllic place of the child's imagination; it emphasizes the discontinuity of childhood from adulthood represented as a spatial boundary—as well as the peculiar elision of puberty in Stifter's depictions of families' youngest members.

The arbor repeats the motif of boundaries and visual evidence, making specific assertions about what these miniature dwellings tell us about the experience of being-child, namely, the affective moments of "delight" in the "refuge." Taken together with the titular occasion of this writing, Stifter's interest in both the drive toward and pleasure in "fencing in" imagines the child's arbor as a wooden grid of order against nature's very wildness.[7] When Stifter's observations turn to grown-up enjoyment of the arbor, however, "the refuge from the open to the narrow and circumscribed" contains the comforting polarity of being able to go from the sublime views obtained in summiting a mountain or looking out from a tower window or rooftop to the feeling of returning to one's small room, cabin, or other enclosed space.[8] Stifter imagines this movement from the wide open space to the cozy shelter as a timeless act of respite—from the ancient Romans to his own day. And the grown-up pleasure of the arbor is not derived from the simple fact of being enclosed, but rather because it enables the perception of the outdoors from within: a play of light and colors finds its way in between the living branches and soft breezes, and the delicate fragrances tickle and delight the senses.[9] The view from within the architectural structure is one of a subject able to glimpse nature, a natural wildness made manageable through the organizing framework of the arbor.[10] The figure of the arbor thus performs one of the essay's epistemological gestures—namely, knowledge through spatial limitation.

In each vignette, Stifter's description attends to how the arbor reveals social difference: how, for example, poets experience the beauty of nature in a manner subtly different from that of the painter. In this movement "from the open to the narrow and circumscribed," a wide range of variations in human life becomes legible as narrow categories: children, poets, old bachelors and crones, housewives, painters, historians, and lovers. Each one finds comfort in the face of whatever demands they encounter: intellectual, physical, poetic, aesthetic. The child's fort, however, neither shares the adult's relationship to the beauty of nature nor imposes visual mathematical order—the containment that makes childhood stand out is not the porous interplay of wild branches and vines trained onto a grid, but rather the sheer joy of enclosure made possible by everyday objects. When the space is too small for the child, they will happily put a fly or beetle inside, imagining that it feels the sense of contentment.[11]

The visions of childhood presented in "The Garden Arbor" not only opens on the child's diminutive rearticulations of adult familial spaces; with his rhetorical questions Stifter reminds us that, for grown-up readers, childhood is easily visually recognizable—everyone has seen children create such spaces for themselves. Stifter's essay also multiplies the *topos* of childhood: The small places that children build and adore make childhood visible through its *difference* from and *identity* with adulthood. The child's fort, in which they tuck themselves or small creatures, can be made of anything outside, and they are equally "cozy" ("wohl") in it: Nestled within it, they make the wider world feel smaller, and remake the adult world on a small scaler. On the one hand, this affective response looks a lot like the "refuge" sought by adults in their own full-size small, intimate spaces. On the other hand, adults delight in sitting under the arbor not only because it is feels pleasant as a sensory matter, but because it also offers specific regulative capacities, filtering and structuring their experience of the wider world around them. Looking out through the tiny spaces, they can see *more* of the world. In quiet contemplation, gaze directed outward through the grid of the arbor, poets and historians alike enjoy a clarity of thought unavailable to them in their chambers indoors: by glimpsing the overwhelming world only through the structure's small openings, they gain inspiration and understanding through the organization imposed by the arbor itself.[12] Childhood, with its forts, thus stands out against adulthood as a spatial phenomenon that reinscribes its own difference—containment against the wilds, and for its own sake.

With the arbor I think we might provisionally say that knowledge in Stifter's world of grown-ups involves, to paraphrase Foucault, the approach of a natural historian, in which areas of visibility are quite literally distributed across a grid. And this spatial framework, used for classification, is likewise repeated by the gesture of sequestration of and boundary for children in their own fort-building. Indeed, in Stifter's fictional world, childhood is both simultaneous and discontinuous with adulthood; other times adulthood finds itself recursively pointing backward toward childhood.[13] And this queer temporality of a gap and return feels less like gradual development and more like a lurch, as the transitions (puberty) never materialize. Stifter severs childhood from any possible contiguity with adulthood, while also instituting a spatial form that organizes and makes visible the characteristics that may be shared. The idea that the arbor is a "fencing in" therefore not only captures the scene of a child imagining their own "little home" ("Häuslein"); it also enacts the separation of childhood—and its recognizability—within its own bounded space. Reduced to a visual phenomenon, we will see that childhood takes on the epistemic qualities of what Foucault described as "classical thought": Just like plants in the taxonomic tables of natural historians, such as Linnaeus, or contained in herbaria and collections, Stifter's descriptive techniques rely on visual representation freed from any "principle of development" or seriality in the temporal sense.[14] Unlike his careful geological studies, which recent scholarship has elucidated in terms of his interest in the unfolding temporalities of earth sciences, for children and the family such visually recognizable epistemic categories exist not sequentially, but simultaneously.[15]

The metaphor of the arbor and the scene of children at play together convey a central focus on epistemological certainty, typical of Stifter's stories, by doubly representing the relationship between surface variables (identities and differences among the figures) and the idea of ordering an otherwise continuous world of infinite variability through tabular—that is, grid-like—organization (adults peering at the world through the holes in the structure of the arbor). While the characters who appear under the arbor can themselves then be categorized by type (old bachelors, poets, painters, historians), they are also enlightened by their encounter with the arbor's grid, gaining epistemic insight into the world according to their interests. Children, by comparison, seem to belong to the version of "everyday life" that Rita Felski has described as "a nonintellectual relationship with the world."[16] Without so much as a before or after, childhood is depicted only as an identical drive to build forts whether "in the haystack" or "out of playing cards on the table,"[17] further underscoring childhood as both universal and perpetual. Spatially contained and decoupled from any expectation of intellectual progression, childhood feels almost like Henri Lefebvre's concept of the "everyday," as childhood's distinguishability through its "little room[s]" of "willow branches" and "miniature house[s] of clay or sticks or pebbles" presents the reader with the strange temporality of "the invariable constant of the variations it envelops."[18] The fact that adults and children share a sense of "refuge" in the "narrow and circumscribed" situates childhood *not* as a developmental stage to be fulfilled in some future adulthood, but rather as a concomitant. In this natural history of the arbor (and the fort), childhood loses its sense of time.

It is by virtue of Stifter's commitment to visual organization that, I argue, we end up with a concept of childhood that sits outside the ordinary chronology of time, at times even violating chrononormative expectations. Despite the overtly domestic themes that we will see in each story about children, in their resistance to conventional temporalities of family these narratives take a queer turn. In the pages that follow here, we will not only see the affinities between Stifter's epistemological poetics and Foucault's characterization of the classical *episteme* (e.g., taxonomies, tabular representations, and cartographic representation), but also how the queer temporal effects of writing childhood *without* the expected linearity and continuity that would connect the past and future also disrupts heteronormative expectations for biological reproduction and familial inheritance. Much like what Foucault describes as the "old flat world" of the preceding centuries' natural histories, where one can be "content with seeing" a world of objects that has been whittled down into recognizable categories, Stifter's children have been flattened and thus freed from, as it were, the problem of real and infinite variation and ongoing change that exists in the world.[19] As a writer, Stifter's epistemological attitude is, as Foucault describes Linnaeus, a "man concerned with the structure of the visible world and its denomination according to its characters. Not with life." Childhood, represented out of time, is thus freed from what Elizabeth Freemen calls "teleologies of the living."[20]

And, as we will see in the pages that follow, the Stifterian obsession with order also produces some queer effects: The child, as the object to knowledge or subject of a "still life" no longer figures as the embodiment of futurity or progress. Immobilized and weird, these fictional children gesture backward, outside of time, and every way except forward. With a playful paraphrase of Edelman, my readings will take up his epistemological-poetic program as itself queer—as refusing futurity—and also reading childhood within this framework as itself linked with transgression, backwardness, the perverse, and the homoerotic.

Indian Summer: Childhood's Time Is Out of Order

Like "The Garden Arbor," the first chapter of Adalbert Stifter's idealistic Bildungsroman, *Der Nachsommer* (Indian summer), opens with a depiction of childhood that mirrors the forms of knowledge and observation characterizing the protagonist's own earliest epistemic approaches on his journey to becoming a natural scientist. The first part of the 1857 novel, which "unfolds in excruciating detail," thus also imagines an analogy between the forms of childhood space and the formation of its inhabitants.[21] The first chapter, "Domesticity" ("Die Häuslichkeit"), links the protagonist Heinrich Drendorf's epistemological concerns for collection, identification, and natural history with the description of the layout and ordered use of domestic space. As a departure from his narratives of "wild" or "natural" children,[22] this book depicts the well-regulated private sphere of bourgeois childhood—indeed, the Drendorf children's narrated existence hardly extends beyond the confines of the family's houses, as they are educated at home, rarely venturing into the surrounding city.[23] Here their lives are circumscribed first by the home's layout and second by the ordered tasks associated with each room:[24] "My father had two children: me the firstborn son and then a daughter who was two years younger. We each had our own [little] rooms [Zimmerchen], where we slept as well as performing assigned tasks which we received even in early childhood."[25] Childhood in the Drendorf household began neatly sorted into spaces by type of life; not only was each location set up for its particular purpose, but each room also reflected the physical attributes of its contents. As in Stifter's arbor essay, diminutive human bodies belong in equally diminutive spaces, as each child occupies their "little room" ("Zimmerchen"). Unlike Stifter's social-pedagogical writings, where he suggests that the child's interaction with their parents could operate as a "fruitful" and "beneficial school,"[26] *Indian Summer*'s early emphasis on the home's layout and usage depicts childhood as belonging to a nursery in which children's spaces are formally defined and largely sequestered from adulthood. The reigning pedagogical aim in the Drendorf house was a kind of precise spatially based system of categorization:

> [Father] couldn't stand "mixed rooms" as he called them—rooms that were used for several things, such as a combination bedroom-playroom or the like. He used to say: everything and every man can only be one thing, but he must be that with all his heart and soul. . . . For example, we children were not even allowed to enter our parents' bedroom. An elderly maid took care of cleaning and tidying in there.[27]

The father's notion of single-purpose rooms is not only evidence of what Beatrice Mall-Grob describes as a pedagogical program of strict paternal order; it also enables the childhood home to preview, as it were, an essential principle that eventually comes to govern Heinrich's grown-up modes of scientific categorization.[28] This principle of organization in childhood mirrors the taxonomic forms of knowledge that order the adult's world; children, like all other objects, belong to what Foucault broadly defines as the "project of a general science of order."[29] This basic formula then comes to dominate Heinrich's own childhood as a whole when, as he recalls, after his father's business grows, the Drendorfs move into a more spacious suburban home, in which his father's logic of avoiding "mixed use" rooms can be enacted to an even greater degree, as entire rooms begin to serve as specialized housing for belongings that become collections.

The new home enables paintings to be displayed in a single room rather than distributed throughout the house. Here, "the floor was covered with a dull colored carpet so it wouldn't detract [beirren] from the paintings."[30] This gallery, while aesthetically pleasing, also indicates its epistemic logic: The space allows one to look at the objects "in exactly the right light" ("in dem rechten Lichte") while also preventing confusion or uncertainty ("beirren") during observation. Allocation of space is therefore part of an epistemological principle of illumination and of visibility. In this way, childhood in the Drendorf home is no different: Just as the principle of resemblance governs the space of containment for childhood (as the small children had their small rooms), paintings are grouped into a gallery, plants into the greenhouse, books into the library, and even decorative furniture has its own "special room."[31] From a jumbled mix of domestic and aesthetic objects "scattered" across rooms in the old house comes the ability to represent family life as a set of collections. The children are permitted to accompany their parents into these rooms on occasion to learn about the world through this categorized inventory—how objects were made, to which place or period they belonged, and the like.[32] With Foucault we might say that the chaos and variability of the world of bourgeois domesticity is thus positively transformed by spatial distribution and containment: The home is organized like a table. And as such, the "linear time of representation" becomes the "simultaneous space" of resemblances.[33] Childhood can be identified by its little rooms in the same way that books, paintings, or plants are featured in classical "unencumbered spaces in which things are juxtaposed"—all of the Drendorfs' things become knowable, as the rooms of the home appear like natural history's "non-temporal rectangle[s]" in which things "present themselves ... according to their common features."[34]

The family's rule that children were not to enter the marital bedroom reinforces the distinguishing boundary of childhood, as they are forbidden from the world of sexuality. There is no in-between, as puberty is effectively elided in *Indian Summer*. Instead, Stifter signals the other side of childhood through the narrator's entrance into those previously proscribed spaces: "As we grew older, we were drawn into more intimate associations with our parents."[35] The invitations into the study and gallery bring with them the pedagogical equivalent of adulthood: Their old teachers were let go; as young adults, the son and daughter begin their respectively gendered courses of study (his sister begins training in affairs of the home, while he is faced with deciding what subject he will specialize in professionally), and those "little rooms" are never mentioned again.[36] At first glance, Heinrich's father and mother each represent the gendered worlds of industry and family, respectively, in ways that accord with Dana Luciano's discussion of "sentimental" nineteenth-century home life (where domesticity finds its meaning as the "true" and "prior" site that recalls Kristeva's "maternal-feminine timelessness"). But here Stifter's commitment to spatial (over temporal) representation of the element of childhood undoes a kind of objectification and spatialization that makes it concomitant within the bourgeois scene, reducing the sense of its "temporal anteriority."[37] The temporality of being-child is not so much the monumental time of maternal care as it is the epistemically simultaneity with all other groups of objects.[38] With the same grown-up vision that Heinrich will employ to observe and record and order the natural world, childhood is provided with no narrative of transition, development, or change—only difference.

As a reflection of the ever-growing class of the European bourgeois family, Stifter's depiction of the Drendorf household not only includes the separation of work life from family life, as the children are neither laboring alongside nor apprenticing:[39] These opening pages of the novel in fact focus on the particularities of the familial sphere, and specifically of the bourgeois emphasis on private life over professional. This is visible in Stifter's attention to the objects and organization of the fictional space, as he carefully renders the familial scene with all the domestic trappings of an industrializing society.[40] Stifter's descriptive attention to the enclosure and separation produced by the protagonist's two childhood homes reflects significant historical shifts in the treatment of childhood during the nineteenth century. The sequestration of childhood in its domestic architectural appearance links the cultural-aesthetic framework of childhood to its epistemological status. As Hans Heino Ewers remarks, childhood was bracketed off not only physically but also theoretically: The child's room functions as one of several indicators of an eighteenth- and nineteenth-century division between "exotic" childhood (in both Romantic and Enlightenment views) and its distant futurity in adulthood. The conventional separation of children from adults evinced the idea that there was something still quite ungraspable about the difference between the two states of human life.[41]

As the novel's narrator, Heinrich, continues to recount his childhood, we learn that although the children were invited into the shared spaces of family life,[42] entrance into the adult realm, such as the father's study, a vault-like room that housed his collection of books, was expressly forbidden. The quasi-cloistered space of the childhood home reinscribes the existing contrast of interior and exterior as the Drendorf home seems to lack windows. There is curiously little mention of typically public or communal spaces—rooms for hosting guests or receiving clients, or even so much as a small foyer or vestibule.[43] Thus, from childhood, the family is represented as itself a sealed space, cut off even from the big city around it.[44] Following the logic of a table, children, represented spatially, occupy a subdivision or a cell of rectangular territory that allows the domestic unit to be identified against the outside, and as pure difference. The nursery is the space of childhood within the observable limits of the table of the family.

The entire domestic scene in *Indian Summer* finds its temporal character substantially weakened. As a classical tabular epistemic representation of space, the two Drendorf houses also allow us to see things with a natural historian's view. Heinrich's father takes comfort in seeing how like belongs with like, as the spatial separation of childhood is less a depiction of relation to futurity and more a means of restricting the infinite contours of reality made available in the chaos of mixed use (when any single thing might at the same time be many things)—which also means restricting the "area of experience" to those identities that observably speak to their univocity. Childhood, defined within "classical rationality," has no gradual connection to adulthood (via puberty) but appears instead as a well-defined static element in the table of the home, saved from modernity's "irruptive violence of time."[45]

Indian Summer's classical deployment of space as a system of knowledge—in layout, furniture, and accessories—is not, however, freed from nineteenth-century bourgeois aesthetics. Instead, Stifter deploys the home's decorative containment as the means by which objects are located as adjacent or separate, and which in turn directly conveys their identity or difference.[46] Here Walter Benjamin's characterization of the bourgeois "interieur" clearly captures the affinity between epistemological and aesthetic practices that Stifter employs in Heinrich's recollection of his childhood home:

> The difficulty in reflecting on dwelling: on the one hand there is something age-old—perhaps eternal—to be recognized here, the image of that abode of the human being in the maternal womb; on the other hand, this motif of primal history notwithstanding, we must understand dwelling in its most extreme form as a condition of nineteenth-century existence. The original form of all dwelling is existence not in the house but in the shell [Gehäuse]. The shell bears the impression of its occupant. In the most extreme instance, the dwelling becomes a shell. The nineteenth century, like no other century, was addicted to dwelling. It conceived the residence as a receptacle for the person, and it encased him with all his appurtenances so deeply in the dwelling's interior that one might be reminded of the inside of a compass case, where the instrument, with all its accessories lies embedded in deep, usually violet folds of velvet. What didn't the nineteenth century invent a casing for! Pocket watches, slippers, egg cups, thermometers, playing cards—and in lieu of cases, there were jackets, carpets, wrappers, and covers.[47]

Stifter's scene of domestic childhood depends on a vision of dwelling that mirrors Benjamin's claim that, in its most "extreme" variations, there is always an epistemic relationship between occupant and home—namely, that the nineteenth-century impulse to encase is, in effect, an aestheticization of the classical forms of knowledge. In essence, the decorative enclosure both refers to and makes visible its contents. In the allocation of space and assignment of form, this decorative drive and epistemological impulse to categorize, to identify, to note are all unified. Like Benjamin's notion of the shell ("Gehäuse"), Heinrich's childhood requires customized storage, where the container doubles as the indication of its contents. Childhood in Stifter's novel appears emphatically as part of its enclosure within a "space of culture" or "world of culture"—and therefore stands in opposition to both the wild, sublime, or dangerous spaces of nature.[48] The Benjaminian shell is also reminiscent of the childlike movement into the fort of his arbor essay, where tiny bodies in their tiny abodes flee "from the open into the narrow and circumscribed." Benjamin not only summarizes bourgeois dwelling as the space where everything has its proper place, each item in its corresponding container; he also describes the intersection of the desire for certainty through a kind of scientific technology, and the drive for detail, as both an essential feature of and an ornament that is germane to Stifter's realist style.

In Heinrich's childhood, the type of cultural industry of encasement that Benjamin reveals functions as a kind of epistemological anachronism, in which the obsession with containment in the nineteenth century enacts the spatialized signification of the classical system of tables. Just as the grammatically diminutive form of the word "room" ("Zimmer") tailors the space, as it were, to fit its tiny inhabitants, so too is the reciprocal relationship of dweller-dwelling that Benjamin identifies also performed by the suffix "chen" in "Zimmer*chen*," as the morphological transformation of "room" to "little room" and repeating the classical immediacy between a graphic or spatial sign (the space of childhood, the "little room") and its contents (the children).[49] Similar containment strategies can be seen across the Drendorf rooms, as the objects of the home are afforded the same treatment. The first home contained a chest for a collection of antique coins as well as displays of antique weapons in the solarium, while the books in the library room were housed inside cabinets whose glass doors were lined with green curtains. In the second home, the room that displayed the fine wooden furniture had a custom-carved wooden ceiling.[50] Each object is housed in a customized container that creates a nesting effect while also telegraphing its contents: Heinrich's father explains in a way that any dwelling ought to correspond to its dweller as the design of this childhood home accounts for its belongings, in its spaces within spaces, to ensure that the objects therein are "obvious"—that they proclaim ("aussprechen") their contents.[51] To paraphrase Foucault's explanation of Linnean taxonomy, they are able *say* what one will possibly *see*.[52] Like showpieces in a vitrine, maintaining "state room"–like tidiness, their contents (and purpose) emphasize the importance of immediately visible correspondence.

Just as in Benjamin's reading of the pocket watch and its case, these are clearly defined interior spaces, not merely associated, accidental, or implicit. Indeed, by demanding univocity from each room, collectively the home appears as a neatly legible table, where visible territories indicate unequivocally both content and meaning. And the space of childhood is no exception to this epistemological framework. In the ordering work of collection and containment we can also see resemblance avant la lettre to the containment work of the "closet": The elder Drendorf's organizing, storing, and displaying delineates what will be "kept 'in'" or "let 'out.'"[53] The home's rooms are like "queer furnishing[s]"—"orientation device[s]" that, as Ahmed remarks, "still 'make room' or clear spaces, in which there are things left for bodies to do."[54] Like the latter-day "closet," the queer work of bourgeois and scientific containment in *Indian Summer* is what organizes what it means to be both "at home" and to be "in the world."[55]

The elder Drendorf's fanatical work of collecting and protecting objects of history has an additional queer bend. As Mike Goode has argued, there is a kind of queer erotics of antiquarianism in the sensory experience of collecting, handling, and apprehending the works of great men.⁵⁶ Heinrich's father, in his obsessive treatment of both the sensuous antique carved objects and the mass of books that he keeps demurely veiled, appears like the "historian" whose "relationship" with his "object always threatens to become carnal."⁵⁷ The father's entanglements with the past end up deploying the entire house into multiple temporalities at once: The timelessness of domesticity and cyclical and eternal time of women's work takes a backseat in a family that seems to be mostly about the men, to wit, Heinrich and his father. Here the home's reorganization feels out of sync with any forward-looking sense of time, as both the antiquarian's collection of the past in the present and the natural historian's impulse toward the nontemporal table both undermine the expectation that family is about futurity. We might say Heinrich's childhood household, to paraphrase Heather Love's allegorical reading of Odysseus, attempts to navigate scientific progress while still looking backward.⁵⁸

Such procedures of collection and identification that poetically produce the childhood home in the first part of the novel are repeated when Stifter portrays the protagonist's first encounters with natural science—that is, his own epistemic infancy, as his earliest scientific procedures follow exactly the classical form of knowledge: observing, collecting, ordering, and map-making. Here, my reading situates the epistemological work of recording the natural world as one which, like Stifter's narrative of family life, is strangely detemporalized.⁵⁹ Even to the extent that Heinrich's stated perspective on the natural world traces new developments in science, which shifted away from strictly atemporal models, such as geology,⁶⁰ the novel's parallels with the novel's first chapter continue to foreground spatial models of understanding, where objects can be represented and distinguished by their visible shapes and boundaries, and not by the passage of time. Like his father's queer arrangement of the home, the grown-up protagonist's scientific impulses to map, organize, and contain—as a form of knowledge—are visible in his desire to create detailed recordings of the objects of nature, after encountering the work of another great man, Alexander von Humboldt's writings.⁶¹ If there is any narrative of reproduction that connects childhood to adulthood in *Indian Summer*, it's a queer one, whose lineage is only male.

Heinrich's own initial interests, which begin with mere collecting and recording, follow the logic of taxonomical classification as he describes animals and plants in detail in "his studies of natural history."⁶² But he quickly shifts from categorizing by feature to creating pictures, as he finds drawing is "even better than description."⁶³ With this discovery, Heinrich's fidelity to the great men of science begins to shift from Linnaeus to Humboldt. Yet his ways of knowing remain nonetheless rooted in the classical age's fixation on the sign, especially as "spatial and graphic representation," exemplified, as Foucault has argued, by the taxonomic table and the "drawing as map or picture."[64] The fidelity that Heinrich seeks is one of identity with appearances, such that his inquiries into the geology of the lake do not epistemically diverge from either his father's ordered collections or his own catalogs, and likewise are less a depiction of a living world over time ("modus vivendi") than a detemporalized representation ("the order of *character*").[65] Here, the protagonist imagines a way to make the invisible bottom of the lake visible through drawing:

> On this occasion I thought if the water were more transparent, not as much as air but nearly so, then you would be able to see the entire basin, not as clearly as in air but in a greenish watery veil. That would be exquisite. As a consequence of these ruminations, I stayed at the lake longer, rented a room at an inn, and made several measurements of water depth at various points whose distance from the bank I had ascertained by a measuring line. I thought, in this way I could get an approximation of the lake bottom's configuration, I could draw it, distinguishing the inner part of the basin from the outer by a softer greenish color. . . . These efforts brought me to a consideration of the peculiarities of earth formations.[66]

Knowledge begins not with the temporality of either history or narrative, but rather with the act of making visible through spatial description. In the double meaning of seeing through "a greenish watery veil" Heinrich describes both what it would be to observe the unobservable depths of the lake floor through the water itself and the medium for such an indirect observation: the topographic map. After taking and recording his measurements, Heinrich begins to draw a green-shaded map that corresponds to the shape of the lake's bottom. The invisible terrain of the lake thus appears as the "greenish watery veil" of his topographic drawing. As Foucault explains, beginning with the seventeenth-century *Port Royal Logic*, "the spatial and graphic representation—the drawing as map or picture . . . has no other content in fact than that which it represents, and yet that content is made visible only because it is represented by a representation."[67] In a similar way, the "greenish watery veil" is both the terrain at the bottom of those watery depths and also the very possibility of its visibility in the map; and it is thus the classical epistemic sign par excellence: "at the same time *indication* and *appearance*." As the narrator here describes his own observations as a natural scientist, it becomes clear that the work of making the world visible through representation mirrors the means by which the entire scene of childhood also can be seen and known. In this novel, topographical knowledge comes into relief through the same contours of the home through the identity of indication (that which it proclaims) and the contours of the observable object itself. On the one hand, as Schnyder and Stockhammer have both argued, the protagonist is a natural scientist whose map-making impulses eventually develop beyond the Linnean system, evidenced by this desire to note the source of each finding and what kind of earth-history might be communicated through it.[68] On the other hand, the work of map-making is no different from the Linnean taxonomy insofar as it endeavors to "cut up the continuum of beings" and "transform" the "sequence of perceptions" into a "picture." The natural historian, like old Drendorf ordering the family home, destroys the sense of chronology and continuity through the work of tabular representation: the sequential work of observing the lake and its surfaces is not preserved in the "immobilized" topographical drawing, whose transparency is only possible outside of real time, in the viewer's imagination.[69] These early explorations can be therefore seen as an analogue to the logic of childhood. Like his vision of and from the arbor of Stifter's own youth, the world of nature looks like the world of childhood: It is something that demands graphical representation. It circumscribes and it is itself circumscribable, knowable as a *where* rather than a *when*.

The reflection we can see in his spatial representation of the watery depths is both of Heinrich Drendorf's own childhood of order *and* the elder Drendorf's philosophy. But rather than creating an easy reproductive linearity from one generation to the next, this backward gesture splits, as it points from a grown man back to his childhood as much as it does to his father. In this queer temporality, multiple eras and generations are, as it were, "sutured together," to cite Freeman's playful expansion of the term "allegorize."[70] Childhood, as part of the world of domesticity (and the chapter with the same name) operates both within the timelessness of women's domestic time, while epistemically relocated out of time through spatial distribution. Freeman describes the ways in which allegorization creates queer temporal effects through the syncopation of narrative, enabling multiple narrative and temporal threads to exist in one—which we can see in Stifter's narration as the work of observation and ordering point the reader both forward (toward the topography of the lake) and backward (returning to the elder's organization of the childhood home).

The space of childhood thus extends laterally, as it were, across time and space from childhood to adulthood and back, as even the would-be moment of adulthood, the announcement of engagement (when the grown child leaves) is marked by the doubling of being-child. Heinrich finds himself with a second father (figure) in his mentor, the Baron von Risach.[71] When Heinrich returns to Risach's estate to announce his engagement, a queer family reunion appears: the two fathers, the elder collector, Drendorf, and the gentleman scientist, Risach, greet each other, exclaiming, "Seldom have I longed to meet anyone as much as you. We have been in contact for so long, and I have loved you for so long through the love of your son."[72] In their longing and letter writing, we might see a version of Sedgwick's queer "tableau of two men chasing each one another across a landscape [in which] it is importantly undecidable ... whether the two men represent two consciousnesses or one."[73] In their shared drives to collect, as Robert Holub has suggested, the elder Drendorf ends up as a "carbon copy of Risach."[74] And, as Ahmed reminds us, the anxiety of sameness has long been depicted as the danger inherent to queerness—here it is in their libraries and galleries that the queer philia and filiation become visible.[75] The epistemological overlaps between the two men, with their art collections and antiquarian libraries, reveal the queerness of fatherly love and how imagined intellectual cross-lineages—a great polyamory with great men of the past!—produce more father figures in the present. Through their epistemic ordering of things in the world, it is futurity—growing up and leaving your parents—that seems lost. In the moment of Heinrich's departure from being-child (announcing the start of his own family), we see instead the queer double gesture of the narrative "cleaving" backward and laterally, an act of separation and sticking fast in the moments where these men "face one another in, precisely and paradoxically, disorienting temporal fissures."[76]

In the preceding sections I have argued that, in emphasizing spatialized forms of representation, Stifter's depictions of childhood do not follow conventional temporalities of linearity and development, and instead present childhood as either timeless, outside of time, or even recursive or backward. Adrian Daub has argued that *Indian Summer* "would suggest that by family we are to understand a broad, knotty, intergenerational formation, not the loving couple."[77] And here I think it is the idea of "knot" that emphatically characterizes the inability to move smoothly forward, to generate new generations. Despite Stifter's own hopes that family would sit above scientific concerns for progress, in *Indian Summer* we find that it is precisely the obsession with knowledge that turns the temporality of family back on itself. By linking childhood with ways of knowing that parallel what Foucault describes as classical thought, as collections, taxonomic tables, and maps or pictures—i.e., ways of knowing that make the world visible through representations of identities and differences—Stifter rejects a vision of the world (children included) as part of narrative of progress, chronology, and development, in favor of one that creates order without an obligation to futurity.

"Tourmaline" and Childhood's "Bad Timing"

In Adalbert Stifter's 1853 collection of novellas, *Motley Stones* (*Bunte Steine*), five of the six tales feature children as protagonists or as key characters.[78] The third story in the collection, "Tourmaline" ("Turmalin"), shares the trope of collection with Heinrich's childhood home, but here it is an excess of things in the home, and out of order, that disrupts the lines of kinship, narrative, and temporality, eventually disturbing and distorting the futurity of the family line. The complex movement between spaces and times that make up the course of "Tourmaline" disrupts the reader's comprehension. Because the connections between events and narrative levels are often belated or only inferred, the problem of *knowing* what has happened is as much thematized as performed by the story. Therefore, I will begin by sketching the story as it unfolds in the text. It begins with a framing narrative: a secondhand description of a gentleman, his wife, and child, who live together in a flat in Vienna. The man, referred to as the "pension man" ("Rentherr"[79]) befriends a local actor, Dall, who later seduces the man's wife. Though it is unclear exactly why, the wife eventually runs off (presumably with the actor), abandoning the pension man and their child. After searching for her in vain, he goes mad and, in turn, abandons the apartment; and, according to the narrator, nothing more is heard of either him or the child. The story then shifts to the inner narrative, a first-person account by a woman who lives in the suburbs of Vienna with her husband and son, and who had apparently also known the actor Dall. She recounts how she encountered a peculiar young girl, whose father, a neighbor's gatekeeper, has died after falling off a ladder and left her alone. Now orphaned, the girl, who is described as having a "big head," possesses an oddly elevated and yet almost completely incomprehensible manner of speech. Taking pity, the woman and her family take her in while attempting to figure out if she has any living relatives who could care for her. Eventually, the narrator uncovers that the dead gatekeeper and the "big-headed girl" are in fact the pension man and his daughter, who had vanished many years earlier (in the framing narrative). The story concludes with a return to the frame narrator, who informs the reader that while the girl "lived in the years to come," by the time of its telling, virtually every trace of the events thus narrated have since vanished, as now "a new row of houses stands where it and its neighbors were, and the young generation does not know what once stood there, and what happened in that place."[80]

In "Tourmaline" we find the familiar realist terrain of detailed depictions of material domestic life: decorated rooms, furniture, and knickknacks, mixed in with scenes of eating, waiting, and observing. Unlike *Indian Summer*, the family scene that emerges is one immediately characterized by a queerness of space and temporality—with Sara Ahmed's sense of queerness the child ends up "out of [the family] line" and with Freeman's "bad timing" of a family that fails to produce its own likenesses.[81] As we will see, the spatial and epistemological framework in this story oscillates between temporalized movement through space and static descriptions of space that can be roughly described according to Michel de Certeau's concepts of "place" (*lieu*) and "space" (*espace*).[82] In this way Stifter's story articulates two modes of storytelling, both of which are, in de Certeau's words, knowledge as "a spatial practice": one of childhood and domesticity where things appear less as a table and more as a tableau, the other of family and queer masculinity, where things appear as mobility and extension.[83] Here the philosophical poetics of childhood lead nowhere as the story of childhood is not one of progress but of errancy and erasure.

The pension man's Viennese flat is a family home so chock full of *things* that rooms feel nearly claustrophobic, or as Eva Geulen describes them, "claustrophilic," as the sheer quantity of everyday objects, the immense detail, shift the mood from typical to strange.[84] The tension Stifter creates out of relatively unremarkable objects and spaces becomes most palpable in their excess, as the Viennese flat is filled to the brim with wall-hangings, tables, and rolling armchairs. This congested scene of bourgeois *interieur* feels like the flip side of dwelling's obligation, the obsessive encasement that Benjamin describes.[85] In this residence, the belongings of the pension man's wife and baby have been sorted together into one wing of the home and presented to the reader in their relation only to one another.

> The wife's rooms were furnished in her fashion. The larger room had dark curtains at the windows, and in it stood soft couches of the same material, and a fine large table, always dust-free and gleaming to a high sheen, with a few books or drawings or the occasional other thing resting upon it. . . . At one window stood an exquisite little sewing table with fine linens, delicate fabrics, and other things for working with, and a small chair in front of it that fit into the window bay.[86]

The passage continues on in this manner, describing each chair, what each table displays and cabinet contains, even the distribution and appearance of the houseplants is described. Here we can read de Certeau's logic of "place" as the spatial structure par excellence for the domestic sphere: "The law of the 'proper' rules in the place: the elements taken into consideration are *beside* one another, each situated in its own 'proper' and distinct location, a location it defines. A place is thus an instantaneous configuration of positions. It implies an indication of stability."[87] The "stability" mirrors the gendered temporality of maternal sensibility—indeed, the rooms are "in her fashion"—and the result is too static and lifeless to feel either like the sacred or cyclical, but instead feels like the routinized space of timelessness.[88] Indeed, even "the large wall clock had no chime, and ticked so softly that it was barely to be heard."[89] Hardly any text is provided for the wife's activities; it takes just two lone sentences to capture the monotony: "In her rooms the wife presided, she looked after the all the child's needs, and occupied herself with work with reading with embroidery with the management of the household and other things of the kind. She had few dealings with the outside world, nor did women often come to visit her."[90]

The pension man's daughter, still a baby in the frame narrative, lived in the mother's "second, smaller room," thus repeating, on a smaller scale, the mother's own timeless and frozen domestic scene. Freeman has suggested that the operations of hetero- and chrononormativity appear through "the gendered double time of stasis and progress, intimacy and genealogy," where women's work in the home serves as the foundation or background for the possibility of men's agency.[91] The logic of place—where things have their "proper" location—situates the child at the center of concentric layers of furnishings and embedding or binding her to the static world of the maternal:

> In the back stood the wife's white bed draped in white curtains. . . .
> Near the bed on a pedestal stood a gilded angel, its wings folded about its shoulders, supporting itself with one hand and gently stretching out the other to hold the tip of a white drape whose lavish folds parted and fell in the shape of a tent. Beneath this tent a dainty basket rested on a table, in the basket a white bed was made up, and in this bed was the couple's child, the little girl by whose side they often stood to gaze
> upon the tiny red lips and the rose cheeks and the little closed eyes.[92]

To borrow again from de Certeau, we might say that the pension man's child, properly located, nested within the folds of the home, is determined through seeing and thus appears as part of a tableau.[93] The narrative perspective here is fixed, and the objects in the room are *seen* as part of field of knowledge and order. Like maps and tables, the static object is not linked with living, moving, or the actions of subject, but rather, with the inert and the dead.[94] And in the "double time" of the story's progression, the childhood home appears ever more lifeless: when the local authorities inventory the abandoned flat, each room and its furnishings are described again, the second time with a layer of dust and an empty crib.[95] What Thomas Elsaesser has suggested about filmic melodrama rings true for the realist efforts of "Tourmaline": namely, that "the function of the decor and the symbolization of objects" is "the characteristic attempt of the bourgeois household to make time stand still, immobilize life and fix forever domestic property relations as a model of social life and as a bulwark against the more disturbing sides of human nature."[96] Despite the chrononormative effects of place—the tableau of domesticity—the mother still leaves, triggering a cascade of unintended effects: madness, poverty, deformity, death.

Both the room's content and object placement reproduce what Ahmed calls the "field of heterosexual objects," where expectations for reproduction appear in and as the "background" which "is not simply behind the child: it is what the child is asked to aspire toward."[97] The mother's grown-up bed is larger—but just as shrouded—and looms behind the crib, just as the mother and father stand over the little girl.[98] The expectation of the child's own heteronormative futurity is part of the domestic tableau. Even the angel in the scene ambiguously represents both the mother as "angel of the house who magically kept things clean" and, in the child's background, as the hoped-for future mother as well.[99] The mother's wing of the home is almost a caricature of conventionality, which stands in stark contrast to the pension man's side of things where the line of sight is decidedly queerer.

If the mother and child belong to description, order, and place, the pension man appears within a narration of movement *through* space. Where the little girl is *seen* like all the things in the wife's wing, the pension man is the one who, following de Certeau, *operates* as a full subject, and thus the reader can recognize his space as a walking *tour*.[100] In comparison with the static timelessness of the nursery, Stifter leans into narrativity in the child's home when it comes to the father's territory. Here directions, movements, and activity dominate, as such dynamic spaces are associated with knowledges of practice or use, and of storytelling.[101] Consider how the pension man's space is actualized both through the narrator's trajectory through the home and emphasis on practices that mark and define its various domestic territories. Beginning with a series of passage ways with iron gates and railings, then ringing to be let in by a servant, eventually the reader arrives at the pension man's apartment, enters through a "brown door," and passes through the "antechamber" before finally arriving in the "large room":

> In this room, all the walls were completely papered over with portraits of famous men. There was not a single patch, not the size of a hand, where the original wall could be seen. So that he, or sometimes a friend, when one came, could contemplate the men quite near or right next to the floor, he had had leather-padded lounges made of varying heights and on rollers. . . . One could roll a lounge to whichever men one liked, recline upon it and contemplate them. For those higher and highest up, he had double-sided rolling ladders . . . which could be

rolled to all parts of the room and from whose steps one gained different perspectives. . . . As far as the fame of these men was concerned, it was all the same to the owner what their life pursuits had been and what pursuits had brought them fame; quite possibly he had them all.[102]

The narratorial movement through rooms and the depiction of movability of the objects in them recall the telling "operation" of a "tour" produced through language. In reference to ordinary language practices, which divide descriptions and narrations of the home into two categories, *tours* or *maps*, de Certeau notes that spatial stories emphasize "either *seeing* (the knowledge of an order of places) or a *going* (spatializing action); . . . it presents a tableau . . . or it organizes *movements*."[103] The technique of the "map" used for the wife's rooms presents objects according to a geographical system, and thus provides a version of the childhood home as a detemporalized "plane projection totalizing observations," belonging to "scientific discourse." With echoes of Foucault's classical *episteme*, de Certeau notes that as with the mapping practices of the seventeenth century, such descriptions of locations in space appear as "autonomous"; they are "constituted as proper places in which to *exhibit the products* of knowledge, [they] form tables of *legible* results."[104] By contrast the "tour," he suggests, belongs to "'ordinary' culture" and recalls the early figural mapping practices of the fifteenth century that emphasized sequential forms such as itineraries, movement, and narrations of actions, and which represented a temporalized, historical journey.[105]

The trope of movability in the pension man's room reinforces the sense of history (over domesticity), and his completist impulse manifested in the collection of "heroes" places him in line with the queer antiquarian father figures of *Indian Summer*. When the pension man befriends a local famous face, the actor Dall, the portraits of great men reproduce more than just history, they are, as it were, an incitement to discourse: The two men are virtually inseparable, spending hours lounging and discussing the portraits.[106] The room takes on a philosophical-poetic caricature of Plato's *Symposium*, as a salon where men gather and recline on sofas and discuss matters of their knowledge. Dall and the pension man make for cheap descendants of Plato's philosopher-lovers, as they are only able to "chat" about the famous faces rather than produce eloquent encomia.[107] Like the paper portraits ("Blättern von Bildnissen") that they are always gazing at, the two "acquaintances" are themselves "bad copies" of their philosophical forefathers.[108] Freeman's characterization of the queer offspring as a "bad copy" works well here, not only in the sense that "a lesbian is a bad copy of a man," but also so in the sense of media (images) that are "inferior derivations and the inheritance of qualities that have no value to middle-class culture."[109]

This gallery of portraits also queers the conventions of family pictures that both Ahmed and Freeman have identified as the visible sequence of heterosexual reproduction. Family trees appear through images of families posed as couples or seated according to age, or where family members' physical resemblances are made visible through serial displays of images.[110] The gallery in "Tourmaline" has no discernible organization, following the logic of sheer collection over linearity. Indeed, the pension man's portraits fail to depict his own child at all (the family's future) and, instead violate "spatial conventions" of genealogy by offering all manner of vantage points, where the temporality of inheritance is scattershot, backward and lateral, as the walls covered in "famous men" utterly destroy the sense of a "simple reproductive sequence."[111]

The failure of family timing, as it were, for the pension man and his family is made visible when the narrator of the inner/embedded narrative discovers that the "girl with the big head and broad features was the rosy infant" and it was the pension man, her father, who had just died, leaving her with no evidence of his estate, and nothing but "a few shoddy utensils, some old clothing, and the beds" and "and a little sack filled with copper coins."[112] Here the queer child is herself also a "bad copy": Now grown and destitute, she fails to inherit the father's defining feature, his pension. Instead, as Eva Geulen has argued, the orphan girl's frozen stare and oversized head points the reader back to the pension man's portraits, while her strangely elevated, literary-sounding diction recalls Dall's "august" theatrical roles.[113] *These* resemblances are queer in that they do all but connect the girl to her mother and father: Resemblance points backward in time, to the objects of her father's gaze and the sound of his "constant" "acquaintance." The child's "bad timing" can, of course, also be read in her features, as "the unusual shape of her head and face" also distorts the temporality of aging as the narrator remarks that it is "impossible" for her "to discern how old she might be."[114] For Freeman, "bad timing" includes all manner of "misfiring of dialogue" and "flat affect," where the delivery of lines produces a "queer accent."[115] Accent, she notes, is not just a spatiotemporal indication; it also articulates the idea of affinity and belonging—that one "shares" an accent by participating in "conventions of timing" (meter, spoken rhythm, prosody).[116] The way the girl with the big head speaks—her accent, as it were—was "so strange" that it was "unlike anything expressed in our everyday intercourse" as it sounded like nonsense that was somehow also in part "sagacious."[117] Just as paperwork has vanished, leaving no role for her as the pension man's inheritor, the girl's speech reveals that there is no community of speakers to which she belongs. With a voice that is both childlike and distinguished, her accent mixes class and genre to impossible effect (as the narrator cannot even reproduce it herself!).

The problem of temporal and spatial disjunctures runs throughout the novella and materializes as gaps in knowledge—or knowledge that appears out of joint. The girl with the big head is the queer failure of the child in the arbor, spending her time in her tiny underground dwelling, staring through the mesh window covers for days on end, watching the shoes and hems of pedestrians outside, and despite the order imposed by the window's grid, her gaze offers no help to her in discerning what is happening out in the world.[118] The pension man never locates his wife; the embedded narrator never confirms the pension man's finances; and the frame narrator is always keen to note how for all the searching and inquiring and conjecture, the primary fate of the pension man is that there is no future for this family. And, of course, the very structure of the novella gestures backward in the anachrony of discovery, retroactively connecting the embedded narrative's "girl with the big head" and the frame narrative's "rosy child." For all the spatial oscillations, in the competing epistemological modes of geography and history, the transition to the inner narrative describes the scandal of Dall, and the pension man vanishing with the child already nods to the threat posed to the fantasy of futurity in being forgotten: "The whole affair had caused a great stir in Vienna; people guessed more or less at the true circumstances, and discussed them for quite some time. . . . But other city affairs intervened, as events always come thick and fast in such places, people spoke of other things, and soon the pension man and his story were forgotten."[119] And even more so, as the story concludes by noting how no one who knew anything is still around—they have all left or died, replaced by a new generation who does not even know *that* anything happened in the first place.[120] The fantasy of futurity is for other families, perhaps, but not this one. This gap in knowledge is followed (and repeated in) both narrative and literal breaks in the text, and when the story resumes, the reader is informed that "a number of years had passed" as the site of narration jumps from the city to the suburbs. The story of the "rosy child" is a queer one, in the Edelmanian sense, in that it is unable to "bring to fulfillment the narrative sequence of history" as there is no one left to tell it.[121]

In this novella we have seen how the figure of the child can also appear as a challenge to the heteronormative assumption that "family is the form through which time supposedly becomes visible as physical likeness extending over generations."[122] In "Tourmaline" there is an absence of visibility (vanishing mothers, children, and inheritances) that makes the family a site of epistemic *insecurity*, and it is the figure of the queer child (the love child of the pension man and all his masculine objects) that appears as the point of failure, or in Edelman's words, "the queer comes to figure the bar to every realization of futurity."[123] All of the epistemological work of observing and gazing, mapping, and telling and retelling (as history and story) that make up the fabric of this novella is not enough to secure the futurity of this family. What the "rosy child" thus makes visible is the fact that pension man's future (being remembered) is not guaranteed, and that the only social world that survives him is also one that also forgets him.

"Limestone" and the Cartographic View of Childhood

If "Tourmaline" is a story in which reproductive futurity is thwarted by, among other things, queer temporalities and the force of forgetting, then Stifter's 1853 novella "Limestone" ("Kalkstein"), which also appeared in *Motley Stones*, presents the inverse: This story presents futurity *only* as memorability with a protagonist who, as an adult, is both childlike and childless. "Limestone" is organized with an additional diegetic layer—with three narrative levels, each one of the nested narratives moves farther backward in time.[124] The novella begins with a frame story, in which friends are engaged in a debate about the nature of human abilities, which introduces the first of the two nested stories, which can be summarized as follows. The novella's main narrator (a friend present for the frame narrative's debate) works as a land surveyor, and he tells of a time when he was assigned to the barren landscape in Corrie Rocks to take measurements to map the region for the state. During this project, he strikes up a lasting friendship with the old country parson, whom he had met at a luncheon some years prior to the assignment. Their friendship begins in earnest when the narrator ends up overnighting at the parsonage because of a sudden storm. The surveyor then gets to see both the priest's life at home and, upon departing the next day, witnesses the town's children wade across a flooded meadow on their way to school. The reader, like the surveying narrator, learns that whenever there is flooding, the priest himself wades out and stands in the deep areas to signal to the children where not to walk in the hopes of preventing a drowning. Over the years, the narrator returns to the parsonage. He checks on his friend during a long illness and eventually hears (the innermost narrative of) the parson's recounting his own childhood, a story that he provides to the surveyor to explain his request: that the latter help ensure that his last will and testament be properly recognized and executed upon his death, as the parson himself had neither children nor surviving relatives to do this for him. Upon the parson's death, the surveyor ensures that the copy of the will—one of three—is read and confirmed, only to discover that his savings were nowhere near enough to ensure the one thing the parson had willed: to build a new school closer to the families, so the children would no longer need to risk drowning.

With its deictic phrasing, the novella begins in the present time of reading, before wending its way backward through narrative levels: "Here I shall tell a tale a friend once told us, a tale in which nothing unusual occurs, but which all the same I have never forgotten."[125] Whereas the pension man's child in "Tourmaline" offers him no prospect of future remembrance, "Limestone" suggests a narrative universe in which the otherwise forgettable story of a childless man will be told again and again in a perpetual (or at least recurring) narrative present. In this way, "Limestone" not only inverts the story of the child-figure (as the parson enjoys no such reproductive future of his own) but also varies the trope of scientific seeing as seen in *Indian Summer*. As the first line and the nested narrative structure already indicate, knowledge and temporality in this novella produce a philosophical poetics of looking back. Between repetitions of the present, depictions of what I want to call uneven time, and the queer figure's storytelling where childhood appears as a "stubborn lingering of pastness," the temporalities of the child and the childlike stand out against the monumental time of the surveyor's geological landscape as well as the futurity of generational time for which the priest's testament would stand.[126]

Like *Indian Summer*, this novella is also filled with tropes of observing and recording, where the epistemic work involves making the otherwise invisible become visible. Here the expectation from the narrator is one both one of "scientific" seeing, in his capacity to precisely measure and reproduce three-dimensional spaces of the world as "miniatures on paper" *as well as* a narrative intermediary, someone with a familiarity with childhood—as he describes himself as a "a great friend of children"—and the character who relates and makes memorable the parson's story of childhood.[127] Though recent scholarship has often focused on the land surveyor as representative of Stifter's interest in the natural landscape and geological sciences,[128] the surveyor's narrative omnipresence emphasizes both the significance of the description of place—that is, the *topo*graphia—and the knowledge and the communication of childhood within a conception of space that corresponds to a Foucauldian "taxonomic area of visibility."[129] Here the tropes of repeating and collecting (critical both to the geometer's work of gathering measurements and reflective of Stifter's own epistemological program in his oft-discussed preface to *Motley Stones*) are also signatures of childhood in *Limestone*, and the basis for the novella's backward turn.

Having "been sent to map out the region . . . [where he was] surveying the hills and valleys so as to set them down in miniature on paper,"[130] Stifter's narrator corresponds to the large-scale map-making undertakings of the Austrian Empire in the nineteenth century. With its tabular recordings of populations, towns, and geographic features, maps like those created during the great Franciscan Land Survey (Franziszeische Landesaufnahme), sought to produce both topographic and demographic images of the Habsburg Empire. These projects followed similar endeavors by the previous Habsburg authorities, thus making the land surveyor's job fundamentally repetitive—both in terms of acts of notation collecting measurements, but also in the sense that someone had already been there and done that.[131] Each successive round of mapping enacted a separation between the given terrain and its residents, and the earth's chronology and local history as such images presented a static snapshot—an image in a series. The Habsburg's projects thus depended on the classical epistemic opposition between the artificially imposed boundaries of taxonomic knowledge and the continuity and chaos of lived reality. That the central narrator presumably was sent to Corrie Rocks as part of such an endeavor makes the aesthetic and epistemological project of the land surveyor (cartography, topography) a germane lens for thinking about the centrality of this structure of seventeenth-century classical thought. The map, like any picture, is a pure sign—a binary, "a relation to an object [thing represented] and a manifestation of itself [an image as object]."[132] As I have articulated in the preceding pages, depictions of childhood in Stifter's prose often involve an organizing gaze that depends on collecting—in this instance, measurements of the landscape—making visible what would otherwise not be perceivable. And here, such an image of the Corrie Rocks region relates directly to the place it represents, while also making visible a view of Corrie Rocks which neither the surveyor nor its residents have ever had. Like Heinrich's lake-veil drawing, such an image is not a representation any individual experience (in time). The map flattens and removes the "real world," as it were, from the linear time of development, transforming "real, geographic and terrestrial space" into a tabular representation of calculable and empirical order: "the analytic one of classification."[133] Although the map itself stands "outside chronology," Stifter's epistemic affinities with the trope of the surveyor thus also trace *backward* through intellectual history (as even his contemporaries had already begun to think in dynamic temporalized terms), while at the narrative level, the surveyor facilitates the reader's view into the past by retelling the parson's story to the frame narrator—thus the novella appears as both epistemic and narrative anachrony.[134]

This tension between the representational space of the map and the "real, geographic, terrestrial space" is particularly evident the morning after the cloudburst. The surveyor recounts the first moments of taking in the flooded landscape, and learning that even in the face of such an extraordinary storm, the repetition of daily life continues for the town's children:

> I walked toward the Zirder to see what effects its flooding had brought, and what changes it had wrought in its immediate surroundings. Having stood a while by the water, and watched it at work, . . . I suddenly experienced a spectacle I had never seen before, and had company I had not yet been granted in this rocky country. . . . As I looked, I saw a jaunty, merry boy crossing the bridge from the far bank, which sloped down into the floodwaters of the Zirder, he knelt and, as far as I could see through my spyglass, untied his shoelaces and took off his shoes and socks. . . . A moment later a second boy came and did the same. Then came a barefoot boy, who stopped as well, and then several more. At last a whole flock of children came walking across the bridge, and when they reached the end of it, they ducked down, just as a flock of birds come flying through the air and descends upon some small patch of ground, and I could clearly see that they were all busy taking off their shoes and socks.[135]

One by one they entered the water, each child routinely repeating the same gesture en masse, as the surveyor learns they must do whenever the Zirder floods their path to school. While the floodplain crossing is in itself extreme in terms of the threat it poses to their tiny bodies, it sometimes constitutes a part of their everyday routine. To counter this threat, they are told to perform this action en masse—and so the rehearsal takes on its multiplicative character. Each child, and there are many, must repeat the action, and this then must be repeated each time there is a storm. Like the insignificant appearances of data that Stifter cites in his "Gentle Law," which are usually overlooked even when they are perceptible, the lives of these children, like the parson's own childhood, play out as ordinary scenes of repetition that occur outside the primary field of (adult) vision. And in calling this scene a "spectacle" ("Schauspiel"), Stifter emphasizes not only its specular quality, but also its distance. It is the surveyor's point of view across the river—as though he were seeing another world—that also constitutes the privileged and rare view of childhood. Even here, those features of the surveyor's vision come to the fore: Focusing by trade on the minutest measurements, scale, and proportion, he is one who observes and records those aspects of the everyday world that go unregistered by most. Like the scientist of the "Gentle Law," he practices a profession consisting in the practice of inverting significance (i.e., the grand landscape understood as the sum total of all the tiny measurements). As we saw in *Indian Summer*, the first glimpse of childhood in "Limestone" shows this trope of doing-again; it too follows the temporal logic of the "everyday" as that of predictable repetition—what Lefebvre calls "monotony"—that also masks the fact of constant change.[136]

Like the temporal distortion of the map, which represents the dynamism of "real" geological space as frozen, childhood appears as its "repetitive gesture" against both the real "variability" of everyday life and the disguising of any temporality of development.[137]

The seemingly abrupt appearance of the parson's unexpected silhouette in the scene of childhood is described thus: "He stood nearly up to his hips. I had not noticed him earlier, nor had I seen him wade in, for my eyes had been fixed on the bridge the whole time, and only as the children moved in my direction had I shifted my gaze to the foreground."[138] When the surveyor and parson meet on the water's edge afterward, the narrator notes that

> as he stood there in the children's midst, I saw that he must have been far deeper in the water than they, for he was wet to the hips and beyond, a depth that would have reached up to some the children's necks. Not understanding the discrepancy, I asked him about it. He said it was easy to explain. The Wenn farmer, who owned the flooded meadow where he had been standing in the water just now, had dug rocks out of the meadow the day before yesterday, and carted them away. A pit was left behind. Today seeing the meadow by the Zirder covered in water, he had thought that the children's path might pass close to this pit, and one of them might come to harm. And so he thought to stand next to the pit, deep as it was dug. The meadow would have to be leveled again; for the water was murky when it flooded, and concealed the depth and the irregularity of the ground underfoot.[139]

Stifter links the scene of childhood with the problem of visibility that runs throughout the stories discussed here. The repetition of children's bodies moving through the water combined with the parson's wet body produces an aggregation of measurements, like measuring sticks or weighted lines, that make the floor of the "murky" body of water visible to the surveyor.[140] What the floodwaters had hidden (change, danger, futility), the children and their childlike guardian reveal with their bodies. At the same time, however, the very topography of the space is presented as *so* dynamic as to be effectively unmeasurable for purposes of map-making: The farmer keeps digging pits in the meadow that the floodwaters then regularly obscure, and then the meadow is graded, thus changing the landscape once again. The Corrie Rocks region resists conceptions of a world governed by natural time, one that is purely cyclical, when human intervention arbitrarily thwarts this, with changes happening in staccato fashion for manmade as well as meteorological reasons. In the aggregate, the children's everyday habit—the repetition of crossing the meadow, under all but the most impassable circumstances—makes the unpredictability of the landscape visible, emphasizing both the need and the impossibility of mapping the space at all.

This scene at the water's edge is also instructive of the parson's childlike character: He looks like them, appearing "in their midst," and he is soaking wet. Both the town's children and the parson, as the story shows, appear almost comical in the futility of their efforts: They take off their socks only to let their skirts and trousers get soaked. The supposed security offered by moving as a group fails to account for the fact that should tragedy befall one (a slick current), it would repeat, as all of them would drown. Their lives are characterized by a kind of repetition without progress: just doing it all over again. As Eva Geulen has astutely pointed out, in Stifter's texts the figure of the child is often characterized as a combination of not knowing (*Unwissen*) and a failure to learn (since becoming knowledgeable would mean no longer being a child), and here the parson is exemplary.[141] When he tells his friend, the surveyor about his life, beginning from childhood, the would-be story of his *Bildung*—his education and development—repeatedly goes wrong, making this innermost narrative one of failure and return.

The parson's story begins before his birth, setting the scene with two generations of tanners. The wealth and commercial success of the family had grown by the time the parson and his twin brother, then children, were being raised and educated to someday continue the family business—not of tanning but of running an entire company that had showrooms for selling goods made by tradespeople in their employ and retailing the goods from other makers. The story of the parson begins largely at home: "I recall from my childhood that our house was very large and spacious, that it had many yards and rooms used for business operations."[142] But the children were housed in their own section of the property: "As the street was noisy, we were put in the back wing, facing the garden, which out father added to the house."[143] Like the pension man's flat in Vienna, this parson's childhood home is unfolded for the reader like a de Certeauean tour, as the parson recounts how the children's rooms were separated by a hallway from the main house and that there were "stairs built in the garden wing allowing us to go straight to the garden and from there to the street."[144] Here the map-making narrator shifts registers to that of the tour, as he retells the words told to him by the parson: This innermost narrative is one of *space*; in contrast to the merely "delimited field" of place, it is a "*practiced place*."[145] From de Certeau we can recognize in the parson's recollection the narrative work of space as operation, movement, repetition, and history—in other words, the space of childhood is not a frozen image, but one that appears as *use*. And the paragraphs that follow are indeed filled with details of how objects (linens and china, desks and school supplies) were used, stored, and cared for.[146] Much like the parson's life in Corrie Rocks, the story and ritual are tightly bound together.[147]

The parson's childhood, however, quickly seems to go off track: Unlike his twin, he is unable to learn to read and write with ease. Where his brother's penmanship was picture perfect ("always even [gleich], and on the line"), the parson's penmanship was all wrong: "never even [nicht gleich], they dipped below the line; they pointed in all different directions."[148] Right away the parson himself notices that something is queer: As a child, his lines do not line up—both literally here when he fails to learn to write and later, when he returns to this wing of the home and the scene of childhood writing.[149] Translating in and out of German, the little parson describes how Greek and Latin texts thwarted all his best efforts, with their words continually refusing to submit to his readings, they too seemed not to "fall in line" ("nicht fügen wollen") or "follow the rules" ("die Regeln . . . waren . . . nicht befolgt").[150] Childhood is not just a state of ignorance (which prevents the parson from taking over his role in the family business); it is a failing to fall in line, and one that repeats, as "several years passed this way."[151] And while his twin, now grown, followed the family line and "took over the management of the business," the parson looped back and returned to the children's study.

Like the repeated touring and mapping gestures in "Tourmaline" (when the authorities enter the home after the disappearance), the parson's story also carefully depicts all the spaces and objects once again as "all had been left as it was" such that, for the reader, even at the level of narration the parson is both telling and doing it all over again. This method of looping back is doubled when the parson, no longer so little, returns to his lessons, and repeats each one until memorized.[152] Here even his eventual success at learning seems queerly timed as he is older now and no longer in line for the family business: All those academic subjects are of no use for this profession, and there is no longer time left for him to repeat his apprenticeship in the business. The parson represents a generation out of joint and is also out of joint from his own generation, having fallen out of line to inherit his father's (and grandfather's) role at the helm of the tannery *and* having run out of time to join his twin in that work.[153]

Once the parson is no longer little, his voyeuristic desires start to look both backward and perverse when he develops an infatuation with the girl who lives in the house behind his family compound—and while she vanishes after a few brief encounters, his interest in the fine white linens that she and her mother washed and hung in their garden persist:

> This woman had a little daughter, a child, no she was a child no longer—I didn't rightly know whether she was still a child or not. . . .
> I so loved to look at her, sometimes I stood at the window and looked

over at the garden where washing always hung on the lines. . . . I was very fond of those white things. Then sometimes the girl would come out, cross the meadow . . . or, though the little house was quite hidden behind the branches, I would see her standing by the window and learning her lessons. Soon I knew the time when she carried out the washing, and I would sometimes go down into the garden then and stand by the cast-iron gate [Gitter]. The path went by the gate, and so the girl had to pass me. She knew quite well that I was standing there; for she always blushed [schämte sich] and walked with more restraint.[154]

The objects of desire—the neighbor girl, the linens—are both visible by looking out of the *backside* of the house, and when he sees her in her house, she is doing what he used to do. The spectatorial gaze in "Limestone" is one that looks backward (both spatially and temporally).[155] Like the parson, with the girl it's unclear whether she is "still a child or not," even though the narrative makes clear she is of age, as a few paragraphs later (once her mother discovers the two have been meeting at the gate between their houses), she is sent off to be married. The scene of childhood looking (through windows and the iron gate, from the study that was just for children) recalls the fort, where the child flees from the big world out there. Here the parson, also still a child/no longer a child, gazes from his fort imagining others were children to play with.

While the neighbor girl grows up, the parson keeps his collection of fine white linens and goes off to seminary—the only education that guarantees he will not grow up to have a family of his own. These linens reappear throughout the Corrie Rocks narrative, like a temporal anchor, or wrench in the works, lodging the past in the present or the present in the past. The figure of the priest as childlike points us backward as it reflects Catholic theology from the Middle Ages. Aleida Assmann has described the ascetic ideal of *Senex-Puer* (the childlike old man), where a tiny childlike body corresponds to both an ascetic denial of the body (here it is the old parson's poverty) as a paradisical state of being and an imitation of God, as well as the image of the angel, for which children are exemplary (as they are "unburdened" by sensual desire, ambition, arrogance, etc.) and which are likewise represented in his celibacy and in the white linens he wears and keeps.[156] By the time the surveyor meets him, the parson's body has grown old: He is now the backward-facing man, who lives like he is still in his childhood home, wearing the garments of his youth.

As the surveyor tells the story of the early days of his friendship with the older parson, his observations of him depict a would-be grown-up home that nonetheless remains a space of childhood. The parson "rented out the upper floor of his parsonage. A man had come along who had held an office and then retired, and was now living off his income in the place of his birth. He had availed himself of the parson's rented room to take up lodgings there with his daughter so that he could look out on the setting in [den Schauplaz vor Auge haben] which he had spent his childhood."[157] The parson's grown-up home is also the site from which another can return to his "birthplace," and just as the parson had gazed from his childhood rooms on the garden below, so too does his renter enjoy having his own childhood view restaged before him. As a "balm" and "delight," the view from the rented room is a "sweet attraction in old age" that returns the adult to his childhood fort, as it were.[158] The spectatorial quality of childhood is not just the idea that childhood needs an observer, as Geulen has noted about the "Kinderfreund" surveyor, who watches the children cross the flooded meadow from afar, but it is also in the backward-looking gesture of childhood: the still childlike parson returned to his childhood room and watched his childlike neighbor from the window, and then the old parson—the *Senex-Puer*—rents his home to yet another old man who is also looking to return to the view of his childhood.

The parson's home also unfolds for the surveyor as a space, in de Certeau's sense: defined by use and repetition: his "practice" ("Gewohnheit") of sitting at his table in the main room by day without candle light (and lighting a candle during storms), taking all his meals at that same table, meals consisting of mostly black bread and milk, and sleeping on a bare bench in the vestibule, each night wearing the same gray woolen nightclothes, and each morning dressing himself in his shabby black clothes in the side room used for storage.[159] The surveyor misses this side room at first, but once the parson shows it to him, he learns that it is filled with dilapidated furniture that store the parson's bread and milk and white linens.[160] The surveyor learns that the parson's practice of frugality and saving every penny had also lead to the repetition of being robbed three times.[161] Collectively, these scenes reveal the parson's character as one which over the course of the text will come to resemble something like "pure praxis"—that is, his habituality becomes *his* defining feature.[162] The repetition of childhood transforms into the parson's daily and lifelong ritual.

The parson concludes his own story by noting that what should now be visible is that no sense of development has occurred whatsoever by remarking: "You see, now I have told you everything, how it has been with me, and how it is still."[163] Eva Geulen's succinct description of the innermost narrative of "Limestone" also parallels the impossibility of development beyond childhood: "It is about a story that never became one, a nonstory of a became-nothing."[164] The temporality of the parson's story is just like his life and afterlife, that is to say, it is one of repetition and failure. Nowhere is this more crystal clear than in the fate of his will and testament, which he asks his friend to ensure is received and executed. After he passes away, the surveyor discovers that the parson had repeated his work, distributing the copies in triplicate. With all that he had been saving, his wishes were that a school be built on the near side of the river Zirder. In death, the parson's childlike studiousness and naïveté became visible: "The accounts from that point to the parson's death were found in his papers. They had been kept with great rigor. From them, too, one saw how diligently the parson had saved. The very smallest amounts, even pennies."[165] Like a child carefully tending his collection of odds and ends, and tallying every coin, but having no idea how much things really cost, it turned out that "the sum that the parson had saved and the sum accruing from the auction of his belongings were much too small to set up a school."[166] In death, the parson finally resembles his childless, bankrupt, and deceased twin brother—neither son having been able to produce a meaningful inheritance on his own. In "Limestone," it is the rich inhabitants of the Corrie Rocks region, and even the surveyor and his wife, who underwrite the eventual construction of a new school.[167]

Even if this is a story about a "became-nothing," de Certeau reminds us that the work of narration does more than reflect the repetition and practice that makes (e.g., the parson's childhood) space *space*. Indeed, narrativity is what "founds" space in the multivalent senses of "authorizing" and "creating," and the "setting and transgressing [of] limits."[168] Storytelling, for de Certeau, is itself a "dynamic partitioning of space" that yields a "frontier and a bridge." We see this interplay of dimension and orientation through the nested connectivity of narration in "Limestone": the frame narrator's retelling of the surveyor's recounting of the parson's act of storytelling of childhood, all of which takes place inside this old-child's home (a residence which doubles as the viewpoint into childhood for his retired renter). As a "frontier," childhood appears in and through each level of the narrative: the childhood room and garden in the home of a family of tanners, the Corrie Rocks children as they cross the flooded meadow, the childlike existence of the old parson in his meager home, and the parsonage that provides the vista onto the renter's birthplace. But through the work of retelling, these spaces constitute the retrospective "bridges" across narrative levels, forming a never-ending backward view of childhood. It is therefore fitting that the novella's narrator concludes by remarking that in the Corrie Rocks cemetery stands the only cross on "the grave mound of the man who established [auf dem Hügel des Gründers] these things."[169] The work of founding ("gründen") is thus not done with progeny, success, or even smarts, but with *story*. Here an otherwise forgettable story cannot be forgotten and is told and retold instead in an endless narrative present.

Stifter's Revolving Worlds of Childhood

In an echo of the opening scenes of "The Garden Arbor," and of the surveyor's cartographic view and the perspective of the big-headed girl's gridded cellar view, the final scene of Stifter's autobiographical text fragment *My Life (Mein Leben)* once again situates the author's own childhood from an enclosed, domestic space. Here, too, the depiction of childhood follows the same tabular impulses that I have argued for in this chapter:

> At this windowsill I also saw what was happening outside, and I very often said: "There goes a man to Schwarzbach, there a man travels to Schwarzbach, there goes a dog to Schwarzbach, there goes a goose to Schwarzbach." On the windowsill I also set pine shavings [Kienspäne] down lengthwise, to be sure bound them to shavings crosswise [Querspäne] and said: "I'm making Schwarzbach!"[170]

As scholars have variously noted, this scene contains and itself performs many hallmarks of Stifter's poetological program: from the repetition and seriality in the young Stifter's narration to the imposition of the grid.[171] What we can now also see here is Stifter's own reflection on the space of childhood as governed by the same regulating gestures of tabular representation and mapmaking, and also the child's joyful gaze from within the small interior of their own miniature creation, like the fort. As was the case with the figures of the surveyor and the natural historian, Stifter's child-self re-creates the world "happening outside" in a way that both recapitulates it while also flattening it. Reduced to its characters, "Schwarzbach" can be identified in classical epistemic form as a pure sign; its appearance and indication are one and the same.[172] The child's Schwarzbach thus stands in disjointed relation to the real geographical historical municipality: miniaturized, on a windowsill, reduced to the image of the intersection, and also outside chronology, and repeatable.[173]

With its anachronistic commitment to classical thought—and the scientific forms of representation that Foucault tells us belong to centuries long past—Stifter's writings on his own childhood and all the strange fictional ones discussed here evince neither stasis nor dynamism. Rather, each mirrors its own "queer affect," what Freeman describes as "the stubborn lingering of pastness (whether it appears as anachronistic style, as the reappearance of bygone events in the symptom, or as arrested development)."[174] Indeed, knowledge and childhood in Stifter's storytelling appear more like "a 'revolution' in the old sense of the word, as a turning back."[175] Similarly, Stifter's child-figures and the figure of childhood that returns even in scenes of adulthood queerly refuse what Freeman calls "progressive logic." Like the backward epistemologies of Stifter's stories, the philosophical poetics of childhood anticipate the images of queer adulthood in "late-nineteenth-century perverts, melancholically attached to obsolete erotic objects or fetishes they ought to have outgrown, or repeating unproductive bodily behaviors over and over" and whose queerness stands opposed to the forward marches of "commodity-time" and "planned obsolescence."[176]

Stifter's characters are already obsolete, and Freeman's characterization of the queer feels equally applicable to all of the figures of childhood we have seen here: the girl with the big head, the pension man, the parson and his tenant, the antiquarian and the child as collectible, the natural historian and the map-maker, and even the child making forts out of everything and anything. As a turning back, Stifter's childhood narratives insist on a temporality that complicates and even resists many of the established scholarly expectations about Stifter's writing. Here children repeat but they never progress, the order imposed on childhood spaces and things fails to produce the epistemological certainty he desires, and the paternally organized families and education produce nothing but queer offspring.

2
Rainer Maria Rilke's Lifeworlds of Childhood

The View from Childhood

Though Rilke is commonly regarded as one of the most important modernist poets, "early Rilke" was, for a brief time, a productive prose author.[1] During the late 1890s, he experimented with a range of prose formats—from lone vignettes to collections of interlaced short stories. By the time he had completed his only novel, *Die Aufzeichnungen des Malte Laurids Brigge* (*The Notebooks of Malte Laurids Brigge*) in 1910, he had shifted almost exclusively to lyrical forms—a shift reflected in the novel's experimental form. As a young writer, he spent the first half dozen years writing numerous short prose texts, some of which focused on depicting children and childhood. Many of these texts share a philosophical quality that overlaps with observations that Rilke scholars have made about the phenomenological quality of his lyrical writing.[2] In the sections that follow, I show that precisely as prose, these texts are able to present examples of philosophical *storytelling*—that Rilke mobilized not only his poetics (which became a mainstay in his lyrical work) but also his sophisticated use of narrative and descriptive techniques to construct fictional worlds that range from realist to fabulist. To paraphrase Rilke's well-known poetic modus operandi, telling stories of childhood feels like learning to see what children see. I will show how such stories contrast the child's standpoint of the *now* of lived reality and worldliness with the future-oriented work of being grown up, engaged in the reproduction of social and religious practices.

The children that appear in Rilke's stories operate as figures of resistance against adult regimes—not in the sense of teenage rebellion but rather like critical reminders of the matter that composes our lifeworld and the very strangeness of its perception.[3] I make the argument that in their apprehension of the world children tell us something about the limits and missteps of grown-up attention. They serve as disturbances to theory: Much like Hans Blumenberg's characterization of the Thracian woman's laughter at the sight of the astronomer Thales tumbling into a well while stargazing, Rilke's child-characters offer the reader a critical reminder of the lifeworld that undergirds reality.[4] Just as the woman's laughter makes perceptible "theory's" blindness to the material world,[5] Rilke's child-figures mark the contrast to their adult counterparts who, like Thales, are the ones caught tragically "looking up" toward an ideal world of morals, values, and manners. In keeping with Blumenberg, I suggest that we "reoccupy" the Thales anecdote once more: For Rilke, children experience the world as a universe of everyday things—the collection of tiny objects in their pockets, the autumnal light as it scatters on the wall, the sunflowers seen from the train windows.[6] They are the ones who notice the absurdity of adult experience; they remind us that we adults have missed what Blumenberg's Thracian woman points out as always "in front of [our] very nose and feet."[7] Throughout Rilke's corpus, children appear as laughing bystanders: They are charged with returning the reader to the world—a "thicket of things"—already in front of them, even against the prevailing adult world of fragmented modern subjectivity.[8] Indeed, Rilke's advice to the "young poet," Franz Xavier Kappus in 1903, includes an aesthetic of rejection of the world of adulthood: "And when one day one perceives that [adults'] occupations are paltry, their professions petrified and no longer linked with living, why not continue to look like a child upon it all as upon something unfamiliar, from the depths of your own world . . . ? Why want to exchange a child's wise incomprehension . . . ?"[9]

Children, for Rilke, are unconcerned with the impoverished world of adult demands. They encounter all the otherwise easily *overlooked* objects around them with an unfettered perception, investing them with their vision, imagination, and reflection. Rather than focusing on the deficiency or naïveté of childhood, writing about children requires attention to the workings of experience; it requires that we ask how seeing the world of objects in experience is connected to its apprehending subjectivity. In Rilke's prose universe, children are not only thinkers of the ordinary world of things, of what we might think of as the lifeworld—the world in front of our noses and feet—they also invite *readers* to consider what it looks like when we are engaged in forms of perception, fantasy, and sense-making. They show us a novel view of the world.

We will see what makes Rilke's experiments with childhood storytelling so radical: His stories and prose fragments run absolutely counter to modern narrative conventions of child-figures that Lee Edelman has characterized as "carr[ying] the burden of maintaining the fantasy of a time to come."[10] Rilke's literary descriptions counter the rhetoric that, for Edelman, exemplifies a ubiquitous heteronormativity which the figure of the child smuggles into social, political, and literary discourses: namely, that the child is the future, children are progress itself, and so on:[11] "For politics, however radical the means by which specific constituencies attempt to produce a more desirable social order, remains, at its core, conservative insofar as it works to *affirm* a structure, to *authenticate* social order, which it then intends to transmit to the future in the form of its inner Child. That Child remains the perpetual horizon of every acknowledged politics, the fantasmatic beneficiary of every political intervention."[12]

Against the appeal of an emerging discourse of futurity, Rilke's prose imagines children that do not serve as mere symbols for cultural, political, or labor progress. They are not indices for ongoing generational reproduction, nor are they a cover for the unthinkability of parental pleasure and mortality. Instead, these children are fully formed philosophical subjects rooted in their own present-time, engrossed in their own cognition. These children radically exist for themselves.

A first example of Rilke's turn to children as queer observers and of his use of philosophical storytelling is the short story, "Wie der Fingerhut kam dazu, der liebe Gott zu sein" (How the thimble came to be God) from 1899. The text follows seven children as they attempt to correct for their parents' failure to see the world's meaning in all the ordinary, little things. The story is told by a first-person narrator who, in the frame narrative, establishes himself as offering something like a God's-eye view, pretending to be a cloud himself as he engages a pair of actual clouds at sunset with his anecdote. This "cloud" recounts the time he observed and overheard the children discussing how to address their parents' shortcomings. The children appear almost as realists—that is, emphatically emerging from within the lifeworld—and with an admonishment of adult epistemological misconceptions and their resulting misplaced priorities. By taking the title and the story's anecdotal form together, Rilke already seems to unite philosophy and poetics in a Blumenbergian manner, while the story's content offers a double critique of adult ways of knowing—children see what the adults do not, and thus are able to lampoon the grown-ups' emphasis on norms and conventions over material conditions, and, in particular, the absurdity of relying on religious ideals of Christianity instead of on the everyday world of lived experience.

This opposition of the real and unreal unfolds as the oldest child in the group, Hans, puts the problem with the grown-ups as follows: "What do our parents do? They go around with cross expressions, nothing is right for them, they scream and scold, but at the same time they are really so blasé; if the world were destroyed, they would hardly notice. They have something they call 'ideals.'"[13] Adults' worries and frustrations are misdirected: With their focus on abstract standards and concepts, they largely miss the very world around them. This is especially preposterous, Hans suggests, as these same grown-ups who are supposed to be responsible for educating children are more concerned with bourgeois conventions and policing shallow norms, such as tipping their hats and laughing when the other is bald.[14] The child's monologue reveals the children's view of adulthood as an ongoing theater of social niceties—or, as Adorno would later remark: "All collaboration, all the human worth of social mixing and participation, merely masks the tacit acceptance of inhumanity."[15]

With a childlike literalism and charm, Hans identifies what is perhaps the most alarming fact of all: that God has yet to be seen among their parents, despite the fact that they all claim to "have" him.[16] Hans speculates that in their "absentmindedness, busyness, and haste," these adults must have lost track of God.[17] The children in this story take up the charge of locating God in order to ensure the ongoing existence of their entire world of things, from the sun rising to the availability of bread.[18] Rilke's child philosopher, Hans, offers a reading of God not as creator but as the lived experience of the prosaic world—a radical view by any church standard;[19] here, God resides in (or as) the things around them. Rilke's child sees the divine *not* as a transcendent, omnipotent being observing a world of his creation, but rather as the very ubiquity and continuity of everyday experience itself. The children decide they will each take a turn carrying and attending to God, but must first determine what kind of *thing* God is.[20] Thus they find themselves faced with "a great quandary" ("eine große Verlegenheit"), the focus of which appears less theological than phenomenological: Which things of experience would be best suited for this task and what would such an experience be like?[21] Hans suggests that "everything can be God" because "a thing, you see, it stays, you come into the room, daytime, nighttime: it's always there, I dare say it can be God."[22] Rilke's philosopher child recasts the divine as the subject's relationship to everyday objects over time.[23] This emphatic interrelatedness of subject and object is repeated with poetic-realist detail when the "cloud" narrator describes the scene in which Hans instructs the other children to empty their pockets to assess which little objects would be best to serve as the "dear Lord":

> Very curious [seltsam] things now appeared: paper clippings, a pen knife, an eraser, feathers, thread, little stones, screws, whistles, little wood shavings, and much else that [the narrator] couldn't identify from such a distance, or where the word for it escaped [him]. And all these things lay in the shallow hands of the children, as if frightened

by the sudden possibility of becoming the dear Lord, and of those that could gleam, gleamed to please Hans.[24]

Rilke's fictional children are described like real ones—their pockets filled with all the detritus of ordinary play. The location of the divine in this odd mix of "things" is itself a bit queer (*seltsam*) as each of these pocket-treasures is taken from elsewhere and thus appears out of place, out of context, out of joint. As the objects in this queer collection lay there exposed, so tiny and trivial, they are also displayed for their double potential: for poetic transfiguration ("to become the dear Lord") and for philosophical exemplarity as an everyday object—available in experience, through sight and touch. Indeed, the relationality between object and subject is evident in the way they "gleam" back at the inquiring child. The philosophical-poetic object—transfigured and exemplary—appears by virtue of the attending subject, Hans.

The final scene of the story rests on a continued play of light and visibility, trading the religious for the phenomenological,[25] while simultaneously reinforcing the *invisibility* of childhood knowledge. After selecting a little silvery thimble—on account of its luminosity—they each take turns carrying "God" in their pockets, until, on the seventh day, little Marie ("Mariechen") discovers the object has fallen out of her pocket and seems altogether lost.[26] She spends hours combing the meadow looking for "a thimble," accompanied at turns by various adults, each of whom gives up when their backs quickly begin to ache from stooping over. Eventually, "the meadow became stranger and stranger in the twilight, and the grass started to become wet." When a stranger returns to walk her home and asks what she's looking for, she replies, "the dear Lord," and he responds with a smile. On the way, he says, "And look here, what a lovely thimble I found today." This quizzical ending presents two possible views of childhood from the only adult character within the cloud's anecdote: (1) the man had been at the meadow already, found the thimble that she'd been searching for someplace else, and returns to give it to her. He smiles when she says she's looking for God in the way that adults trivialize the seriousness of children's interests; or (2) the man happened to have found a shiny thimble someplace and offers it, knowing that children are easily pleased by trivial objects. What both readings share is a dismissal of the enterprise of childhood. The child's "searching for God" in the meadow is the child's work of deciphering what makes the world the world; it is an enactment of a philosophical practice in which things and their observers are already messily entangled in the world. But like Blumenberg's critique of theory's own blindness, the adult sees only the inconsequential business of childhood—conveyed with a condescending smile.[27] The children's insistence that there is a truer knowledge available through material experience—which trumps the adult world of manners—remains ignored, save for the omniscient view, narrated from above. On the second reading, the recognition that children are delighted by little things ("a lovely thimble") relegates childhood attention to easy enchantments and whims. In either reading, Rilke portrays the adult as failing to recognize the philosophical capacity that children possess. We can extend the comparison with Blumenberg's Thracian woman to say that the children in Rilke's story are similarly injected into the scene of philosophy by their recognition of their parents' stumbling and failing. To paraphrase Paul Fleming's summary of the woman from Thrace, the philosophical incisiveness of these children issues from their multiple functions and positions: Although at first appearing as mere members of the lifeworld (they are just kids), the children are also spectators and theorists (*theoroi*) (looking for God in a thimble) who belong to the scene of philosophy of the lifeworld—in other words, "by representing their lifeworld, they are standing in for and, thus, also outside of it."[28]

In contrast to the world of adults, the world of children is marked by their attention to ordinary experience—from the little objects that distinguish themselves as they glimmer to the distortion and indistinguishability that happens to the meadow as the sunlight fades. Children transform the scene of knowledge from concepts (God, ideals, norms) to quotidian experience (glimmering thimbles, grass at dusk). In the latter, as Edmund Husserl suggested, we are given the world of objects only in profiles—that is, as partial and variable (*Ideas*, §41).[29] Rilke's child-figures subvert the romantic notion of childhood as a nearness to God, pointing instead to their subjective fields of perception, where ordinary life appears as the now of determinate experience. What this story shows is Rilke's tendency to foreground childhood experience as both poetic and as philosophical: Child-figures convey the metaphoricity *and* the phenomenology of the everyday world. Grounded in the encounter with materiality—found and recovered objects, scraps of paper, and feathers—childhood is set against the prevailing cultures of adulthood and family. Indeed, the child's wandering in the meadow while bent over and staring into the grass appears queer—both in the sense of a queer sight (to behold) and taking a queer line of sight (perspective that seems out of line with that of the grown-up world.[30] We might therefore also characterize the critique that Hans lodges against the parents (which gets Marie into the meadow in the first place) as a refusal to grow *up*, to following their line of thinking. Recalling Kathryn Bond Stockton, here Rilke's queer child-character grows "laterally" rather than up, staying put, looking down or sideways at the world of things, and lingering with childishness.[31]

Like Sara Ahmed's philosophical example of the "happy baby," Rilke's child-characters also suffer from the "problem of character" in ways that traverse assumptions about childhood in general and fictional child-figures in particular.[32] "The idea of character," in Ahmed's example, is not just "an idea of consistency": It is an attribution that comes to have a reality of its own; it is the "expectation of consistency" that organizes the child-subject's experience of themselves as much as it orders the perceptions of them by adults.[33] Thus, as Ahmed notes, whenever the "happy baby" cried, "he was out of character."[34] In their failure to adhere to adult regimes of knowledge, and in their willingness to explore alternative theories, Rilke's depiction of Hans and his friends includes within it the somewhat Lockean attribution that children are "plastic," as their "minds" are seen here to be "easily turned, this way or that, as water itself."[35] But this characteristic of childhood is also precisely what enables Rilke to deploy children as intervening in the misguided situation of adulthood. Rilke's children do not depart from the expectations of the child as easily delighted by unimportant objects while also taking the trivial far too seriously. Instead, the "force" of these characterizations is made visible when the grown-up appears. Reading with Ahmed, we can see Rilke's portrayal of the adult's "investment in character," attributing little Marie's unbroken attention to the trivial (the thimble) as the reification of what is attributed to childhood (the adult smiling at her frivolousness).[36] Crucially, by centering children first as independent of their adults, Rilke's cloud fable also *resists* the sentiment of this characterization and instead allows the reader to imagine children not as on the way to knowing but rather as already serious critics and as theorists of ordinary experience. Children, to return to Blumenberg, are naturally suited phenomenologists, interested as they are in the "science of trivialities."[37]

"Seeing more; not more than seeing": What Children See in "Pierre Dumont"

If Rilke has generally been regarded as a poet rather than a narrative writer, it was partly because the bulk of his prose work was written in the first decade of his career, and partly because his prose, in retrospect, bears so many of the aesthetic hallmarks of his subsequent lyrical projects.[38] Although he wrote some eighty stories between 1893 and 1903, their genres remain difficult to taxonomize. While Rilke himself referred to them as stories ("Geschichten"), novellas, and sketches ("Skizzen"), these brief narratives are sometimes furnished with only minimal elements of plot: Some, like the above-discussed "How the Thimble Became God," are easily identified as a short story within a collection, while others are so plot-bare that they might be better characterized as anecdotes, miniatures, scenes of the everyday ("Alltagszenen"), or what Bernard Dieterle broadly describes as "narrative figments" ("Erzählgebilde").[39] These stories, and in particular the depictions of children's experiences, make use of this relatively plot-poor impressionistic genre in ways that center on the phenomenological capacity of narration, while also eschewing a future-oriented arch that conventionally teleological narratives employ to frame the present-time of ordinary experience. As we will see, Rilke's fictional scenes, or "narrative figments," share a set of affinities with Husserl's phenomenology and with Blumenberg's subsequent interventions. Rilke's famous poetic motto from the *Malte* book—"ich lerne sehen" (I am learning to see)—which articulates the protagonist's and poet's task of an ever-more capacious seeing, as well its correlative in his writings on painting and sculpture—"simply seeing" ("einfaches schauen")—reflect Rilke's desire to develop a "craft" of poetic writing that more adequately captures the world of visible phenomena.[40] Antje Büssgen has rightly emphasized that Rilke's aesthetics are grounded in the notion that people are simply "eye-people" ("Augenmenschen"), that they are profoundly oriented toward and affected by optical phenomena. As a writer who describes his own "intellectual acquisition of the world" as "so fully employ[ing] the eye," Rilke's characterization of his own philosophical-poetic project approximates the work of phenomenologists like Husserl and Blumenberg, for whom the task of philosophy is, in some ways, merely rendering the world into language, and for whom *seeing* and being able to adequately *describe* what one sees are the critical acts.[41]

In this section, I read Rilke's stories of childhood as grappling with the challenges of phenomenology at the heart of both Husserl's and Blumenberg's theorizing: with the problem of seeing as linked with literary and artistic expression; and with the idea that the proper domain of philosophy is the description of our experience and the things contained therein, rather than the articulation of metaphysical and ontological trajectories. Just as Husserl and Blumenberg do not present us with fully consonant philosophical approaches or stable assumptions, and, taken individually, their philosophical corpora are not always internally coherent, so too do Rilke's depictions of childhood shift in their emphases. In view of this fluidity, this chapter moves freely between Husserl and Blumenberg, as their overlapping concepts serve to provide helpful phenomenological idioms for drawing out the philosophical stakes in Rilke's prose. Rilke's writings on childhood share the aims (and challenges) inaugurated by Husserl and encapsulated in Blumenberg's posthumously published reflections on the work of the phenomenologist: that is, as one who is engaged in the "description of phenomena . . . on the basis of intuition [Anschauung] and its evidence," but for whom this practice is understandably complicated by the "difficulties with language" whenever one tries "to translate [umsetzen] intuition into description."[42] In Rilke's attention to describing the children's perceptions of the objects in their often strange and expansive lifeworld, the work of describing childhood thus seeks to address this "oldest problem in philosophy."[43]

A brief prose text, "Pierre Dumont,"[44] written some time before 1894, provides us with an example of the ways in which Rilke's philosophical poetics of childhood rely on conventions of narrative fiction to capture precisely these concerns. Before proceeding, however, it will be helpful to first outline relevant moments in Rilke's essay "On Landscape"[45] that provide us with a provisional framework for a philosophy of description as spectatorship, and the co-emergence of seeing subject and seen object. Alongside what Michael McGillen calls Husserl's and Blumenberg's forms of "phenomenological description," Rilke, I suggest, must be read as working out the ways in which children's experience of the world relies on a painstaking portrayal of the relationship between optical phenomena in space and the significance of the finitude of human visual perception prior to the supplements of rational and conceptual knowledge.[46] In the essay, toward the end of his prose period, Rilke reflects on the way landscape paintings convey something more general about the way we see the world. He laments "how poorly one sees the things among which we live," but that it is the perspective of the newcomer, the stranger, the view from a distance, that make our perception of the "objective as a grand, present reality possible."[47] There is a parallel between the possibility of landscape painting in "On Landscape" and the phenomenological attitude of the child, who makes the world visible as a philosophical object in all its strangeness. With a sense of spectatorship that is not bound up in the act of assigning meaning, Rilke's small spectators instead find themselves to be indeed "among the things, like a thing," and thus also marked as the ones who are both seeing and seen.

In "Pierre Dumont," Rilke introduces his titular protagonist as a "tot," barely eleven years old, riding the train with his widowed mother to a military academy.[48] The story itself appears through a mixture of atmospheric prose and the pained dialogue between a mother and her child as both try to hold in their sadness at separating.[49] Without disturbing the metaphorical content of this moody depiction, we can see how Rilke's narrative figment deploys the conventional techniques of prose fiction to show the world as it unfolds in concert with the child Pierre's own inner life. In narrating Pierre's experience of and in the lifeworld, Rilke imagines the child as able to "simply see" the landscape in ways that his mother does not. The child's vision exemplifies Rilke's aesthetic project of learning to see insofar as his visual experience encompasses the ordinary world in its entirety without imposing rational selection, as landscapes dotted with both rural flora and industrial pollution.[50] Here, the "unremarkable" is as worthy of representation as the "great"; the full potential of aesthetic spectatorship encompasses the "entire world itself."[51]

As the child, Pierre, gazes out the window at the passing countryside, the world unfolds for him, and—to paraphrase Husserl—it does so as a correlate of his own consciousness (*Ideas*, §47). Objects move into the range of his perception from, as it were, the background and beyond the frame of the window, that is, from a horizon of that which is yet to be perceived.

> Meanwhile, Pierre stood at the window and looked out at the scenery. They were nearly at the station. The train traveled more slowly and rumbled over the railroad switch. Outside, green embankments, wide expanses, and tiny cottages slid past. Giant sunflowers with their yellow halos stood guard at their doors. The doors, however, were so small that Pierre thought he would probably have had to stoop to even be able to enter.—Then even the cottages vanished.—Black, smoky warehouses arrived.[52]

Although the landscape's details would have been impossible to register at full speed, the child staring out the window of the train as it approaches the station enables him to contemplate the objects easily.[53] With the slow movement of the train, the grassy fields and various buildings each move, in turn, into, and then out of Pierre's "field of the focus of [his] attention" (*Ideas*, §45), and thus we see Rilke's prose presenting the reader with a picture of the natural world as it is given to the experiencing subject. The Husserlian thesis that things are nothing more than things of actual or of possible experience, is legible in the interdependency between Pierre's consciousness and the objects depicted outside the train. The subjective character of the objects is emphasized as the scale of the sunflowers against the little doorways is given in proportion with Pierre's own supposition that he would need to duck under their looming blossoms. This speculative digression richly renders the child's mental activity as part of what Husserl describes as the "indeterminate but determinable horizon" of experience (§47): The tiny cottage doors and the oversized flowers already "point beyond themselves" to the "possible experience" (§47) of trying to enter the cottage and needing to stoop. In this first register, Rilke's philosophical poetics makes Husserl's doctrine legible[54]—the use of serial exposition, on a basic level, supplies the poetic effect of movement as well as the phenomenological arrangement of objects moving in and then out of a subject's field of perception, and thus also of his determinate experience.

In a second register, Rilke uses the narration itself to construct a consciousness that undergirds this seriality. By using what Dorit Cohn termed "psycho-narration" and "narrated monologue," Rilke is able to convey Pierre's "mental activity"—to use another of Cohn's terms—as the horizon of possible objects in such a way that the narrative fabric interweaves the content of the child's cognition with the forward movement of the story.[55] Although at first glance the narration is poised to keep the protagonist at an objective third-person distance through the exposition of the train's movement, upon closer inspection the reader finds Rilke beginning to alternate between two narratological techniques representing what Cohn calls "figural consciousness" or "figural mind."[56] As the passage continues, and the flora and cottages come into focus, the focus shifts between the objects as Pierre perceives them from the vantage point of the passing train (e.g., "green embankments," "tiny cottages," "giant sunflowers") and the work of Pierre's own fantasy ("The doors . . . were so small that Pierre thought he would probably have had to stoop to even be able to enter."). The moment of imagining is inseparable from the child's contemplation of the cottage doors; narrated monologue and psycho-narration work in concert to infuse the objectivity of narration with the child-subject's own sensory and inner experiences that together produce this particular world as it coasts past. The appearance of narrated monologue—the effect of "pensée avec"—fruitfully troubles the very difference between objective and subjective.[57] Thus, in this vivid scene, the phenomena seen from the train as it approaches the station continually and inseparably implicate the attending subject, the child Pierre.

The apparent ambiguity at the narratological level poetically solves one locus of philosophical difficulty in Husserl's own thinking—namely, the tangled relationship between imagination and perception, on the one hand, and the theoretical provocations of landscape spectatorship, on the other.[58] This is particularly pronounced in Blumenberg's account of the notes Husserl took while on vacation in the countryside that "describe the characteristic features of the form of experience called 'landscape' as the peculiar interrelatedness of actual perception and the becoming-image of that which is perceived."[59] In the scene, where Rilke's writing moves between narratological techniques, we notice how landscape perception becomes image, as things move in and out of the picture frame of the passenger window. What for Husserl was the troubling *in*distinction of the role the imagination imparts, for Rilke, is a kind of verisimilitude in his portrayal of childhood experience. In notes for an unpublished manuscript on fantasy and perception from around 1906, Husserl contemplates the scene of the world in terms startlingly close to Rilke's depiction of Pierre's vista from the train:

> Why does nature, a landscape, act as an "image"? The houses "little houses." These little houses have (a) an altered size in comparison with houses as we ordinarily see them; (b) a more shallow stereoscopic quality, altered coloring, and so on. Like toy houses, they are apprehended in a manner similar to that in which we apprehend images.... We take the appearances of the village ... for the nonpresent possible present, for the appearances that we would have, if, etc.[60]

Rilke's prose can capture how distant objects are enlivened as Pierre's imagination joins in, how the child's fantasy and perception work in tandem to produce the details of the lifeworld visible from the train window and flattened as if an image. It conveys the child's inattention to (or ignorance of) the optical illusion of depth and size, and the incredible "nonpresent" but "possible present" that his image-like-intuition enables. The "giant sunflowers" take on their divine quality and their saintly "yellow halos" safeguarding the cottage entrances because of their relatively impossible height—and the doors *look* so small because of their location even further away from the child-viewer. In an act that is freed from rational, aesthetic conventions of perspective, Pierre speculates that "they were so small that ... he would probably have had to stoop to even be able to enter"; it is as if he were regarding their size as the *image* of small doors rather than the depth of field of those faraway portals.[61] Together, all these objects become part of the child's "picture" of the landscape, one that exemplifies a "fundamental question" of phenomenology, namely, whether one should regard fantasy as *interrupting* perception or whether the imagination *always* contributes to the nexus of connections to reality.[62]

The way that Rilke describes Pierre's perception of the scale of the sunflowers in front of those distant (and therefore tiny-seeming) cottages suggests it is the latter. In Blumenberg's coinage, this simultaneity may be thought of as "concentric layers of fiction and fact" ("[die] konzentrische[] Einlagerung von Fiktum und Faktum").[63] The ordinary world of objects (flowers and doorways) in Rilke's story is not first optically perceived and then fantastically varied; rather, Pierre's world consists of both at the same time. The *fanciful* aspects (e.g., the haloed appearance, their guard-like posture before the doors, and miniature height of the entrances themselves) are inextricable from the *optical* ones (e.g., the yellow petals, the depth of space, and distance from the cottage doors). The lenses of fiction and fact are overlaid to produce the fullness of the child-subject's world. Rilke's imbrication of philosophy and storytelling offers an alternative to the comically detached spectator-philosopher (*theōrós*) who, like Aesop's astronomer and Blumenberg's midcentury high theorist, stumbles against the lifeworld, having missed what was right in front of him. Instead, the lifeworld of the titular child spectator in "Pierre Dumont" emerges seamlessly through acts of seeing and contemplation (*theōría*) in which perception (*Faktum*) of the close at hand *and* fantasy (*Fiktum*) of the distant coalesce. The child, ever the phenomenologist, practices something quite close to Blumenberg's own dictum: "seeing more, no more than seeing."[64]

Rilke's poetics of the eye-person ("Augenmensch") takes a final turn in the last scene of the story, after his mother drops Pierre off at the academy barracks after dinner. Describing Pierre's gradual awareness of his mother's growing absence as she vanishes in the distance, Rilke once again emphasizes the relationship between an object's scale and the perceiving child-subject. This time, however, Pierre, is not projecting himself through fantasy, but instead becomes aware of the distortion ("Bilddehnung")[65] of his mother's figure as she recedes into the distance. Rilke narrates both the moment of childhood separation anxiety and the changes to the "optical subject's" field of vision ("Blickfeld") as the object of attention moves away.[66] Rilke's precise description is as follows: "At the gate, [Pierre] looked around once more. He saw the tiny black shape [die kleine schwarze Gestalt] there between the trees in the twilight [den verdämmernden Bäumen] and hastily choked back his tears."[67] As his mother begins the walk back to the train station, the image of her becomes ever less clear. The increasing remoteness of her body is given as visual *in*articulateness, reflecting the real conditions of optical perception through the atmosphere over distance. As with the surrounding scenery, the evening landscape, Pierre attends to the ever-decreasing visibility ("verdämmernd"). Thus, the affective moment of "missing her" is mapped onto a waning optical registration; Rilke narrates Pierre's reaction in a way that—to paraphrase Blumenberg—requires seeing more: that he isn't able to really see her.

There is a second philosophical-poetic valence to the scene of the child attending to a distant (beloved) object: the role the sensibility of objects plays in the production of the world of experience. As Pierre casts his attention toward his mother as she leaves, and experiences the failure to see her well, Rilke not only displays his phenomenology of narrated "things," he also describes with great narrative economy the relationship between movable bodies, the perception of clarity, and the *sense* that something has vanished. Husserl imagines that if one were to move beyond the "sphere of [peak] optical clarity [Sphäre des deutlichsten Sehens]" through increasing proximity, then either the improved close-up comes at the expense of the object as a perceivable *whole* (the closer one gets, the less one can see the rest of the object) *or* the limits of optical clarity are in fact haptic as one literally bumps into the object with one's nose.[68] By contrast, there would seem to be a nearly infinite distance from this point of peak clarity in the opposite direction—at least until it disappears from sight.[69] Rilke narrates the retreat of the figure of the mother—"the tiny black shape"—into the distance; to borrow Blumenberg's phrasing, her body is perceived just as it approaches the "zero-threshold [Null-Grenze] of an object's disappearance from [this] sphere of experience."[70] For Husserl, this point of disappearance ("Null-Grenze") "corresponds kinesthetically to infinitude [Unendlichkeit]"—a "dramatic" phrase that, in Blumenberg's reading, describes the point of insensibility just prior to the mobilization of memory as the object moves out of view.[71] The mother's eventual vanishing is indeed merely the fact of her no longer being within optical range, but Husserl's phrasing, however imprecise, conveys the very experience that brings tears to young Pierre's eyes: the *feeling* of his mother being gone. In recounting the moment *before* complete nonvisibility (when her body eventually would be obscured by a building, the train, the horizon, etc.), Rilke's representation of the child's separation anxiety focuses not on the sentimental work of tarrying in memory, but on the phenomenological attention to distance and on the role sensibility plays in the construction of experience.

I have argued that Rilke's scenes of childhood deploy narratological and descriptive techniques that depict the child's encounter with the ordinary world in ways that convey both the aesthetic activity of "simple seeing" and what Blumenberg abbreviates as "seeing more." In these miniature character studies, Rilke not only renders the phenomenological complexity that undergirds these unassuming sounding phrases with the difficult nuance of perception and fantasy; he also overcomes a critical difficulty that Blumenberg identifies in Husserl's own thinking, namely, the overreliance on the examples from ideal, instead of real, nonidentical subjects. Blumenberg notes that although individuals' experiences of the world can be described as universally limited by the nature of finite human intuition (e.g., that we can only see a limited number of faces on a die at any given moment, or that the interiors and exteriors or front and back sides of an object are not ever simultaneously available from any subject position),[72] in reality there are neither universal subjects nor universally available intuitions. There is, I want to suggest, always enough ordinary, particular detail, a kind of naturalism or even realism, with which Rilke invests each of his narrative figments, to yield descriptions of *individual subjects*. "Pierre Dumont" is not an Aesopian fable or an everyman's tale, but instead offers the reader *Pierre's* afternoon experience on the day his mother drops him at the academy, with the granular detail only Rilke's prose could provide.

The conclusion that Blumenberg draws from the difference between a philosophy of ideal spectators and a phenomenology of individual perception encapsulates the very indispensability of poetics for philosophy that Rilke's text demonstrates:

> In the strict sense, there is no transmissibility [Übertragbarkeit] from one subject to another. The medium of description must always be engaged [eingeschaltet], the instrumental sense of which consists solely in one person's given intuition inducing another person's, which in turn produces that one intuition which brings about agreement to the description. Description is the means, not the end.[73]

In "Pierre Dumont," the work of the literary text is the description of one individual's intuitions (Pierre's) of the world. This narrative figment *engages* the "medium of description" in the phenomenological sense. From the moving objects seen from the train, to the projection of himself among the sunflowers, and to his mother's appearance as a mere speck on the horizon, we, the readers, are Pierre's "other" subject. This task of making present the intuitions of an other makes a demand of the child-figure—a demand that imagines the child a subject of the now, a figure of the present. At first reading, Pierre's predicament of returning to the military academy and leaving his mother and childhood home behind reinforces the social expectation of reproductive futurity we might have come to expect. However, Rilke's writerly focus on the now-time of being-child offers a queer challenge to this expected temporality of childhood. As a phenomenological subject, he is immersed not only in the stream of his own consciousness (e.g., recalling the delicacies of past holidays) but also in the finely attuned range of his own visual field during the moments of experience. "Pierre Dumont" therefore resists the view that childhood is merely the tabula rasa readied for social formation (military academy, adulthood); it represents childhood instead as a state of being in which one is *already* fully equipped to know one's lifeworld, and ready to tarry in their own world made of fiction and fact. Not yet hindered by adult practices of selective seeing, a child need not "learn to see"—the child is already "seeing more." Thus, as the prose writer of childhood, Rilke takes up the philosophical work of *description*.

Playing Dead: Childhood Reflection

For Rilke, the aesthetic work of spectatorship requires a capacious range of visual objects to properly capture the world as it is. As we have just seen, in "How the Thimble Came to Be God" and "Pierre Dumont," child protagonists Hans, little Marie, and Pierre exemplify the practice of seeing the world as it is, especially the "unremarkable" things that it comprises. As Rilke's later descriptions of Paris in the Malte-novel make clear, however, "simple seeing" also includes those things that adults selectively look away from—the "ugly" side of life. His prose work on childhood around the turn of the century takes up this project avant la lettre: stories such as "Das Christkind" (The Christ child) align the child with everyday scenes of poverty, illness, violence, and death while emphasizing the darkly romantic imagination that allows children to look directly at the grimmest moments of the everyday and to transfigure those same objects through their cognition.[74] As we will see, through the concurrent topoi of death and perception, and through decisive shifts in narrative focalization, Rilke's stories undermine the conventional role of the child as the paradigmatic figure of futurity. Operating in violation of Lee Edelman's now classic reading of nineteenth-century sickly child-figures, such as Tiny Tim,[75] Rilke's texts offer no Scrooge-like adult protagonist whose orientation is salvaged and redirected through a revitalized commitment to reproductive futurity. With heavy-handed religious imagery, Rilke not only depicts the impotence of bourgeois religious sentiment, but also envisions how child-characters reconfigure the rhetoric of the everlasting into that of the finite and immediate present.

In his 1893 Christmas tale, "The Christ Child," Rilke narrates the demise of the impoverished and abused young protagonist, Elisabeth, after she suffers hypothermia in the woods on Christmas Day. The exposition of this quasi-naturalist narrative is chronologically disjointed. The frame narrative takes place after her death, as the children in the pediatric ward watch the nurses remove her bed linens. This is then followed by the (earlier) inner narrative of Elisabeth's Christmas celebration, in which, after fleeing her abusive stepmother, she imagines a joyful and abundant holiday with her deceased mother in the snowy woods. The little girl receives a few coins from her father and buys herself "a pair of candles; a colorful and long, glittering garland; matchsticks; and a huge, heart-shaped Lebkuchen" and then heads to her favorite spot in the forest by a weathered wayside Madonna. Here, she decorates a small fir tree with the finery and candles, and, gazing at the glow, falls into a reverie of a cozy Christmas with her mother (the Madonna), before falling asleep in the snow.[76] The story resists Edelman's thesis that the Child provides adults with the fantasy of survival, as here Rilke queers the conventions of child-figures by linking her with death and finitude—indeed, in her failure to feel the cold at all, with the resistance to her own survival.[77] The connections to paternity and reproduction are all dead ends as the "woodsman's daughter" dies in the woods under a small fir tree. And although the vision of reproductive motherhood is doubled in the dead mother and the Madonna, there is no resurrection, but rather the repetition of maternal death as the child freezes with hands folded—like a wayside Mary figurine—in pious repose.[78]

Rilke's frame narrative begins with the freshly inked entry of her death in the hospital's registry: "'Deceased' was listed with indifferent, brutal letters, damply aglow in the thick, green hospital house-book. On that same line, it continued: 11th Floor, Room 12, Number 78. Horvát, Elisabeth, woodsman's daughter, nine years old."[79] In stark contrast, the concluding lines of the story establish this as merely one of two parallax views (adulthood and childhood perception): as two orphan children report to the pastor the scene of Elisabeth asleep in the snow when they find her: "We saw the Christ child—in the middle of the forest. [The child] lay near a gloriously luminous little tree and rested. And it was so beautiful, the Christ child—so beautiful . . ."[80]

Rilke narrates the woodland Christmas festivities with careful attention to the child's cognition. In Gérard Genette's terminology, this focalization on the child[81]—and this shift in information and perspective that centers "little Elisabeth"—is precisely what turns the frozen and derelict landscape into the fantasy of holiday splendor and motherly warmth. It is this narratological technique that makes Blumenberg's "concentric layers of fiction and fact" visible. As the objects of perception are simultaneously recast with the fantasy of the child-subject—just as we saw above in "Pierre Dumont"—the world of the child protagonist appears through this composite cognitive process. We can take, as a further example, the scene of the winter landscape as it unfolds outward from the point of view of the child protagonist:

> Then she bit heartily into the Lebkuchen heart and stood with her cheeks full so near to the glowing fir tree that the reflection of the radiance sparkled in her pure eyes.
>
> The entire, vast forest seemed to celebrate. The tall black firs stood in a broad circle like awestruck supplicants and marveled at the little insignificant sapling, like people beholding a miracle child. Even the distant stars appeared to huddle together over the spot to avoid missing any of the show, and to be able to tell the dear Lord and the angels and little Elisabeth's good mother what a good child [braves Kind] she was.[82]

Once the third-person narrator notes how the makeshift Christmas tree's glow is mirrored in the child's eyes, the focalization follows this specular gesture by reflecting her view of the trees as they tower over her and the sapling, and the way the stars appear to her. The entire environment appears to possess a tender regard for her—one that echoes her wish expressed by an earlier look she gives the little statue: "She cast a playfully reverent glance at the stone-Madonna, as if to convey: I am good, aren't I? You didn't expect me today."[83] This subtle shift places the reader's perspective in line with the child's—seeing the vast scale of the forest and winter sky unfold as the horizon of *her* experience, and the wistful fantasy of likewise being seen in return. From her central viewpoint within the forest and in mirroring the small sapling, Elisabeth emerges within the landscape as both spectator and storyteller. Rather than mere personification (the poetic work of grown-up authors for grown-up readers), we see the depiction of childhood reality that involves ordinary objects that are both *present* (trees, stars, the sky) and simultaneously *represented*—they become characters that tell a story.

The resulting concept of reality hovers between play and dream. In this narrative figment, Elisabeth occupies contrary roles at once: spectator and creator, character and audience, observer and interpreter, while her experience of the world retains the Husserlian conditionality of being "as if it were a 'picture'" ("als ob sie ein 'Bild' wäre"). In this way, the child protagonist "fictionalizes" ("fingiere") reality in such a way that it is then taken as an image in which that same reality would be represented."[84] In the aesthetic re-presentation of the forest glade qua nativity scene, Elisabeth is both viewer and character: like the specular sapling, she is at the center of the scene—the "miracle child" they all gather around and the titular "Christ child" found by others. She is the object of both spectatorship *and* narrative as the figures above crowd around to see her and to tell of her good deeds.

Child-subjects, it seems, possess a kind cognitive ambidexterity—one that is philosophically enviable, yet darkly so. In a posthumous observation titled "Reflection" ("Reflexion") Blumenberg declares that children are ever ready to adopt an adult-like seriousness in matters of play. He recounts a scene from Mark Twain's "A Tramp Abroad," in which the narrator recalls two children engaged in a pretend game of "silver mine." Here, the rivalry of who will play which parts in this drama of dangerous labor results in one child taking on both the role of the miner, who falls to his death, *and* of a member of the search party seeking (his own) corpse.[85] This playful anecdote from Twain provokes Blumenberg's own ironically serious reflections on the absurdities of philosophical thought. Twain's child-character experiences himself as an embodied subject in everyday life, but with his "death" he can engage in reflection on himself in a truly detached way, as object. With gallows humor, Blumenberg identifies the flaws in a philosophical conception of reflection that requires one to become one's own "pathologist": "The lethal plunge/case [Fall] leads to theoretically optimal conditions for reflection." Children, however, in their serious unseriousness, easily move from one position to the other; they are endowed with an unfettered vision of the world, and of themselves in the world.

Although the frame narrative of the "The Christ Child" centers on the protagonist's corpse, her capacity to view herself "as if an image" is what permits this form of reflection.

In "The Christ Child," Rilke shows how children engage in image-like experiences of the world: Through their creative capacity, they emphasize the moments in which we encounter the world "as if an image." Like Blumenberg, Rilke experiments with literalizing the limits implied by such forms of reflection. The child in this story does not represent an adult spectator's own wished-for futurity—her father, the woodsman, does not get to see himself perpetuated through her future. Instead, her imaginative spectatorship brings forth death. Like the boy in Twain's "silver mine," she enacts the very finitude implied by any "true" moment of philosophical reflection. The story, alluding both to the titular nativity scene and to fantasy reenactments of bourgeois Yuletide celebrations, repudiates the expectation that Edelman sees exemplified by, for example, Dickens's *A Christmas Carol*: "Christmas . . . stands in the place of the obligatory collective reproduction of the Child, the obligatory investment in the social precisely as the *order* of the Child, which demands our collective assent to the truth that the Child exists to make flesh."[86] In Rilke's holiday tale, the child does not signify the collective investment in heterosexual reproduction, but rather the *a*futurity—the radical present-time—of childhood reflection.

Toy Souls: What Children Apprehend

After viewing Lotte Pritzel's exhibit of highly stylized wax dolls, Rilke wrote his 1914 essay, "Dolls," in which he speculates that Pritzel's creations were not at all like children's toys, that indeed these figures must have existed under the precondition that the "world of childhood was already over."[87] Rilke then quickly digresses from this assessment of Pritzel's delicately costumed figurines and turns to a rumination on the messy and brutal existence of ordinary childhood dolls. Though his essay does not take the form of narrative fiction, the tone of his prose is equal parts child's reverie and belated adult observation. In this relatively late example from the period well after he had switched to lyrical forms of expression, Rilke still employs the philosophical-poetic approach to childhood perception that I have shown to be operative in "Pierre Dumont" and "The Christ Child," writing in ways that charge the forgotten objects of childhood with phenomenological significance and that reflect the now-time of childhood temporality. This late approach to childhood, however, remains far more ambivalent in its deployment of the technique of "simple seeing": On the one hand, the naturalist impulse to see without selection is made available in the adult's view of the bedraggled toy; on the other hand, the child's aesthetic vision sees the ephemeral "doll-soul."

Alternating between childhood's enchanted vision and the belated adult's horror, Rilke's description of this quintessential child's toy follows the differing outcomes of object apprehension. In particular, the child encounters this object without the later knowledge—that is, it lacks the future view of the decrepit uncanny object, as well as the hindsight of unsatisfying encounters upon childhood's end when the beloved object fails to appear enlivened as it once did. Rilke scholarship has tended to focus on the adult experience of the uncanniness of the doll and the ways in which it marks the boundaries of the child-subject.[88] I argue that in this relatively late essay, the child's encounter with the doll involves the "double perceptual appearance" that Husserl associated with apprehending art and representational objects, resulting in a more complex nexus of fantasy and perception than seen in, for example, the above-discussed story, "The Christ Child."

Rilke's account of the belated adult perspective of this toy conveys a kind of detached revulsion, attending to the sticky, snuggly, even violent handling of it by the child. To the adult, the doll object refuses to appear as the once-enlivened companion. Imagining one's own weathered and lifeless childhood doll in adulthood provokes abject horror:

> It would almost enrage us with its dreadful, turbid obliviousness; the hate that surely always constituted a part of our relationship to it, would spike. [The doll] would lay there unmasked before us as the gruesome foreign object on which we wasted our sincerest warmth, as the superficially painted drowned corpse that let itself be lifted and carried by the flood of our affection until we dried off and forgot it in some thicket.[89]

For the adult, a once-loved doll reveals itself as having only had the surface appearance of something living that, returned to mere object state, reemerges as inanimate and strange. The grown-up's sharp awareness that there's *nothing there* is rendered as the experience of the doll as a body thick with the nothingness of forgetting. What then was the appeal in the first place? How was it ever that we "wasted" "warmth" on it? How could this carcass have been buoyed by anyone's affection? Even in Rilke's ambivalent—if not hostile—telling, there is indeed an alternative experience of the doll, the one seen *in* childhood.

The child, through their imagination, fills this humanoid object with so much subjectivity that it become a "conspirator" and "accomplice" ("Mitwisser," "Mitschuldige").[90] The doll of childhood transcends its lifeless object body (the belatedly appearing "water corpse") through and with the child—a doll-subject appears jointly "with" ("mit-") the child. Rather than reminiscing, Rilke begins to speculate about how the doll comes to have its soul. This genesis he locates in the child's fantasy and storytelling capacities:

> Like in a test tube, we mixed into [the doll] what we experienced without realizing it, and we watched it change colors and come to a boil there. In other words, that, too, we fabricated; [the doll] was so bottomless without fantasy that our imagination became inexhaustible with it . . . but I cannot help but imagine there were overly long afternoons in which our double fancies ran out and we suddenly were sitting across from each other and expecting something from it.[91]

Here the scene of animation always threatens to collapse, revealing the empty material body. Rilke envisions the child's experience of the doll as the possibility of seeing something (or someone) where there is nothing. Speaking from his belated position, he goes on to emphasize how at some point the child becomes aware of this, and disenchantment becomes permanent: "But we soon realized that we could not turn [the doll] into a thing or a person, and at such moments it transformed into something unknown, and everything familiar we suffused and showered it with became unrecognizable in it."[92]

This process of seeing what was not there is cast, from the adult's hindsight, both as a kind of pitiful waste and as a romantically ephemeral orientation in the world.[93] In view of Rilke's earlier prose, we can see here the remnants of the idea that writing about how children experience the world requires thinking about ordinary experience as such. From his retrospective position, Rilke equates the doll's silence and emptiness with all the eventual heartbreaks of adult life more broadly and speculates about such moments.[94] The recognition of the doll's inertness is the hallmark of the departure from childhood. And yet the child's sheer capacity for attribution—that is, the ability to pour both story and soul into the lifeless material—resembles the basic contours of aesthetic perception: the ability to see content in representational art, for example.

If we consider what occurs when we cognize referents in figural image-objects, such as sculptures or photographs of people, we can make sense of the doll-soul in a new way. In working to give an account of imagination and its role in apprehending signification, Husserl provisionally suggests that there is a moment of "conflict" between the perceptual object (e.g., the bronze material shape or photographic paper) and the "nonpresent subject" of a "human figure."[95] To make this paradox more vivid, Husserl parenthetically adds that this is also how children "apprehend" the human figure in dolls.[96] In other words, children's ability to perceive a confidant of their own making in an otherwise lifeless object, provides, for Husserl, the philosophical example for understanding what signification (Bedeutung) is.[97] The child's natural relation to the doll tells us something fundamental about how it is that we can see something that is not there *in* the thing that *is* there. We find that Husserl's own working through of the cognition of the absent signified aligns with Rilke's own frustration with locating the unlocatable doll and its spirit. In appended notes from 1905, Husserl phrases the problem as follows:

> (Indeed, does the image-object apprehension as such belong essentially to image consciousness? Can I not say: The material of sensation is immediately apprehended there as re-presenting the subject? No, that won't do.)
>
> Hence the "nonpresence" of the image object signifies [bedeutet]: It appears as present, but is a *semblance* [*Schein*]. It is not compatible with what is actually present: It is mixed with the latter; it is filled with contradiction (with conflict).[98]

This conflict Husserl contrasts with the otherwise straightforward "phantasy image" in which there is a present material object of perception; the doll, like a bronze figurine, involves two simultaneous "perceptual apprehensions": (a) one belonging to the "sensory and perceptual reality" and (b) another to the "phantasy world,"[99] the latter being the character represented *by* the physical object. I want to point out here two ways Husserl's notes track with Rilke's account. First, for Husserl there is a nonpresent figure ("das Nichtgegenwärtige") in what is "actually" present; in Rilke's essay, there is "something . . . invisible" ("etwas . . . Unsichtbares") in the doll body, which he disparagingly refers to as a "pelt" ("Balg").[100] Second, the material experience of the object (the "pelt") is not a re-presentation or re-appearance of another subject (e.g., another child, an "accomplice"), as the apprehended "subject" is not present; instead, it is merely a frustratingly fleeting "semblance." Childhood makes the foundational "conflict" of the aesthetic gaze visible. Rilke's description of the locational difficulties mirrors Husserl's own attempts to account for the apprehension of something whose material substance and conceptual referent are not one and the same object appearance. Rilke sees the cognitive labor on the side of the child that apprehends a fugitive *sujet* whose apprehension requires a "mixture" (to paraphrase both Husserl and Rilke) with the perception of a present object, the motionless doll's body: "Only you, doll-soul, we could never really say *where* you actually were; whether you abided in [the child] or in the sleepy creature across from him."[101] As Husserl suggests, some of the sense of conflict that arises because there is a "double perceptual apprehension" of objects that otherwise "stand in rank and file with other perceptual objects [and which] belong to perception's field of regard."[102]

In his essay, Rilke inventories the range of objects that belong to the child's "field of regard," and which together yield the larger aesthetic universe of the childhood nursery. The child's "double perceptual apprehension" of toys produces the "authentic, nearly visible soul" of "the great, brave rocking horse," the "genuine soul of the streetcar," and the "inexhaustible soul of the picture book."[103] But for Rilke, the adult view of the doll, with its human-like form and metaphorical capacities, makes for a most unnerving mortal image: a human semblance decaying from within, as the moth larvae that had lived inside leave after consuming the doll's fabric interior.[104]

In this way, the doll essay is very much in keeping with his early prose works as an experiment in what Judith Ryan characterized as "his narratives' common aim to explore human psychology and its manifold variants,"[105] but with a decided focus on that particular phenomenological conflict that is the signature of aesthetic perception—on what Blumenberg characterizes as the perception of a reality consisting of both fiction and fact.[106] The doll and its soul—its semblance—requires a kind of belief in (or positing of) signification that, as Rilke tells it, is quite unique to children. And with adolescence comes the cessation of this capacity to transfigure the doll to nonpresent presence (soul) from mere uncanny corpse (pelt).

This phenomenological work of childhood experience also explains the utter queerness of children's comfort with dolls in the first place. We might think of the work of signification in seeing the doll's soul—an Other, just like themselves—as, to quote Stockton, "metaphor, which itself is a sideways accretion: the act of imagining oneself as something else."[107] In this way, the queer child's work of "seeing" the doll figures them as "having a knack for metaphorical substitution, letting one object stand for another, by means of which they reconceive relations to time" and that "riding on a metaphor they tend to make material," they "imagine relations of their own"—they "delay; swerve, delay."[108] Neither looking ahead to their own death (the corpse) nor lamenting the loss from adulthood, the child's ghostly partner seems perfectly ready for the queer kinship the child finds in the doll (conspirator and accomplice). As a child's early love, the doll makes for a queer partnership—one that leaves nothing but food for moths in its future. The doll, to paraphrase Stockton, is thus the metaphor for the very appearance of childhood in all its temporal strangeness.[109]

The Fantastic World of Childhood in the "Notes" and the *Notebooks*

Thus far I have argued that what has often been described as the "naïve" and "romantic" encounter in Rilke's portrayals of childhood can instead be read as evidence for a deep awareness of, and sensitivity to, the child's capacities for apprehension through both perception and fantasy.[110] The technical sophistication of Rilke's experimentations in depicting reflection rivals the technicality of key concepts in Husserl and Blumenberg's philosophies of phenomenology. In the following section, I argue that even in the comparatively minor roles that childhood plays in two of his lyrical prose (or prose poetic) texts, "Notes on the Melody of Things" ("Notizen zur Melodie der Dinge") and *The Notebooks of Malte Laurids Brigge (Die Aufzeichnungen des Malte Laurids Brigge)*, children are shown as subjects richly endowed with capacities to imagine and intuit the ordinary world around them. In each case, we will see that the material world of childhood—the domestic interior—is a creative landscape for the child; more important, Rilke's techniques of description tell us something of the nexus of consciousness to reality, and they highlight, in their attempt to translate intuition into description, the fundamental incommensurability between philosophy and poetics.

In his 1898 "Notes on the Melody of Things," Rilke sketches two children as distracted readers in a cramped room. Here, the wider possibilities of an imagined space spring from the material lifeworld of the domestic enclosure. Such spaces inhabited by children are not static, but rather malleable under the force of imagination. In a scene that resembles a scene of poetic production, the child's own subjectivity as self-reflexivity gives shape to the image of the child as writer:

> xxx. I want to suggest a rather small example:
>
> Evening. A small parlor. At the table under the lamp sit two children across from one another, reluctantly leaning over their books. They are both far—far [weit—weit]. The books cloak their escape. Every now and then they call each other, in order to avoid losing themselves in the vast [weiten] woods. In the narrow room, they experience colorful and phantastic fortunes. They fight and triumph. Return home and marry. Teach their children to be heroes. Even die well.
>
> I am idiosyncratic enough to regard this as plot [Handlung].[111]

Rilke proposes an interrelationship between the given space of material appearances and the child's peculiar intuition of it, and the dialogic of fantasy and poesy that is built on subjective freedom places the possibility of poetic production firmly on the side of philosophy.[112] The scene of "reading" is instructive of fantasy's character as the progression moves from outward or objective appearance (two children sitting opposite each other, etc.) to child-subjects with lively interior experiences that project beyond the framed space. The space of narration, as well as the narrated space, are self-contained in the brevity of description, set narrowly between the narrator's interventions. The story thus appears as "narrow" as the parlor itself. Fantasy's appearance in the narration, however, quickly revises the narrowness of the "small parlor" as only a provisional form of containment. Although this simple scene ("Evening. A small parlor.")—with its nod toward staging and setting—takes place within a discrete space (locatable in a home, in a room, at a table), the children are projected out far from each other, as well as far from their room ("weit—weit"). More than a simple juxtaposition of an ordinary scene of reading with the extraordinary production of the fantastical space of imagination, this makes (the) room for an invented space, a vast universe of the imaginary, as it overwrites the narrowness of both its textual and architectural limits.

In keeping with Husserl's remarks about the incompleteness of mere fantasy—its discontinuities, insufficient, and imperfect forms[113]—the prose text too is formally fragmented and abbreviated. Indeed, the scene of childhood fantasy shares what we might call the "protean" character of all pure fantasy, in which something new constantly emerges.[114] From each moment arises a new fantasy space as the child's story unfolds in protean fashion; the result is something that can be taken for "plot." The space of the "small parlor" seems to demarcate the edges of the children's world and the multivalent site of childhood experience. Precisely this tension, visible in the relationship between the materiality (of the home) and the ideality (of childhood), lies at the core of my argument.

This fragment characterizes the family space as both the bourgeois room of leisure (the kind of "small parlor" that would have a table for reading, card-playing, entertaining) *and as* a childhood space of discipline and the labor of education (where children sit "reluctantly leaning over their books"). Following pedagogical doctrines, they are sequestered in their nursery. In this vignette we see that Rilke's aesthetic theory depends on place, for the children's parlor provides the set of objects against which fantasy, like perception, unfolds: "Without this rather dark background, through which they weave their fables' threads. How differently the children would dream in the garden."[115] Sara Ahmed, reflecting on the phenomenologist's philosophical starting point, asks a similar question: "At what point does the world unfold? Or at what point does Husserl's world unfold?"[116] She imagines this world as follows:

> The familiar world begins with the writing table, which is in the room: we can name this room as Husserl's study, as the room in which he writes. It is from *here* that the world unfolds. . . . In Husserl's writing the familiar slides into the familial; the home is a family home, a

residence inhabited by children. They are in the summer house, he tells us. The children evoke the familial only through being "yonder," being at a distance from the philosopher who in writing about them is doing his work.[117]

For Rilke's children in their parlor "it is from *here* that the world unfolds" as well. And it is from that "family home" that they do their own work of going "yonder." The scene of the philosopher at his writing desk finds its analogy in the children in their nursery, likewise bent over their tables and under their lamps. The distance of childhood from adulthood that Husserl himself notices (they are part of *his* background) is shown here from the other end: children, lost in their thought, leave the room behind ("far—far")—it is part of *their* background. We might overlay Ahmed's description of Husserl—the philosopher figure—with the children in Rilke's "Notes": "The family home provides, as it were, the background against which an object (the writing table) appears in the present, in front of [them]. The family home is only ever co-perceived, and allows the philosopher [children] to do [their] work."[118]

We can say that it is by virtue of the quotidian space of the home that the children are able to imagine themselves within such a fantastic aesthetic framework, for which the narrator is "idiosyncratic enough to regard . . . as plot." Only in *this* parlor can nonaction become action, can plot become story. From nothing comes something (new); Rilke renders a scene of genesis—an epic tale that is called up ("rufen") from the most banal circumstances, aesthetic pleasure invoked in the face of obligation and boredom.[119] From line to line, the fragment performs the crucial ambivalence of imagination, where a single image explodes with possibility. Childhood becomes the site of antinomy: stasis and action (sitting/battling); containment and expansion (parlor/forest); prosaic and epic (children/heroes). The magic of childhood is the simultaneity of each of these—the most remarkable springs forth from the unremarkable. In this movement from reading to daydreaming, we can see what Gaston Bachelard's "topoanalysis" has also shown: the home's "felicitous space" furnishes the poet with a "universe" of being, with which the child-subject transforms an ordinary room into something much more.[120]

The conditions of nineteenth-century dwellings as they appear in Rilke's work make the epistemological and aesthetic consequences of this "small example" legible as rooted in spatial perception. Recalling the Latinate origins of "text" (*textilis, textus*), Rilke continues in the subsequent fragment, xxxi, that it is *where* the children are that provides the material for poesis: "in the yellow canvas of this parlor evening . . . it is not irrelevant whether one is stitched in silk or wool."[121] Rilke makes it explicit that the parlor is the substance from which the tapestry of their fantasy is woven, reiterating that the matter *matters* with regard to the imagination and the scene of fabrication. It is only under *this* hanging lamp that *this* story of battle and victory could ever be imagined. Indeed, the thrust of such a simple scene is explicit: Art must have its roots in the material. The otherwise flattened universal child-subjects come alive at the moment when their imaginations are activated in response to the parlor. To borrow from Aristotle, Rilke seems to portray a partial dependence of *phantasia* (imagination) on *aesthesis* (sense perception), which thus transforms mere child-types into active, thinking child-subjects with the capacity of *nous*.[122] These subjects are constituted by their ability not only to perceive, but also to manipulate sense experience as representation. At this juncture, Rilke's portrayal of the relationship between imagination and sense perception is still unclear: How does the imagination respond to the encounter with everyday things, with what Husserl calls "transcendent objects"? How does the poetic impulse issue specifically from the *child's* intuition of space? For Rilke, poetic representations are akin to ordinary intentional acts—the mental images produced by attending to sensible objects. He thereby turns the child-subject into a poet through the rewriting of quotidian space, through the transfiguration of the child's lifeworld—the parlor—into the realm of imagination. Crucially, this transfiguration depends on the unavoidably *incomplete* representation of objects through intuition (i.e., perception, *Anschauung*). Rather than thematizing the role of fiction vis-à-vis the partiality of memory (as Goethe does),[123] Rilke suggests that it is the limitations of sense perception that make way for poetic production.[124]

If we recall the *Reformpädogogen* of his time, Rilke's insistence on visual perception plays on the scene of learning, turning the narrow discipline of training oneself to see into the practice of exercising the freedom to see (as we have just retraced in the "Notes," where drudgery becomes the delight of *fabula*).[125] These scenes of childhood do more than reflect historically shifting ideas at the intersection of pedagogy and aesthetics, such as the de-emphasis of academic style or a strict sense of mathematical rationalization in favor of the uncontaminated "primitive" view.[126] Like John Ruskin and his invocation of the "innocence of the eye," Rilke participates in a complete rethinking of the subjective power and significance of childhood.[127] To further explore how Rilke stages the home through the eyes of a child, let us now turn to representations of the limits of perception in Rilke's longest prose text, *The Notebooks of Malte Laurids Brigge* of 1910. In the scenes of Malte's childhood, Rilke vividly describes mental acts relating to things in space, or what Husserl calls "transcendent objects" (*Ideas*, §41–44). By reconsidering Malte's obsession with "sehen lernen" along the lines of Husserl's notion of intentionality, it is possible to demonstrate how this learning leads to a rejection of the rational apparatuses that develop after childhood.[128] For Rilke, seeing has the potential to become a poetic procedure, demanding a peculiar attitude of consciousness of (or attention to) seeing *as if* unburdened. The poet, like Husserl's philosopher, must learn to see, or adopt the attitude of a child.

Extending Käte Hamburger's argument that Rilke's poetry indeed reflects a Husserlian approach, the legibility of the world in his prose texts seems to fall along phenomenological lines.[129] In contrast to the intentionality presented by the "lyrical I" in his poems, Rilke's child-figures render their world anew through mechanisms of intention—and, even more so, through misperception (or infelicity). As we will see, this provides an analogue to Rilke's thinking about the relationship between subjective experience, fantasy, and poetic potential. The architecture and "canvas" of the home and its objects are not to be read as forms of containment, but rather as metaphors of bracketing. This method of bracketing or "parenthesizing" objects of consciousness that Husserl advocates—viz., "exercising the phenomenological epoché" (*Ideas*, §32)—emphasizes a certain purposeful limiting of subjective perception, in contrast to the "natural attitude" toward the "givenness" of the world (things perceived as "at hand"). Like Malte's desire to "learn to see," the *epoché* also demands a deliberately naïve position in which one strives to forget learned attitudes and determinate knowledge. Just as Husserl suggested that one be "shut off from any judgment about spatiotemporal being," Rilke's child-figures also seem to practice a version of this ubiquitous parenthesizing, in which the "entire pre-discovered world ... as it is actually experienced" may be subject to unbiased circumscription (§32). The child's eye strips away learned assumptions, giving unfettered access to the subjective and poetic world. My analysis will claim that the child-subject offers a unique window into how perception, imagination, and subject formation operate in a constellation, intimately linked to aesthetic production in general, and literary-poetic production in particular.[130] By examining scenes from *The Notebooks of Malte Laurids Brigge*, we will see how a nuanced representation of spatial perception establishes the child's banal encounter ("free from judgment") as the catalyst of poetic impulse.

Let us turn to a detailed rendering of space in Malte's recollection of the Brahe home he visited as a child. The organization of it appears incongruous: a mazelike space, disjointed and impossibly circuitous. I want to argue Rilke's narration simultaneously depicts two forms of what Husserl called "Egoexperiences": adult memory (of childhood) as well as (childhood) perception. In arguing for the former, I remain consistent with Rilke scholarship (i.e., this scene makes the difficulties of memory legible and places his work in line with Proust's) while also wanting to draw out the author's phenomenological sensitivity to the *present*-time of fantasy consciousness that appears while remembering past perceptions and in the perception of presently present objects. I will offer a second reading to show how this fantasy work of memory *also* contains the present moment (in the past) in which the child Malte's perception of the home's interior takes place.

For Husserl, we may recall, mere fantasy (imagined objects) and memory (real objects recalled through fantasy) share certain characteristics. Like perceptual appearances, things produced through fantasy appear to us through the form of real objects in the perceptual field (e.g., they can be viewed from only one side at a time).[131] However, objects of fantasy ultimately always lack a relative degree of information that would be expected with perceptual objects—in other words, our minds cannot provide the totality of possible adumbrative views and instead yield objects that appear for us as "phantom-like" in their visual saturation, or whose shape remains an "imperfect plastic form" with "unsteady contours" that are "filled out with nothing, with nothing that one would assign as a defined surface."[132] With this in mind, let us follow how Rilke's narrator Malte describes the interior spaces of his childhood with a sensitivity to precisely this phenomenological character of fantasy:

> As I find it again in my retrieved childhood memory it is not a building; it is completely divided up in me: a room here, a room there, and a piece of corridor that does not connect these two rooms but is preserved by itself, as a fragment. Everything is scattered around in me in this way: the rooms, the staircases that unrolled downwards with such great complexity, and other narrow, spiral staircases whose darkness one negotiated like blood in the veins; the tower rooms, the balconies suspended high up, the unexpected high platforms onto which a small door pushed me out: all that is in me and will never cease to be in me. It is as if the image of the house had fallen into me from an infinite height and shattered on my ground.[133]

In this passage, the architecture of the house mirrors the instability of mental (re-)presentation—but in my reading I am focused less on the fallibility of memory or the psychical fragmentation, but instead on the careful reflection of the "discontinuity" that Husserl thinks is part and parcel to all fantasy.[134] As a "childhood memory," the parts of the house that are poetically representable by the narrator do not produce the totality of an original, complete structure, reflecting the notion that the work of memory is *also* the work of fantasy. The disjointed appearance of the staircases and passageways conveys the complexity of the home's interior but in such a way that the "imperfect form" lacks connective structures that enable three-dimensional space to make sense as it would in the perceptual encounter. And indeed, this image of the home is distinct from the home itself as, in Malte's words, this is the version that is "in [him]." As a phantom of the actual perceptual home, this space appears to the first person-narrator as "shattered" and "scattered." In this way, the present-tense of the first line ("I find it again") is instructive as we see how Rilke resituates the scenes of a childhood long past in the *now*-time of its reoccurrence in the act of recollection.

As a narrated memory of Malte's actual experiences as a child, this passage conforms to Blumenberg's hybrid characterization of perception for which I argued earlier in the case of *"Pierre Dumont"*: that the world of childhood appears in "the concentric layers of fiction and fact."[135] The home depicted here is the one of young Malte's perceptual attention, in which the work of the imagination occurs simultaneously with perception. The passage conveys the child's experience of a home whose looming scale, mazelike layout, and peculiar rules of etiquette converge to make the Brahe home ungraspable without fantasy's supplementation. In the novel, we learn that Malte has limited access to certain rooms, some only at appointed times. Without free range of the building, for the child many of these spaces fail to "connect" to each other systematically to create the sense (or *Sinn*, the sense data that undergirds meaning) that an adult easily makes of an entire house. The generally dark and almost nightmarish nature of the house squares with both the child's funereal encounters with the Brahe family and the way that fantasy and perception work together to shape the way in which the child conceptualizes object of experience.

Here, it might be helpful to bring in Stanley Cavell's description of how a child's perspective troubles the completion—or felicity—of naming things, precisely when those things rest on a concept or mental image that remains unclear, incomprehensible, or outside of one's experience. Indeed, Cavell points to the child to demonstrate how the construction of sense and space are dependent on one's relative position:

> For example, if you are walking through Times Square with a child and she looks up to you, puzzled, and asks, "Where is Manhattan?," you may feel you ought to be able to *point* to something, and yet at the same time feel there is nothing to point to; and so fling out your arms and look around vaguely and say "All of this is Manhattan," and sense that your answer hasn't been a very satisfactory one. Is, then, Manhattan *hard* to point to? . . . It feels hard to do . . . when the *concept* of the thing pointed to is in doubt, or unpossessed, or repressed.[136]

The ability to conceive of the totality of a structure—to re-present it—is, at least in part, a question of perspective. The rendering of a discrete space hinges on the creation of a mental object—Cavell goes on to tell us that it might require the view from a plane in order to see and name the object, "Manhattan." We can easily imagine that a child who has seen only Times Square will have a very limited notion—perhaps just as wild and incomplete as Malte's picture of the Brahe home. Cavell's example reminds us that if the certainty and capaciousness of the child's mental image could only be assured with the aid of an airplane, then an element of "indefiniteness" will persist.[137] Rilke's child-figure, Malte, reveals that even interior spatial arrangements are "hard" to fathom without additional experience. Rilke's haunting image reflects the same kind of epistemological anxiety *about* childhood intuition that one would feel when "pointing" to a Manhattan that would nevertheless remain "missing" for the child. It draws our attention to the child's "indefinite intuition," made visible in the home's disjointed representation. Significantly, the aesthetic quality of the passage issues precisely from this impartial and infelicitous intuition: The perspective that would be uncanny and disturbing in an adult here transforms the ordinary encounter into a poetic one.

Through Malte's insistence that such images of the room are located "in me," we are shown the perspectival limits of an individual intending child-subject; intention is described as a specifically mental event.[138] The transcendent object (the house) appears to be complete precisely insofar as it is broken up into pieces ("completely divided up in me"). We can read this as a phenomenological claim: Although the object *is* constituted in the moments of its intention, it is also determined by the scope of the child's movement through the space.[139] As Husserl notes, the unity of any three-dimensional object in space arrives through the perspectival accumulation of perceptions of it, through adumbrated perception (*Ideas*, §41). The consciousness of something physical as a mental act of representation is sense-producing; it is the institution of subjectivity vis-à-vis the object. In Rilke, the child-subject appears as the producer of objects, where the constituting of the house (as object) is *also* the constitution of the subject through narrative (or, as in the "Notes," through "Handlung") and through text-image making.

Rilke seems to agree with Husserl that the shape of everyday space cannot be taken for granted as a fully representable totality. Indeed, the child's perception of space seems to be open to expansion, exclusion, and deformation. If we look closely at the description of the dining room in the Brahe home, Malte's recollection of the room posits a relationship between the finitude of a child's intuition (à la Cavell) and the poetic image of an irrational space:

> This high, as I imagine vaulted space, overpowered everything: with its darkling height, its never quite visible corners, it sucked all images

out of one without giving one a tangible substitute in return. One sat there as if lamed: completely without will, without consciousness, without desire, without resistance. One was like a blank spot. I remember that this crushing state at first almost made me sick to my stomach, a kind of seasickness, which I overcame only by sticking out my leg until my foot touched the knee of my father, who was sitting opposite me. . . . And after several weeks of desperate endurance I had, with a child's almost unlimited adaptability, become so accustomed to the uncanniness of these gatherings that it was no longer a strain to sit at a table for two hours; now they even passed relatively quickly, because I occupied myself by studying those present.[140]

This passage reveals Blumenberg's "concentric layers of fiction and fact" as a palimpsest of subject positions: The disorientation and anxiety of space that the young Malte experienced is layered over with the rational commentary of an adult Malte.[141] The overwhelming height and impressiveness of the space appears in relation to the child-figure, but the inserted suspicion that the room is "as I imagine vaulted . . ." does not belong to the child-figure. Though this belated architectural identification interrupts the child's view of the room, it also offers us a helpful contrast with the adult Malte's interposition of a ceiling metaphor as a decisive resistance to metaphors of infinity and epistemological uncertainty.[142] As the young Malte's initial, "mere" perception of the space renders only limited features of the room's construction, it also shows no interest in aristocratic or bourgeois discourses dealing with the aesthetics of such a marked enclosure.[143] This child-figure asks us to peel away symbolic aspects of the room's design; the *perception* of space is most noteworthy here.

Perceived by the child, the room is neither borderless nor shapeless but rather lacks all determinate or rational spatiality, and the disorientation of the child-viewer becomes visible as the corners of the room withdraw into darkness. This produces "a kind of seasickness" as the space ("Raum") is imagined to be incomprehensibly expansive. Without a horizon, the space begins to swim; young Malte reaches for the touchstone of his father's leg to steady himself. The ordinariness of a vaulted ceiling is transformed into a perception of excess—"übel"—that is so extreme as to produce nausea.[144] The apparent absence of the ceiling's limits begets even more absence. Projected into the child's own subjective boundaries, formlessness and vast emptiness reproduce themselves: "One was like a blank (*leere*) spot." The interaction of raw sense experience (*hyle*) with mental form (*morphe*) (*Ideas*, §85) draws this self-presentation of the dining room inward.[145] The object of sublime expanse is reproduced, as it were, *in* the intending subject. Like the fantastical expansion of the narrow children's parlor in the "Notes," Malte's inversion of space follows Rilke's narrative of poetic imagination: An ordinary domestic interior is opened up in the child's perception, and then, following the logic of *horror vacui*, Malte's "this crushing (vernichtende) state" of retreating walls becomes a creative source of obsessive childhood production and reproduction. Malte, the narrator, thus begins to busy himself by populating the room, filling the void with family members and ghosts.

The perception of the ordinary dining room can also be seen as an optical drama. As a metonymy of both the limits of visual perception and the poetic value of childhood experience, the play of light and dark in the room serves as a reminder of an epistemological problem. Indeed, the term that appears frequently in the text with regard to both childhood and darkly visible (or wholly absent) aspects of the home is "unaufgeklärt" (unenlightened, mysterious). In this passage, it is shorthand for the unlit corners of the ceiling, but when Malte elaborates on the poet's need for a well-seasoned life, his list includes "the childhood days, that are still unenlightened."[146] For Rilke, this chiaroscuro-like effect is more than just having a taste for the poorly lit; the dark corners of the home—and similarly, of the poet-subject—are sites where rationality loses its hold and the play of imagination does its work. The lines that precede the description of those high ceilings bring the tension of darkness-enlightenment and perception-imagination to the fore. This vaulted dining room, though used every evening, seems to have no existence in the daylight or in relation to daytime:

> The only thing that is wholly preserved [ganz erhalten] in my heart, so it seems to me, is the great hall in which we usually gathered for dinner every evening at seven. I never saw this hall in daylight; I don't even remember whether it had windows or what they looked out on; every time, whenever the family came in, candles were burning in the heavy sconces, and within a few minutes one forgot the time of day and everything one had seen outside.[147]

Though Rilke's child-subject describes for us the *partial* image of the room, it is nonetheless explicitly characterized as a *complete* image of a room ("ganz erhalten"). Like a young philosopher's assistant, he carefully brings our attention to the way in which childhood intuition reveals the effective edges of sensory information (*hyle*) at work against the accumulated experience of the adult mind—that which could fill in the dark spots within the child's "horizon." With regard to the *young* Malte's perception, the *rest* of the room cannot be co-intended: the absences of light, visible windows, or a ceiling that connects to the tops of darkened walls are precisely *not* taken for granted. The intervention by an adult Malte of "suspected vaulting" highlights exactly this difference. The phenomenological *epoché*, however, demands recognition of these shadowy absences. As we have already seen, an object's unity in space has a perspectival limit. The unity of objects in space only appears to us as what Husserl calls "abgeschattet" (adumbrated), where the single identity of a manifold thing is synthetically available only to the extent that it can be intuited via possible perspectival positions (*Ideas*, §41). Malte's view here is of portions of a room in which windows simply are not visible. This shadowiness of intention is as legible in the term "Ab*schatt*ung" (and even in the English ad*umbra*tion) as it is in the Brahe's poorly lit dining room. However, the unavailability of any given aspect of an object to intuition does not affect the possibility of that aspect having a mental "form" (*morphe*). Indeed, Rilke's notion of the poet's "unenlightened" sight is revealed—literally and metaphorically—as the partial depiction of the room. This produces the relationship between the "physical" or "transcendent" room (with windows of a certain number and kind) and the apparently windowless, phenomenal or subjective room, which, to Malte's young eye, remains inexorably ambiguous.

Rather than simply reading this as an intermingling of interior-exterior tropes,[148] we should ask: How is it that the demand for poetic response arises from this shadowy, indefinite, and ambiguous experience? It is the child's ability, and even propensity, to *misperceive* that provides space for the imagination and creative production. While this work of poetic prose can be read generically as an aesthetic experiment, the child's explicit attempts to render a coherent lifeworld also require a generative (i.e., poetic) response. To explain how the imagination fills in missing or inconclusive sense data, let us consider Dagfinn Føllesdal's discussion of Joseph Jastrow's famous duck-rabbit image[149] to illustrate how the mind productively accounts for deficient and ambiguous sensory impressions (*hyle*):

> In the duck/rabbit case, this was obvious, we could go back and forth at will between having the noema of duck and having the noema of a rabbit. In most cases, however, we are not aware of this possibility. Only when something untoward happens, when I encounter a "recalcitrant" experience that does not fit in with the anticipations in my noema do I start seeing a different object from the one I thought I saw earlier. My noema "explodes."[150]

The purpose of Jastrow's image is to illustrate the ways in which prior experiences shape noematic sense: In Malte's case, it is his lack of "architectural" experience that prevents a categorical or nominal response, producing instead a "recalcitrant" effect. We can see in the duck-rabbit image that ambiguity itself produces a manifold of mental activities. The child-subject Malte is predisposed to this kind of "explosion" of noemata. Neither could he have cause to cointend an invisible ceiling, nor would such a ceiling be automatically affixed to the sense (*Sinn*) of "being-vaulted"; it is rather the sensory (visual) data that institutes the production of multiple meanings (*Sinne*). Just as the sublime scale of the dining room produces a kind of nausea in him, so too does it yield an excessive need to "fill in" missing data. Limited hyletic data thus afford a capacity to *see* more. In essence, the narrower the "anticipation," the greater the need for "filling" activities; accordingly, the lion's share of labor must fall on noetic components like imagination.

Rather than simply suggesting that it is the life of pure imagination in children (and poets) that is so productive, Rilke shows us that imagination in fact responds to the instability and contingency of connections between sense data and mental activity. In the image of the "windowless" dining room, what we see is one moment of a child's "recalcitrant experience"—where the given information allowed for an ambiguous multiplicity of noemata (because he never saw the room by day, he could not remember any windows). The original image of the dining room suddenly was *more*: a room both with and without windows, whose possibly infinite expanse could never be pinned down in a single, stable image. Not only the scale but also the shape of the room could be imagined, reimagined, or left as whole *and yet* still be only "partial." Like the ambiguities in the simultaneity of Jastrow's duck-rabbit, Malte's impressions of the room are both unified (in its dim sublimity) and also multiple (What time of day was it outside? Which way did the room face?). Malte's young mind had to fill in those empty spaces with manifold possibilities.

The structure of the child's world that Rilke offers us through the representation of experience as the bracketing of spatial perception now appears as experimentation (returning us to the notion of the *epoché*). In this way, reflection on the act of making meaning (*Sinn*) is starkly thematized. The imagination does more than simply "fill in" the holes (*horror vacui*), it makes room for the possibility of poiesis. If this network of stairs and hallways is akin to the body of the dweller, then the sublime possibility and multi*valence* of space reveal the explosion of possibility in the child's fantasy. By reading these structures in the quotidian scenes of childhood and the home, two crucial aspects of Rilke's work become legible: (1) the child is an intending subject, constituted along phenomenological lines; (2) through representation that operates between material intuition and noematic activity, the child-subject is revealed as poet-subject.

Rilke's space of childhood—whether impossibly large or claustrophobically narrow—is open to poetic revision. It is not a failure of memory or the anxiety around empirical fidelity that causes such rewriting to occur, it is rather the child-subject's experience of each space. Through their subjective freedom, the child-figure's material encounter with the limits of a bourgeois interior initiates poiesis: The banal canvas of the home becomes the landscape of epic fantasy. Confronting the sublime shape of a room that escapes a child's knowledge and prior experience, Rilke locates the catalyst of poetic experience at the intersection of the child's ambiguous perception and the responding mental activity, imagination.

The "Notes" and the *Notebooks* both linger in the child's experience of the world in a way that not only produces a poetic subjectivity that Rilke contemplated in his aesthetic writings, and both fragment series and the novel resist easy temporalities of progress or even progression. The scenes of childhood are not linked to growing up in a linear way: Those little vignettes have no before or after; and little Malte only appears erratically in unpredictably recurring passages, after some section breaks but not all. Childhood is always out of joint with a grown-up narrative. With the sudden starting and stopping of childhood, Rilke's narration follows a disordered chronology that allows for the expansive now of time, perception, and imagination while foreclosing the idea of sequence and even causality.[151] Childhood does not serve to provide fullness or meaning in adulthood. Indeed Malte himself remarks that for the adult childhood is elusive and useless.[152] Instead, children appear as an irrational interruption, as figures who, as Ahmed says, "make things queer" by "disturb[ing] the order of things" and where "the effects of such a disturbance are uneven, precisely given that the world is already organized around certain forms of living—certain times, spaces, and directions."[153] The philosophical capacities of representing childhood produce other queer effects: with Stockton, we might say that children in *The Notebooks* and the "Notes" do not "grow up" but "grow sideways" where the lateral movement of perception and imagination make the "width" of their "experience or ideas" visible and thereby "[bring] 'adults' and 'children' into lateral contact."[154]

"Wise incomprehension...": On the Model of Being-Child

In the preceding section, I have argued that Rilke's prose treatment of children's perception and phenomenological intention is particularly shaped by a certain resistance presented by objects in the lifeworld, and that childhood's nonunderstanding is a productive and vibrant driver of fantasy. In this way, Rilke's child-figures experience the world in ways that feel akin to Blumenberg's notion of "pensiveness"—a term he uses to describe the kind of philosophical thinking that finds its roots in the frustrating "incongruity" between a fable and its apparent moral.¹⁵⁵ Pensiveness denotes a kind of thinking that operates with a sense of "space for play" and produces a more robust view of the world because it tarries in the difficult areas between "meaning and meaninglessness."¹⁵⁶ Indeed, we have seen this modeled across Rilke's prose work: in the divine thimble, the impossibly giant sunflowers and tiny cottage doors, in the puzzling semblance that appears in the nothingness of the doll, and finally in the fantastic bivalence of domestic spaces. Rilke's prose is peppered with romantic references to childhood as the exemplary model for poetic production: for example in his *Letters to a Young Poet*, he advises that the aspiring poet re-create the inner liveliness of a child's "wise incomprehension" ("weises Nicht-Verstehen") as a resistance against the "paltry" ("armselig") busywork of status and career.¹⁵⁷ But his call to embrace the child's way of resisting understanding takes on the character of pensiveness—a philosophical-poetic standpoint that, in view of what we have seen in the preceding sections, finds ample agreement with Blumenberg.

Let us return to the Thales anecdote—itself an object of pensiveness, and an infinitely applicable philosophical story about philosophy itself—that I noted at the start of this chapter, to now "reoccupy" it in such a way that it captures the task of childhood in Rilke's storytelling. I suggested by way of analogy that, just as for Blumenberg the Thracian woman's laughter discloses the absurdity of theory embodied in the tumbling astronomer Thales, Rilke's child-figures interrupt and critique the normative discourses of adulthood. Children, like the Thracian woman, not only remind us of the here and now, they belong to ordinary worldliness; adults, like the ancient astronomer, are oriented toward both spatial distance and temporal futurity.¹⁵⁸ In this reoccupation, as it were, the Thracian woman appears as a queer figure—crossing class, regional, and cultural boundaries—whose laughter intervenes and disrupts like the well that trips Thales in his contemplation. Rilke's child-characters likewise cross boundaries of narration, their appearance indicating how the present disturbs the easy forward gaze of adulthood. In contrast to what Dana Luciano calls the "chronobiopolitics" of the nineteenth century, Rilke's child-figures resist the "anterior" and eternal time of the home and the futurity of childhood as "investment"—instead they appear invested in their own present; they dally in their own wayward time, the nonprogressive time of sensation.¹⁵⁹

What we see in Rilke's writings on poets and children is that his view of human cognition aligns with Husserl's in key ways, in particular in the shared regard for acts of seeing as an intuition that produces a legitimate claim about the world even as it often involves deficient, or otherwise "imperfect," representations of things in the world.¹⁶⁰ In Rilke's prose we find poetically articulated the awareness of an incommensurability of the world as we perceive and imagine it with our attempts to describe it—an awareness that unites the long history of phenomenology leading up to Blumenberg's own critiques. Rilke's stories about children model this view of philosophy as a way of thinking in and of the lifeworld—attuned to what surrounds us but with a willingness to see things as if anew. We hear this echo in Rilke's advice to the young poet: "Why not then continue to look like a child upon it all as upon something unfamiliar, from out of the depth of one's own world?"[161]

In reading Rilke as a thinker of perception, fantasy, and sense-making, I claim that his philosophical storytelling makes the heady work of phenomenology more legible and more accessible. Thinking about how children think takes us out of the "busyness" of grown-up life and helps us see what it means to *see more* of the world around us. Husserl notes in the introduction to *Ideas for a Pure Phenomenology and Phenomenological Philosophy* that it is the philosopher who is herself "learning to see." As Rilke's stories make clear, this is something children already know how to do, and it is the work of literature that allows us to understand their "wise incomprehension."

3
Walter Benjamin's Small Worlds of Childhood

Children's Play and Reflections of the World

In a passage from his unfinished literary montage, *The Arcades Project* (*Das Passagen-Werk*), Walter Benjamin ruminates on the ways the French philosopher and early socialist Charles Fourier imagined utopia resting upon the "model of children's play."[1] "The Fourierist utopia," Benjamin writes, "is the image of an earth on which every place has become an *inn* [Wirtschaft]. The double meaning of the word "Wirtschaft" (i.e., farm, inn) blossoms here: all places are worked by human hands, made useful and beautiful thereby; all, however, stand like a roadside inn, open to all.... On that earth, the act would be kin to the dream."[2] In his playful reading, the child's business of play, creativity, beauty, and democratic hospitality come together with dreams: The material and the fantastical are one. What will be instructive for us, however, is that in this critique of extant industrial bourgeois alienation Benjamin casts the child's attitude as one that is both novel and *world-making*. The utopia evinced in children's play features the multitude: encompassed by an entire world, itself filled with smaller worlds—inns or farms, places of creativity, beauty, and dreams.

Inspired by Fourier, Benjamin offers his own incredible vision of innumerable small worlds—each *Wirtschaft* filled with activity, together forming a utopian earth—that exemplifies the idea that childhood is itself a "microworld" or "microcosm" which could critically intervene in material history.[3] This fragment also supplies us with a glimpse of a paradigm that reappears frequently throughout his oeuvre—one that makes children's knowledge and perception intelligible. Benjamin's philosophical poetics of childhood centers children as philosophical subjects in their own right and imagines children's experience as already complete in itself. In the above passage, the utopian critique of bourgeois alienation relies on descriptions of the radical now-time of childhood cognition during play. With his emphasis on the world-building quality of childhood work, Benjamin disrupts assumptions that writing about childhood means representing the activity of growing *up into adulthood*. His attention to the fullness of childhood experience queerly resists what Kathryn Bond Stockton later characterizes as childhood's tendency to be "relentlessly figured as vertical movement upward."[4] Indeed, the utopian image of childhood is so expansive that "up" would not account for the universe it already contains. Here, and throughout his corpus, Benjamin carefully attends to the child's experience of their world on its own terms. Children appear not as future adults (and bourgeois subjects); they are, instead, instructive to adults, as their utopian character appears precisely in how they already *are*. Benjamin's recurring depictions of children warrant a thorough reexamination—one that moves past the idea that children appear primarily as indices for or phases of belated adult subjectivity. This chapter makes the case that Benjamin's child-characters are meaningful both in and because of their radical present-ness, in contrast to conventional interpretations of his work as about memory and nostalgia, in which child-figures would be incomplete, only to gain their full meaning as futurity.

In this passage on Fourier, it is the child's capacity to experience a whole world—and in its order—that retains something of the greater universe beyond it; as Benjamin writes, this is a "Leitbild"—that is, a "principle"—which is "realized" in children's games.[5] This representation of both utopia and children's play recalls the metaphorical labor that Leibniz's *Monadology* (1714) once provided Benjamin in his early writing. The monad, Leibniz theorized, is the fundamental substance or unit of which he theorized all beings in the world consist, each reflecting the universe—each from its particular vantage. We see Benjamin envisioning childhood play as sharing the monad's principle of expression, such that "Fourier's utopia," "the world," and all the little scenes of "Wirtschaft" together recall Leibniz's own marveling at how a microscopic ecosystem contained within a drop of water expresses the whole of creation.[6]

In the "Epistemo-Critical Prologue" of his habilitation, *The Origin of the German Tragic Drama* (1924), Benjamin introduces Leibniz's monad in an attempt to articulate the proper shape of philosophical thought through a dialectical definition of the "idea." In what will come to be seen as a hallmark of Benjamin's writing, Leibniz appears here through paraphrastic practice rather than as direct quote. Benjamin reformulates the following metaphysical proposition on divine creation as an epistemological and ontological assertion about the idea: "This interconnection . . . of all created things to each other, and each to all other things, brings it about that each simple substance has relations that express all the others, and consequently, that each simple substance is a perpetual living mirror of the universe" (§56).[7] Benjamin's prologue repurposes this figure of thought as an "image" which "contains the world," whose very representation is that of the world in "abbreviation."[8] In this paraphrastic gesture, Leibniz's description of the limitations of individual monadic reflective abilities (§60) reappears as the "indistinct abbreviation of the rest of the world of ideas" insofar as "every single monad contains, in an indistinct way, all the others."[9] Benjamin's explicit invocation of Leibniz's *Monadology* in this passage, in conjunction with his clear appropriation of the monad as model for the idea, serves as provisional evidence of Benjamin's familiarity and engagement with the basic structure of Leibniz's monad despite there being little surviving evidence of his having studied Leibniz directly.[10] It also exemplifies what I show in this chapter to be Benjamin's paradigmatic attempts to articulate the relationship between human cognition, especially intellection and imagination, and its representation in spatial and specular language, by employing both philosophy and poetics.

Benjamin seems to not only have been struck by the similarity between the structure of the monad as philosophical thought (idea), but also the necessity of spatial metaphors for representing philosophical concepts in general. It is Leibniz's concept of perceptual distinctness as it appears in the *Monadology* that, in my reading, informs and shapes Benjamin's writing on childhood to a significant degree. Larry M. Jorgensen has elucidated this notion of "perceptual distinctness" in Leibniz in terms of what contemporary Leibniz scholarship calls the "universal expression thesis (UE)," the symmetry and transitivity among perceptions, representations, and their objects.[11] Universal expression requires that "each substance have an internal structure that preserves the correlating structure of the universe" and, at the same time, that its perceptual distinctness be tempered by each monad's point of view, such that "qualitative" differences in what is preserved arise based on an individual monad's point of view.[12] Benjamin returns again and again to the expansive capacity of the monad to express the whole universe, while forgoing Leibniz's conceptualizations of memory and consciousness.[13] Something akin to the thesis in Leibniz's 1714 text appears to provide a framework for describing scenes of childhood perception and knowledge formation as well as the necessity of their (poetic) representation. Benjamin's depictions of childhood cognition capitalize on the underlying principle of *structure preservation*, whereby both reasoning and perceiving express or re-present some or all aspect(s) of an object.[14]

Benjamin remained intrigued by both the metaphorical potential of what we today call "universal expression" and the phenomenological aspects embedded in the necessary distinctness afforded by point of view.[15] In his writings on children and childhood, his use of the monad becomes particularly evident, as the child-subject is depicted in a world with all the poetic realist attention to material detail, but where such prose reveals the wider prosaic world. Benjamin exploits these literary depictions of the everyday to emphasize the monadological structure of cognition as an interplay of perception and imagination. In this chapter I demonstrate how Benjamin's often experimental prose vignettes reimagine the literary enterprise as one of universal expression, portraying the experiences of the child-subject by continually borrowing from Leibniz and thereby imagining the child and their activities as "perpetual living mirror[s] of the universe" (§56).[16] In some cases, it is also in virtue of Benjamin's poetics of form, his use of what Gerhard Richter called the "modernist Denkbild" (thought-image), or aphorism, in his reflections on the child-subject that serves as a contemplation of ontology—a response to the question of what is, and of the representability of the world to ourselves, in both form and content, as a picture of cognition in general.[17]

As in this first example on Fourier, I am not going to be making hard-line claims that Benjamin was somehow an idealist. Rather, I analyze how his portrayals of childhood, by grappling with a dialectical view of the material and ideal, elevate the child-subject. Benjamin's philosophical poetics of childhood emerges as an organizing principle of representing childhood subjectivity, in its nearly systematic affinity and analogy with the monad. Moving beyond recent readings of his idiosyncratic monadology (e.g., an "immanent infinity"), I do show that Benjamin repeatedly characterizes not only the child's perception and imagination but also the relationship between child-subject and the world of material objects as monadological by emphasizing how *internal* particularity or singularity reflects and, in a way, also guarantees the multitude of the *external* world.[18] Scholars such as Samuel Weber have tended to regard Benjamin's monad as representative of autarky and immanence (complemented by indirect relationality in its "constellation" with others) in his conceptualization of the idea.[19] By contrast, others such as Paula Schwebel make the case that Benjamin's "distort[ion]" and "historical mediation" of Leibniz's *Monadology* provide a way for him to describe the melancholy response to secular modernity.[20] This chapter therefore expands on this recent scholarship in its suggestion that, as a philosopher in his own right, Benjamin turns to the rational metaphysics and theologically oriented language of Leibniz to create his own philosophy of material life while affirming the conditions of modern secular thought.[21]

Benjamin's extensive corpus of writing on childhood, ranging from commentaries on children's illustrated books to detailed scenes of his own childhood growing up in Berlin, has been characterized as a quasi-Proustian project on memory and the passage of time.[22] His posthumous memoir, *Berlin Childhood around 1900* (*Berliner Kindheit um 1900*), has come to be regarded as part of a long-standing engagement with belated representations of "a lived event" ("ein erlebtes Ereignis"), a problem which occupied a number of his essays.[23] And perhaps because Benjamin also frequently wrote on the twin issues of memory and temporality, scholarship has largely overlooked the possibility that his writing on childhood presents an altogether different approach to the lived event: that is, as the forms and limits of human perception and cognition in the moment of experience. This chapter proposes just such a reading of Benjamin's writings on childhood.

However, recovering such a critique requires, perhaps counterintuitively, a willingness to relinquish the commonly held view that Benjamin's writings on childhood are always primarily about childhood's forward-facing value to adult memory and the aesthetic representation of that belatedness. Instead, I show that Benjamin's writings on children and childhood express a larger philosophical undertaking in human perception and cognition, and one that only becomes *a*chronologically visible alongside his idiosyncratic deployment of Leibniz's *Monadology*—as what Samuel Weber describes, writing of early Benjamin's interest in the monad, as a way of capturing how "phenomena represented in one idea reflect, in a discontinuous, abbreviated . . . manner, other ideas, which together constitute the 'world.'"[24] This chapter traces what I see as the far-reaching consequences in Benjamin's engagement with Leibniz's philosophical metaphor, as the influence of his reading of the *Monadology* echoes throughout his writing on childhood experience.

By reading Benjamin's writings on childhood with an eye toward the appearances of monadic expression, we see him working to understand a range of phenomena, from perception of objects in everyday life to his thinking about poetic writing as a technology of philosophical representation. My aim is not to address every mention of childhood in Benjamin's corpus, nor to suggest that the monad serves him as a theory of everything, but rather to show that his repeated return to representations of childhood produces a paradigmatic account that is both epistemological and phenomenological in nature.[25] In other words, Benjamin is interested in the way that children experience and come to understand the world around them on the basis of something like Leibniz's structure preservation (i.e., translating and transporting of features) in monadic perception that thus demands an attunement to poetic representation.[26]

Benjamin, like the other two authors examined in this book so far, turns his attention toward the relationship between representations of childhood and ordinary experience, and, again, we find the result is something unexpected.

In his attention to the moment of experience, the present time of perception, children cease to appear as temporally future-oriented signifiers, such as the "not-yet" of adulthood or the "before" to the coming-of-age novel's "after," or as only arriving belatedly to meaning as memories or nostalgia. As I have argued throughout this book, this emphasis on the "now-time" of encountering the material world and the present-ness of cognition offers a radical departure from conventional accounts of childhood as they are removed from, to paraphrase Lee Edelman, the logics of familialism and reproductive futurism. Benjamin's depictions refuse long-standing literary and philosophical traditions in which children appear as signifiers of the production of the social fabric of the bourgeois family unit or as necessary operable figures in its perpetuation.[27] Indeed, they appear detached from the entire "vertical" or straight project of the family as such—neither as objects of parenthood nor as future reproducing adults themselves. In this regard, it is no surprise that, like Fourier, Benjamin focuses on the child's *own ways* of being, precisely as a counter to the default processes of existing modes of adult social reproduction. Rather than represent children as the "fantasy of futurity" of the persistence of the current social reality (or even of a single family),[28] Benjamin's texts embrace the epistemological value of children as subjects who have a specific knowledge and have a unique purchase on the material world in which they are present. It is in *this* utopian spirit—one that envisions something *other* than a future promise of more of the present—that Benjamin sees the radical, and I argue, queer possibility in children's thinking.[29] Benjamin's narratives of childhood appear in relation to his writing on the power of the domestic interior as both index and effect of late nineteenth-century culture. The aesthetics of childhood is understood as part of the larger domestic phenomenon of bourgeois life. Childhood spaces are not only subject to the historical materialist critique of culture evident in his writings on design or architecture; they also show Benjamin to be attending to human subjectivity, in particular as the interplay between material perception and a transcendental view of imagination. Children also fascinate Benjamin as epistemological subject matter because they belong to the past. This temporality is not early nineteenth-century Romantic inaccessibility;[30] instead, the utopian possibility in the child's small worlds recalls what José Esteban Muñoz (after Bloch) calls the "no-longer-conscious" of nonlinear time.[31] And, at the same time, because children are embodiments of our very capacity to learn and to know, they offer the queer attitude of hope that is precisely *not* tied to a heteronormative futurity.[32] Like Stifter and Rilke, Benjamin roots his philosophical poetics of childhood in a distinctive representation of material in space. Whereas Stifter looked backward to the Enlightenment and Rilke's philosophical poetics of childhood anticipates twentieth-century phenomenology, Benjamin allegorizes Leibniz's early eighteenth-century metaphysics, such that the *Monadology* comes to serve as a kind of figural framework for childhood intuition and the necessity of poetic language for its representation.[33]

The pages that follow are organized into five roughly chronological sections. The first section examines what I describe as Benjamin's early observational strategies and articulates why we should see this as part of an emerging paradigmatic use of Leibniz's *Monadology*, albeit stripped of its original theological stakes. We will see how Benjamin uses the monad as a philosophical reference for articulating how much finer (i.e., nearly absolute) childhood capacities to perceive, imagine, and understand the world are. The second section examines both published and unpublished fragments to show how Leibniz's philosophical rhetoric of scale informs not only Benjamin's literary depictions of childhood in a crucial way but also his turn to the poetic use of technological mediation in writing about childhood. The third section focuses on the generic questions raised by his use of aphoristic expression and miniaturization, the ways in which both specularity and scale integrate his epistemological with aesthetic concerns, to essentially suggest that the monad permeates his very practice of representation. The fourth section takes up his unfinished memoir to argue that here we find a kind of late-stage, perhaps more fully developed, philosophical-poetic project of childhood. The fifth and final section reflects on how we might rethink of the work in his corpus as producing, to borrow from Agamben, a *paradigm*: that is, as a form of knowledge made visible by virtue of the collective effect of intersections between Leibniz's *Monadology* and Benjamin's vast array of childhood texts, and one which insists on a queer temporality of its reading.

The chapter as a whole thus argues that Leibniz's monad is a critical component of the philosophical paradigm that Benjamin's work produces, one that reaches well beyond his early explicit endeavors at theorizing conceptual thought as such. Indeed, in his essays on and depictions of nineteenth-century bourgeois childhood, Benjamin creates what amounts to an entire cryptomonadology. Collectively, his writings on childhood undermine the assessment that his use of Leibniz, like his philosophical strategy more broadly, is merely the result of being a "lyric thinker" who borrowed suitable "metaphors . . . of systemic totality."[34] In the pages that follow, we will see Benjamin's systematic return to the ideas he seemed to have largely abandoned. Rather than revealing a corpus that is dilettantish in its engagement, we will instead see how such deployment (or exploitation) of certain metaphorical tendencies in Leibniz enables Benjamin to elevate the child-subject out of the discourse of mere nostalgia or innocence, and into the pantheon of philosophers.

Leibniz's *Monadology* and Childhood Intuition in Benjamin's Early Essays

Children are an occasional but consistent subject matter within Benjamin's early critical essays and fragments on aesthetics and the imagination. Some of these texts center on children's visual perception in ways that intersect with both historical and contemporary discourses of painting and color, and a range of benchmark theorists of the child's naïve and nonconceptual aesthetics, from John Ruskin's mid-nineteenth-century ideal of the "childish perception" of color to early twentieth-century painters such as Kandinsky and Klee.[35] Over the course of the decade, Benjamin began what would become an oeuvre-spanning process of experimenting with both the poetic process of depicting how the seeing child might appear combined with *what* children see. In his earliest writings, Benjamin takes an observational stance, describing children in their ordinary lives, taking notice of them in acts of perceiving and understanding the phenomenal world. In these texts, children appear as Gaston Bachelard had described them—still tethered to the world around them.[36] Adults, by contrast, appear limited by habit or in the habit of limiting their own cognition—driven by impulses toward finitude, order, and efficiency. Children, therefore, express the human capacity for a much wider range of possible perceptions and, accordingly, of understanding.

Gershom Scholem not only captured Benjamin's particular attentiveness to children as subjects but also saw that the stakes of childhood perception and cognition were not just a matter of aesthetics. In an essay on the intellectual significance of his friend, he writes that

> one of Benjamin's most important characteristics [was] that throughout his life he was attracted with almost magical force by the child's world and ways. This world was one of the persistent and recurring themes of his reflections, and indeed, his writings [on childhood] are some his most perfect pieces. . . . works dedicated to the as yet undistorted world of the child and its creative imagination, which the metaphysician [Benjamin] describes with irreverent wonder and at the same time seeks to conceptually penetrate.[37]

Child subjectivity falls under what Scholem rightly saw as Benjamin's primary domain of interest: namely, a "philosophical experience of the world and its reality . . . the meaning of the term *metaphysics*."[38] What Scholem and scholars since then have overlooked is the inextricable relationship between Benjamin's poetic-aesthetic experimentation and the development of this idea of metaphysics.

In his essay "A Child's View of Color" from roughly 1914, Benjamin remarks that children seem to differ from adults in their capacity for distinguishing an "infinite range of nuances" through individual senses, such as sight.[39] The child, he tells us, therefore experiences color not merely as that which "cloaks the surface of phenomena," but rather, in virtue of their detailed sense of color, they view the color of objects not as an "isolated" phenomenon but as part of a continuous or interrelated cognition, fused with the "world of imagination."[40] Benjamin's account depicts the child's perception-imagination in such a way that is already suggestive of the monad's structure: Namely, the finite sensory experience of a substance's color is linked to—or, in his words, secures ("sichert")—the infinitude of an entire "world." Leibniz provides an analogous characterization of cognition in ordinary encounters: "We ourselves experience a multitude in a simple substance, when we find that the least thought we ourselves apperceive involves a variety in its object. Thus, all those who recognize that the soul is a simple substance should recognize the multitude in the monad" (§16).[41] Over the course of several texts on children's perception and imagination, Benjamin develops the same symmetry that Leibniz seeks to establish between the material makeup of the universe, on the one hand, and the composition of the human soul (or mind), on the other.

Childhood cognition is, as Benjamin sees it, fused with the imagination, and thus transforms material encounters into a dialectic of particular and universal as isolated objects of cognition and as the simultaneity of a whole world to which such objects might belong. In his 1924 essay, "Old Forgotten Children's Books," Benjamin's repetition of the Leibnizian monadic structure not only enables him to present the dialectic of the child's productive "play," which enables individual perceptions to yield their own small world; it also elevates the child as one who is able attain something shy of a God's-eye view.

> [Children] feel irresistibly drawn to detritus [Abfall] generated by building, gardening, housework, tailoring, or carpentry. In these waste products, they recognize the face that the world of things turns directly and solely to them. In using these things, they do not so much imitate the works of adults as bring these residual materials and waste products [Rest- und Abfallstoffe] together in a disjointed, new relationship with one another. Children build their own world of things for themselves, a small one within the large one.[42]

The child's encounter with the material world illustrates a crucial difference in intuition: that which appears to adults as purposeless, indeterminate, or without order—in other words, our trash—is the substance out of which children realize their creative capacities.[43] In this essay, children see the world as constructed like Leibniz's monadic conception of matter, where each minimal physical unit "express[es] the whole universe" (§65) as if it contained within it "a garden full of plants, and a pond full of fishes" (§67).[44] In Benjamin's telling, children are able to engage with a world that is, like the "subtleness" of Leibniz's "imperceptible" (§68) monadic one, and thus largely unavailable to adults.[45] In the passage above, children perceive ("erkennen)" the ordinary overlooked and discarded object as the matter which makes up the *real* world itself. Like the divine view of the monad, the child also sees that "there is nothing fallow . . . nothing dead in the universe, no chaos, no confusion except in appearance, almost as it might appear in a pond at a distance, where we might see the confused and, so to speak, teeming movement of fish in the pond, without separately discerning the fish themselves" (§69).[46]

Benjamin depicts the child at play in a way that is, oddly, not all playful. Their serious regard for a world overlooked by adults is emphasized through the rhetoric of trash or waste in German: "Abfall-." With its multiple resonances of being cast off, dropping off, and disappearing (or even a religious "falling away"), this term depicts the child as not only noticing the value of such debris but in fact retrieving, reviving, or renewing it—thereby affirming their position in analogy with the absolute creative and epistemological capacities that Leibniz assigned to God. All that which is cast off or hardly regarded by adults is, at the same time, the unmediated experience of childhood perception of the phenomenal world (the "face [which] turns directly and solely to them"). In this passage, Benjamin refashions the child as a creator of things much as Leibniz describes both the monad and the nature of all of creation, namely as the "small world" within a "large one." Childhood play thus embodies the power of the divine, by virtue of which putatively "fallow" objects of ordinary adult activities become the enlivened substances which make up the small worlds of childhood. With the particular rhetoric of *Abfall*, Benjamin fills the child's world not only with revitalized waste, but also with that which "falls away": Ripened fruits and their seeds as well as fallen leaves are all litter that feed and give rise to new life.[47] The temporality of the fallow and revitalized objects of childhood play move between the cyclical (nature) and monumental (divine), but also the particular contingency of the child's own present.[48] The queer time of play thus refuses the industrial time of work by taking up its refuse, while moving beyond the anterior time of home and the eternally recurring time of season and family, and dallying instead in its own "disjointed" time of novelty.[49]

The relationship of small worlds to larger ones that childhood play creates, in turn, echoes the universal expression thesis. This idea, in which some structure is preserved across scale and location, is one that easily speaks to the work of poetics generally, and metaphor, in particular, as philosophical principles.

In this way, Leibniz's UE also undergirds the world of childhood, which is likewise governed by the flexibility and portability of relationships and features. In Benjamin's essay, the child is therefore able to appear as the Leibnizian divine not only because of their unique capacity for perception, but because the child's "world of things" issues from their capacities for metaphorical creation. It is instructive that, as Benjamin continues in this same passage, he emphasizes that the child's dexterity to transform everyday material scraps is the same ability as that which affords them intellectual and imaginative powers. The microcosmic expresses, as *metaphor*, the monad's capacity to contain (in reflection) "an entire garden full of plants, and a pond full of fishes" (§67),[50] and, as if by extension of universal expression (as the preservation of structure with infinite perspectival variation), the child, in Benjamin's view, is thus able to build a microworld by repurposing and reanimating leftover images and motifs, as storytellers:

> Children thus produce [*bilden*] their own small world of things within the greater one. The fairy tale is such a waste product—perhaps the most powerful to be found in the cognitive life [*geistigen Leben*] of humanity: a waste product that emerges from the growth and decay of the saga. Children are able to manipulate fairy stories with the same ease and lack of inhibition that they display in playing with pieces of cloth and building blocks. They build their world out of motifs from the fairy tale, combining its various elements.[51]

With its play on image (*Bild*) and imagination (*Einbildung*), this passage emphasizes the involvement of the child's transfigurative perception in their creative capacities in the practice of world-building (*bilden*).[52] Benjamin links the production of worlds—*poiesis*—with the child's imagination, and simultaneously reminds the reader that, like the child's play with scraps, these larger story-worlds are built from fallow bits of saga. We see here three features of childhood: First, child's play reveals a material world missed by adults (overlooked as waste); second, such play can be understood as the creation of fairy tales, which are themselves the castoffs from the otherwise proper saga; and third, the "small world" of childhood appears when these unrelated and neglected units ("building blocks," "waste products," "motifs") are both preserved and brought into novel configurations. In the multivalence of *bilden* (as forming, composing, shaping), narrative and poetics are the point of access for other worlds. They are the means by which childhood appears for the grown-up, just as it serves the child's own reflective activity.

By imbricating the child's recognition/seeing with storytelling, Benjamin also makes a case here for an emphatically perspectival reading of children's cognition. Let us recall Leibniz's own characterization of the monad as that which constructs a difference between divine knowledge and the individual reflective capacity of each monad to perceive the world: in other words, the relationship between individual substances that collectively make up the universe and the vast multiplicity within the universe itself. Leibniz proposed that each monad would need to contain the "perception" of the infinity external to itself in order to be entirely sufficient (i.e., nothing would enter or exit), but that distinctiveness occurs because each reflection must also be in some way deficient or partial such that no one monad would also be an identity with the absolute knowledge of God (§60).[53] To illustrate this, Leibniz famously imagines the monad's partial—but nonetheless true—reflection as one of any number of infinite possible (and distinct) spatial perspectives:

> Just as the same city viewed from various directions appears entirely different and, as it were, multiplied perspectivally, in just the same way it happens that, because of the infinite multitude of simple substances, there are, as it were, just as many different universes, which are, nevertheless, only perspectives on a single universe, corresponding to the different point of view of each monad. (§57)[54]

In Leibniz's telling, each monad is both limited and distinct in its own potential perception of the totality. His metaphor for the monad's perspectival perception (the view "from various sides") recalls the Husserlian "adumbration" of objects in Rilke's child-subject.[55] Yet the world-building child-subject in Benjamin's essay not only aggregates adult detritus into an entire world; they also translate the material through their own perspectival shift, and thus the construction of their smaller world repeats the Leibnizian finitude of related-yet-discontinuous monadic perspectives. In Benjamin's cosmology, children "don't so much imitate the works of adults with these things as place these residual materials and waste products in a disjointed [*sprunghaft*], new relationship with one another." Children thus appear like Leibniz's God: they create a world out of simple substances—viz., things whose value and contents are invisible to adults—and they organize them in such a way that both preserves some structure (as motifs) and echoes the distinct, separate yet connected views of each monad to the whole of the universe. The child's divine-like creativity in Benjamin's essay is ultimately both the poietic process of creating new stories from abandoned motifs and the perspectival capacity to "build . . . their world of things," one that is also out of line or out of joint. Thus the scene of childhood mirrors the intersecting grounds of metaphorics, epistemology, and metaphysics set forth in Leibniz's *Monadology* as both set about in their own respective nonlinear ways.

From the position of third-person narrator, Benjamin can only describe the totality of the child's work—the construction of "a small world within a large one"—from the grown-up perspective, that is, without any access to the detail of the microcosm. And so from this standpoint, he also elevates the present-ness of childhood experience: not only that which is present (the detritus, the discarded and otherwise overlooked). The adult can therefore reflect on the no-longer-conscious only as the temporality of the emphatically present now-time in which both childhood perception and childhood *poiesis* operates. While these early depictions of the child, which I am calling observational essays, seem to accept that the "pond full of fishes," so to speak, remains imperceptible to any adult onlooker, over time Benjamin's writing on childhood shifts toward increasingly poetic narrative strategies to articulate the child's perception of an otherwise invisible world. As I will show over the course of the remaining sections of this chapter, this emphasis on poetics also affords him greater freedom to contemplate the role of metaphor in the philosophical capacity of children as subjects as well as the figure of childhood as a philosophical metaphor for possible forms of cognition in general.

Technologies of Representation in "Portraits of Children" and "Enlargements"

During the period between 1923 and 1927, Benjamin began to experiment with novel approaches to writing and conceptualizing childhood. In a series of sketches, he no longer depicts children as figures on the margins of adult life occupying an invisible domain. Instead, he makes childhood visible in its details with brief vignettes featuring children as central protagonists of their own scenes, engaged in ordinary activities. When the vignettes were published in his aphoristic collection, *One-Way Street* (*Einbahnstraße*),[56] they could be counted among the exemplary experiences of modernity, with all those grown-up topoi that would come to define his corpus, such as architecture, the postal service, writing, and print. Whereas his early essays on childhood report generalized observations of how children cognize (e.g., see, recognize, imagine, understand) the world, each of the six aphorisms in *One-Way Street* portrays a single child by interweaving a literary realist description of bourgeois childhood with highly poetic language that articulates the dialectics of creativity as perceiving and understanding.[57]

In a note to himself during the draft stage of the project, Benjamin indicates the technical stakes in the belatedness of representing childhood. In a brief fragment titled "On the Portraits of Children in 'One-Way Street'" ("Zu den Kinderporträts der 'Einbahnstraße'"), Benjamin records what he sees as the critical task at hand for these aphorisms.[58] In an echo of the note's heading, which already nods to the theme of photography that would eventually frame the entire set of vignettes, he reminds himself of the challenge that children pose to every project of representation: "What must by all means be thought out is whether this is not an expression for the incomprehensible earnestness of childlike intuition: that it knows nothing but totality."[59] How can childlike intuition—in its authenticity—be depicted? What would it mean to say that children know—that is to say, recognize—*only* the totality? In repeating the forms of intellection and construction discussed in the preceding section, the task of writing any individual scene of childhood unavoidably involves confronting the whole of experience; children, this suggests, are like Leibniz's monads, where each one "express[es] the whole universe" (§65).[60]

Benjamin's brief note ends with a fragmentary quote that encapsulates the problem facing the author: "Here, just this sentence from Berthold Auerbach's: Writing and Nation . . . : 'In later years, this small world is' . . . 'no longer comprehensible as a whole, it always points the beholder to the larger one.'"[61] In citing Auerbach's 1846 text, Benjamin emphasizes that the adult writer's epistemological challenge posed by childhood directly affects the possibility of its poetic representation. In his own awareness that what must be surmounted is the belated position of his own perspective, he contemplates what Bachelard later observed. These "portraits of children," he hopes, will be able to adequately achieve the model of two worlds ("a small one and the large one") and, I think, their philosophical analogues, in the monad and the universe. This note, therefore, reads as a variation of what occupied him in "Old Forgotten Children's Books": Namely, that, in contrast to the child's view, the adult capacity for perception (reflection) and recognition (knowledge) is finite and impoverished, always overlooking the small worlds. How then can an adult properly write on children as subjects?

In the published depictions of childhood in *One-Way Street*, we see that Benjamin proposes a twofold solution to this problem. The child's perception is so totalizing that the entire contents of the world are containable within their cognition. Rephrased in the terms I have been using thus far, if the perspective of the child's world is like Leibniz's description of the divine or absolute view of each monad—which contains what amounts to "an entire garden full of plants, and a pond full of fishes" (§67)[62]—it appears for the child that the contents of that small world are entirely knowable. How then might one depict this? Like Leibniz, Benjamin too takes recourse to metaphor. And, like the contrast that Auerbach draws between how and what children "grasp" ("erfassen"), on the one hand, and grown-up cognition of one's "later years" on the other,[63] the task of representing childhood will not only need to address intellection but also scale.

In the published version of these "children's portraits," Benjamin must abandon what I have described previously as an observational stance toward representing childhood, and he turns instead to a philosophical-poetic approach in order to address this issue. This shift results in a more decisive employment of metaphors (e.g., of photographic reproduction) as if to counter the notion that, unaided, adult perception is unable to see the "small world" of childhood. Here the "portraits" of children can be understood not just as depictions of a frozen moment of the private sphere.

In *One-Way Street*, Benjamin organizes six scenes of nameless young school-age child engaging in ordinary activities under the heading "Enlargements" ("Vergrösserungen"), a move which immediately positions representations of childhood as matters of visibility and scale.[64] This time, however, it is the very representational capacity of textual depiction that recalls the monadological conception of a "small world within a large one." The size of the child's world is so small that it could be framed, like a portrait. As we will see, this image of the small world that demands an enlargement to be legible makes sense. We can read this shift in language from the general notion of "children's portraits" (ambiguously unclear as to painted or photographed) to a specificity of the technological language of enlargement.[65] In line with other concerns about technological mediation, we also see some sense of this in his essay on photography (1931), published only a few years after "Enlargements." In this essay, Benjamin describes how this "most precise technology can lend a magical value to its products, such as a painted picture can never again have for us."[66] What interests Benjamin is the photograph's unique capacity for "slow motion and image enlargement" that make the otherwise imperceptible perceptible.[67] The temporality of the children's portraits as enlargements is one of suspension (stopping to look at childhood where it is rather than as an index of the future), and as extreme slow motion they offer the reader a dilated time, such that the contents may be more easily registered.

The camera, he suggests, is also more closely related to medical or scientific forms of seeing, which make microscopic structures and cellular anatomy visible, as "photography discloses in this material physiognomic aspects, image worlds, which inhabit the smallest things, interpretable and latent enough to have found a shelter in daydreams."[68] Photographic representation is therefore not only a kind of world of its own—one of image—but it also contains and makes those "smallest things" available to both perception and cognition. With a hint of Leibniz's language of monadic reflection, poetic writing serves as the "technical aid" of enlargement that makes these invisible and rich worlds of childhood "interpretable." Benjamin's conception of the "enlargement" deploys photograph's capacity to uncover a microscopic yet replete world of things.[69]

These "portraits" of children thus do not emerge here representative of the straight time of family life (i.e., as a material representation genealogy or objects of future family memories) as these figures do not appear as anyone's children.[70] Here, the technology of poetic enlargement dislodges childhood from its conventional place as visual evidence of family lines.

Benjamin's productive conception of enlarging technology is a revaluation of Siegfried Kracauer's earlier characterization of what Kracauer considered to be the impoverished cognitive value in a photograph.[71] In Kracauer's phrasing: "In photography the spatial appearance of an object is its meaning. . . . The photograph captures [its object] as a spatial continuum from any one of a number of positions."[72] Benjamin, it could be said, adopts the first of Kracauer's ideas, that is, that photographic technology replaces ephemeral artistic meaning with objects that have been made available to perception by virtue of their spatial appearance; this, in turn, produces a world in which the contents are all the more visible. The second part of Kracauer's proposition seems to us now already baked into Benjamin's conception of childhood: it recalls both Leibniz's characterization of individual monadic reflection of the world as distinct perspectives of an object in space (§57).[73] In light of its heading, each vignette in the series of "Enlargements," be it of a child reading or playing, is therefore announced as a spatial appearance in Kracauer's sense as well as something assisted by a microscopic operation in Benjamin's sense.

As a paratextual component, the heading "enlargements" (rather than "portraits") frames these brief depictions, and it alerts the adult entering this text that, in contrast to mere observation of children, the aphorisms that follow involve a technology (*technē*) of writing that makes their contents—childhood—accessible and knowable (*epistēmē*). The work of enlargement is the representation of an object as both slow time and as impossibly pure spatiality, or as Kracauer acerbically suggests: The photograph is a "stockpile" of its contents.[74] This strictly epistemic view of childhood perhaps closely approximates part of what Benjamin thinks children do or how they perceive. As readers of Benjamin's writings on the child's gaze have remarked, Benjamin's child is almost Romantic, because, unlike an adult, the child cognizes objects in a way that is "nostalgia-free."[75] To paratextually describe childhood as a series of "enlargements" is not only to ready the reader for a spatialized view of objects made more readily visible; it is to underscore that the *technology* of writing is what will overcome ephemerality, belated unintelligibility, and nostalgia—to mimic, as it were, the experience of childhood *during childhood*. What we will see now in the aphorisms themselves is thus not only the representation of the child's experience as spatial, but also a poetics of the present moment, as time made still, or as pure space, operating out of time.

Let us consider, for example, the second "enlargement" in the series, with its subheading, "Tardy Child" ("Zu spät gekommenes Kind").[76] This aphorism is written in the present tense and narrates a child's late arrival at school. From the first line, the text resists both easy nostalgia for the past and ephemerality as the reader is thrust into a radical present as the clock that governs the queer time of childhood appears frozen: "The clock over the school playground seems as if damaged on their account. The hands stand at 'Tardy'("zu spät"),"[77] Like its subheading, the clock that the child encounters reads not a time but simply the adjectival status of being tardy or even *too late* ("zu spät"). The text proceeds with the child's movement through the school's interior halls, the space of childhood appearing though the child-subject's own attentiveness to sound, sight, and tactility: "And as they pass in the corridor, murmurs of secret consultation come from the classroom doors. . . . Or all is silent, as if they were waiting for someone. Inaudibly, they put their hand to the doorhandle. The spot where they stand is steeped in sunlight. Violating the peaceful hour, they open the door."[78] The alternation of chatter and silence unfolds a continual now-time of the experience of movement through the space of a hallway, as the child passes each classroom. Here Benjamin's poetics—with its technical capacity to, as it were, "enlarge" childhood—extends the subjective intention of the school's space, thereby making it available to the adult reader.[79] In its palpable anxiety and focus on the moment of disruption effected by arriving late to school, the scene depicted is not really one of belatedness, but rather the perception of being radically present and spatially located.

At precisely this moment of breathless anticipation—as the child opens the door—the sound of the teacher prattling on metaleptically shifts the narrative from classroom space to the grown-up world of labor: "The teacher's voice clatters like a mill wheel; they stand before the grinding stones. The voice clatters on without a break, but the mill workers now shake off their load to the newcomer. Ten, twenty heavy sacks fly toward them; these they must carry to the bench. Each thread of their little jacket is flour-white."[80] The grade school classroom, a small world of its own, suddenly appears for us as the bustling world of mill work. Though the shift is by way of simile (the teacher's voice is *like* the clattering millwork), the child's perceptions directly enable the small world of the classroom—in a monadic reflection—to perceive the "large world" of grown-up labor. Indeed, what the child hears ceases to be the teacher at all, but rather the rhythmic noise of the machinery. Childhood experience is organized with a kind of poetics of the *Monadology*'s universal expression, whereby the "clattering" ("klappern," "klappernde") is the transitive structure preserved across both the small world of the child's classroom and the larger world beyond.

It is not only monadological space but also time out of joint that Benjamin's philosophical poetics makes accessible. In the queer crossings of the classroom and mill, and of childhood and adulthood, the child-subject resists the imposition of chrononormativity, to paraphrase Elizabeth Freeman, as the child's productive capabilities in the now-time of experience, dreamily refuse to be neatly integrated into the masculine time of progress:[81] The play and interplay of temporalities overrides the linear productivity of arriving on time or clocking in. The reader is able to enter a classroom that has been enlarged—and slowed to a standstill—making the intersecting sensoria and the monadic temporality of childhood perceptible. As in Leibniz's *Monadology*, in which "the present is pregnant with the future," this small world of childhood already contains a view of the totality.[82] The ambivalence of the child's "little jacket" coated white presumably from both the dusty classroom chalk and the clouds of the millwork's flour opens up a queer temporality insofar as the present subsumes both past and future. Although this scene surely also contains a critique of the "millwork" of schooling and the invariability of labor (for young and old alike), what matters for my reading here is how the now-time of monadic experience also *already* contains a future. The simultaneity of perception undermines the notion of coming of age, in which the child would appear as a signifier for a fragile future whose fecundity needs constant assuring. Instead, Benjamin's philosophical poetics of childhood foregrounds the capacious present time of experience over reproductive futurity: the child is neither the locus nor the guarantee of heteronormative futures but rather an access point for imagining childhood knowledge and perception as totality. Much like the *Monadology*'s metaphysics of time, the future is already part of the infinite beyond that is contained within each monad in the present.[83] And so the "tardy" child arrives in their own queer time, in an expansive present that simultaneously expresses times prior to and after.

The fourth vignette in the series of "enlargements" has the subheading "Child Riding the Carousel," and here Benjamin portrays a child's first ride on the carousel, with the opening and closing lines again providing an embodied account of the child's movement through space. The middle portion of the vignette follows the child-subject as their spatial perception transforms into imaginative cognition. Using a third-person narrator, this entire episode is nonfocalized with an emphasis on the child-subject's perception of the event. It exploits the "small world" of the carousel, with its animals and scenery, as a recapitulation of the "large one" in which the ride is physically situated. Rather than only presenting the reader with another example of "lived experience," this aphorism modulates between the now of finite childhood perception and the infinitude of childhood cognition.

Like the phenomenological technique that recalls Rilke's child-subject in his novel *The Notebooks of Malte Laurids Brigge*, Benjamin carefully constructs subjective intention as the attention to and cognition of the carousel in space. For example, the opening lines depict how the carousel appears on approach from a low angle of view—viz., that of a small child. First, the reader encounters the platform's movement in close proximity to the ground beneath it, then the narration, tracking the vision of the child approaching the relatively huge carousel, takes notice of the animal figures soaring high above, at "the height which, in dreams, is best for flying."[84] Benjamin depicts the subject's bittersweet experience of motion: "Music starts, and the child moves away from their mother with a jerk. At first they are afraid to leave her. But then they notice how brave they themselves are."[85] The movement that the text narrates articulates both the child's own embodied perspective of motion through space in the growing distance from the mother, and in the detail of the mechanism's bumpy start. Looking out as the ride proceeds, the appearance of the stationary objects standing around the carousel are represented from the moving child-subject's perspective, as the trees appear to "line the way."[86]

The vignette is organized in a way that is similar to that of the tardy child: like the protagonist crossing the threshold into the classroom, once the carousel ride itself is underway, the space of the carousel transforms. The child suddenly feels themself enthroned and reigning "over a world that belongs to them" and from their seat on the carousel, they glimpsed "the top of a tree emerging from the primeval forest . . . exactly as [they] saw it thousands of years ago."[87] The magical realism of the carousel's feature and its environment creates a specular relationship between the "large world" with, for example, the trees on the property surrounding the carousel appearing as a whole forest or jungle from the riding child's view. With its echoes of divine rule, the explosive capacity of the child's cognition of the "small world" on the carousel repeats the Leibnizian relationship of monadic perception insofar as the carousel is recapitulated in childhood cognition as a whole "world" which belongs to them.

What may be less obvious upon first read, and particularly in translation, is the rhetorical strategy in which the macro view of a carousel (itself a huge round crown shape) is mirrored in the child's view of the carousel ride and also contributes to a representation of the kind of knowledge children may possess. The repetition of the carousel's physical, circular shape begins with the language of enthronement as a metonym for a crown ("Krone"), followed by the appearance of the "Wipfel" (tree top), which is also a synonym, in German, for "Krone" (e.g., "Baumkrone"). And in describing the child's fantastic journey around, Benjamin proposes that the philosophical child's "wisdom" is made real and *circular* like an "eternal recurrence of all things" amid a Dionysian "frenzy" of the sound produced by the booming orchestrion, which is, itself, the *"crown* jewels" (*"Kronschatz"*) at the center of the ride.[88] With all of this pomp, Benjamin announces the child as philosopher.[89] The tropology of macro and micro crowns and turning wheels is less a claim about a conception of time that is circular, but rather a form of knowledge that demands representation of a de-temporalized or cross-temporalized and totalized conception of experience. The wisdom of the child is its radical openness to all and across time. The child, to paraphrase and amend Benjamin, knows only a queer totality. Like the spatially contained but temporally transcendent scenes of school and work in the "Tardy Child," the carousel, too, encompasses an eternity and stakes its affinity with the poetic-philosophical rhetoric of Nietzsche. The depiction of the carousel itself captures the philosophy as the crown-shaped carousel stands in for the large world that encompasses the small world of childhood, itself filled with the infinite conceptual lushness of a monad.

In this section, I have considered the conceptual work and queer temporal work that photographic enlarging technology does in *One-Way Street* and the switch to poetic narrative that Benjamin makes in a series of vignettes. In its analogy to the way that Leibniz describes imperceptible infinity contained within the monad's finite structure, these "enlargements" allow Benjamin to experiment with a concept of scale and spatiality in philosophical representation. The epistemological capacity that Benjamin attributes to the child in his earlier writings leads to the problem of perspective. From an observational standpoint, adults simply don't see what they do! Theorizing childhood cognition, the ability to see both the small and large worlds, as it were, demands a different representational strategy, evident now in this series of "enlargements."

In his turn to poetic representations of space—e.g., rooms, halls, cabinets, and carousels—the "Enlargements" attempts to solve the problem of perspective by imagining the child's cognition as the perception that ranges across temporality or chronology. Here I share Tara Forrest's assessment that, for Benjamin the camera is uniquely able to expand "subjective intention."[90] However, as this present chapter shows, the limits of perception and experience (and accordingly also cognition) are a function of adulthood as such, and for which poetic writing offers a response. The now of childhood experience occupies the same space as the future of industrial labor and the past of primeval nature. With "Enlargements," Benjamin gestures back to his earliest work on Leibniz, as his depiction of the child's cognition comes to resemble his characterization of the idea in *Origin of German Tragic Drama*: Any phenomenon must have within it "all history" and where "historical perspective can be extended, in the past or the future, without being subject to any limits of principle."[91] The representation of phenomena in childhood requires spatial metaphors to represent extreme historical transcendence and totality, and thereby reinforces the claim that philosophical capacity of the child-subject may be almost absolute.

"Multum in Parvo": Aphorism, Miniaturization, and the Project of *Berlin Childhood around 1900*

> There are animals in the world much larger than ours are, as ours are larger than those tiny animals of the microscopists, for nature knows no boundary. And . . . there could be, indeed, there have to be, worlds not inferior in beauty and variety to ours in the smallest motes of dust, indeed, in tiny atoms.
> —LEIBNIZ, WRITING TO BERNOULLI[92]

The spatial paradigm of childhood depicted in the series of six "Enlargements" continued to influence Benjamin's writing well after the publication of *One-Way Street*. Starting roughly around 1932, Benjamin began developing the first of several versions of his memoir, *Berlin Childhood around 1900*, where the philosophical-poetic form used in the "Enlargements" would come to form the bulk of a new text dedicated to excavating his own youth.[93] And, with varying degrees of alteration and preservation, many of the same vignettes also reappeared—a practice that Michael Jennings has argued is intrinsic to the resulting photographic character of Benjamin's writing in this period.[94] However, unlike *One-Way Street*, which, as a whole, was neither exclusively interested in depicting childhood, nor consisted entirely of these realist-style vignettes, Benjamin's project in *Berlin Childhood* was to be a book-length study of childhood composed of somewhere between thirty and thirty-six short, self-contained, prose texts, each ranging in length from a single brief paragraph to an extended scene described over five or six paragraphs.[95] While Benjamin seems to have abandoned the specific language of photographic "enlargement," a draft of the preface he wrote for the so-called "final version" of his memoir indicates that representing childhood remained tied to the idea of a technological and epistemological use of minute scale.[96]

In this preface, which situates the collection's emergence in exile during the Nazi regime, Benjamin describes the project as a "process of inoculation" in the face of the real likelihood that he would never return to Berlin and in anticipation of his own nostalgia for the loss of the place of his youth.[97] He writes that he "deliberately called to mind those images which, in exile, are most apt to awaken homesickness: images of childhood. [His] assumption was that the feeling of longing would no more gain mastery over [his] spirit than a vaccine does over a healthy body."[98] Benjamin's hope was not that the power of childhood would ameliorate potential suffering; in other words, childhood is not a salve that can be conjured and applied belatedly to an adulthood in exile. Instead, it is *writing* childhood that yields a prophylactic awareness of an entire microscopic universe of activity, where the resulting aphorisms reflect "miniaturizing technologies."[99]

With his writerly attention turned solely toward childhood, Benjamin signals to his reader that rather than the fuzzy effects of photographic enlargement, his reader should expect this monadology of childhood to be something made sharply visible, as if through a microscope. Without departing from the trope of mechanical seeing, Benjamin's invocation of childhood as inoculation suggests that techniques of representing it open up radical new possibilities for the far-reaching potential of human perception and its consequences for epistemology. Much like the revelations by seventeenth-century microscopists (contemporaries of Leibniz, such as Robert Hooke), Benjamin's project illuminates childhood for an entire world that the adult eye, a stand-in for the naked eye, would be "otherwise blind to."[100] Benjamin's technique of writing his own childhood reminds us of Susan Stewart's characterization of this once novel technology as "open[ing] up significance to the point at which all the material world shelters a microcosm."[101]

Benjamin's mobilization of acts of writing childhood so as to mount an effective defense depends on a model of the subvisible.[102] Childhood is again rich with an infinite regress of scale where the activity cannot be seen without technological assistance, but rather than depending on the ability to make something visible with the language of photographic *enlargement*, the idea of "inoculation" preserves the small world as it is. Reminiscent of his observational writings, in these new texts children once again appear uniquely able to perceive an otherwise *unseen* yet rich, animated, and *independently meaningful* world. He returns anew to the central appeal that Leibniz makes about the structure of the world, exemplified as in even the tiniest and otherwise *empty-appearing* drops of water the reality that God had left no space empty (§67). *Berlin Childhood* metaphorizes the optical technology of Leibniz's day, namely the microscope and the world of microbiology that it inaugurated.[103]

Although it is not clear exactly how detailed Benjamin's own understanding was of the specific biological concepts undergirding common types of immunization in his own time, this expression of his hopes for the protective effects of *Berlin Childhood* suggests that he was familiar with the basic principles of the technology of vaccines available in the late nineteenth and the early twentieth centuries. These relatively early, yet modern, and widely used vaccine types are commonly referred to as "whole cell" vaccines, as they contained complete cellular samples of a virus or bacterium that was either dead or alive yet severely weakened (attenuated). These vaccines work by awakening enough response to develop immunity, at least theoretically, while minimizing the risk of infection. As a metaphor, whole cell vaccines also contained the image of microscopic mastery, a technology of miniaturization.[104]

During Benjamin's lifetime, whole cell vaccines were used against diseases such as cholera and rabies. The late nineteenth century, the time of his own childhood, still saw the use of *vaccinia* (against smallpox) which entailed infecting small children with live cowpox. However, due to variables in production, its efficacy occasionally left the vaccinee insufficiently immune.[105] And although smallpox vaccination was statistically quite successful, there were still thousands of cases where inoculating children led to live infections, which in turn meant suffering, disfigurement, and sometimes blindness or even death.[106] An analogical expression of this anxiety around the risks of live infection appears in Benjamin's analogy, noting the risk and rewards of writing as a process of immunization.[107] By working with "images of childhood" that were likely to provoke nostalgia, he could hope that it would produce *just enough* of a response to be protective, without his own "longing" ("Sehnsucht") proliferating and ultimately "gaining mastery" ("Herr werden").[108] However, this immunological view of childhood also recasts the scenes of childhood themselves as antinomies of potency and impotency, recalling what Samuel Weber describes as the Leibnizian "detail" that first interested Benjamin in the monad.[109]

Benjamin's explanation of the hoped-for effects of writing childhood, this medical metaphor for writing, also traces a line back in time to the original appearance of Leibniz's monad in *Origin of German Tragic Drama*. Sam Weber's classic reading of the multifaceted appearance of the "detail" as a "'microstructure' of knowledge" in Benjamin's conceptualization of baroque allegory and Leibniz's monad highlights one such avenue.[110] A brief detour via Weber makes the value of Benjamin's metaphor of microscopic technology all the more legible. Allegory's antinomy, in Weber's reading, hinges on the detail's "function": that it makes a remarkable shift from apparent insignificance to an exegetical "prop of signification" ("Requisiten des Bedeutens") that illuminates that which is sanctified.[111] The parallax nature of the detail means that the world in baroque allegory is both not so strictly dependent on it ("aufs Detail nicht so streng ankommt") and yet also only gains its full potency through the interpretation of such detail. And this ambiguous character of the *detail*, Weber notes, is embedded in the word itself as something "detached," having been being cut from elsewhere while still integral to the production of meaning of the world in baroque allegory.[112] For Weber, the detail's function in Benjaminian allegory corresponds backward to Leibniz's use of "detail," where it serves as the principle of differentiation by which a monad can be distinguished from other monads, all while continuing to reflect everything else around them.[113] Leibniz's detail, "as detached, becomes capable of 'mirroring' or 'representing' that from which the monad has separated itself [i.e., all other monads, all of creation]" and is thus also responsible for each monad's "autarky."[114]

The principles of human vaccination, established in the nineteenth century,[115] can also be described like Weber's reading of the monad, because just as Benjamin regards allegory like a microstructure of knowledge, the metaphor of immunization corresponds to microstructures in science. Unlike an aspirin or antibiotic (interventions that counter symptoms or destroy an invading pathogen), the immunological efficacy of vaccines occurs precisely because they contain minute quantities of complete cells of a virus or bacteria that have been cut off from the infection where they originated. Individual whole cells are "autarkic" in that they provide a complete set of information, while also "reflecting" or "mirroring," as it were, the original infection from which they have been drawn. Once recognized by the body's immune system, however, they are unable to become a widespread infection and instead remain isolated immunological remembrances ("details") within the system. In a concrete sense, inoculation provides the body with a kind of microstructure of knowledge—and the immune system retains the monadological "idea" of the pathogen. In the task of representing childhood, Benjamin allegorizes that writing itself is doubly *allegorized* in this same manner. The philosophical-poetic power of childhood not only operates with a certain immunological (im)potency but is also governed by the same logic of the baroque detail: Child subjects see the very ordinary—the insignificant—and *also* the way the ordinary contains, within itself, entire worlds. Inoculation, in the double sense of Benjamin's deployment of it here, belongs among the variations of both "autarky" and "microstructure" that Weber describes.

This work of miniaturization and the microscopic, like enlargement before, comes to form the basis for the specific literary theoretical assertion that Benjamin is testing out here—and which he perhaps now thinks may be successful—for addressing the problem of representing both the past and childhood in particular.[116] In his preface, Benjamin observes that in contrast to the richness available in the actuality of the present—the "continuity of experience"—the memoirist is left to grapple with details that have since "recede[d]" ("die biographischen Züge . . . ganz zurücktreten").[117] However, with *Berlin Childhood*, he embarks on an "effort to get hold of the *images*" ("*Bilder* habhaft zu werden") in which the experience of the big city finds expression in a child of the middle class ("in einem Kinde der Bürgerklasse sich niederschlägt").[118] Details of ordinary experience that vanished in memory are perhaps made accessible through *the child's* capacity for expression. In other words, the success of this technology—these small fragmentary, aphoristic texts that make up the manuscript—depends on the same idea of universal expression that I have shown to be at work in earlier writings. Thus the child's experiences not only reflect the larger world (here, the city of Berlin) but also provide a specific representational possibility: making images of experience accessible. By turning to the child as the form of expression, Benjamin hopes that writing can now do what memory alone cannot.

Unlike his early published passages depicting children, this preface tells us exactly what scale of perception the collection's writing entails, and, above all, what aphoristic writing on childhood enables. Writing understood *as* microscopic activity leaves the size and scale of childhood wholly undisturbed—this small world doesn't need enlargement. The reader is invited to think of writing as the means of accomplishing that which Benjamin marvels at in his early essay "Old Forgotten Children's Books," namely the ability of children to register the imperceptible. The mode of autobiography in *Berlin Childhood* becomes the technology of making the invisible (i.e., childhood experience) visible (as images he can get a hold of). In the same way Leibniz had regarded the subvisible as a world not only unseen, but also one that—save for the microscope—could only ever be imagined by way of metaphor. We recall that Leibniz explained the infinitude of even the minutest volumes of water or tiniest nooks in natural world as something that "can [each] be thought of as a garden full of plants or a pond full of fish"; though they "are not *themselves* plants or fish, they *contain* other organisms, but usually ones that are too small for us to perceive them."[119] What for Leibniz is a matter available by way of analogy and imagination, can at times be *seen* and indeed confirmed as true by the technology of the microscope.[120] The facticity of such a spectrum of scale affirms Leibniz's project in the *Monadology*: securing God and his creation, the natural world, as infinite against the limits of human [technological] perception.[121] The new world opened up by microscopic seeing reminds one that there will always be a whole world beyond our view. Benjamin's metaphor of the vaccine can be understood in a similar way: The idea that childhood can be made visible through a technology of writing does not undermine the special status of childhood perception. Rather, it underscores its difference.

What then is this "miniaturizing technology" of inoculation? It is more than just the use of smaller, short-format prose. As aphorism, these vignettes recall a kind of Romantic totality—small and fragmentary, but self-contained and yet also paradigmatic. We might think here of the Schlegels' enigmatic formulation: "A fragment, like a miniature work of art, has to be entirely isolated from the surrounding world and be complete in itself like a porcupine."[122] Though Benjamin had begun to use this format in the early versions of this material in "Enlargements" in *One-Way Street*, it appears that he came to understand this writerly work that might finally address what he had previously described as the challenge posed by "childlike intuition," namely that it "knows nothing but totality."[123] The formal program calls to mind Benjamin's own paraphrasing of Leibniz's *Monadology*, where each aphorism "render[s] this image of the world in its abbreviation."[124] This formal strategy reflects a mimetic aim that operates on multiple registers, which, Anja Lemke argues, assumes that the signifying power of resemblances extends beyond the letters on the page, whereby various relationships of resemblance within the semiotic framework of the text mirror the world as a whole, a capacity made legible through literary figuration.[125] Although Benjamin's generic approach has shifted from observation (of childhood experience generally) to memoir (of his particular childhood), his reliance on aphorism emphasizes the philosophical metaphorics of universal expression as texts on childhood always preserve and communicate something about the greater world in which childhood takes place.

Brevity in writing allows Benjamin to mirror in the form of the object that "incomprehensible earnestness of childlike intuition: that it knows nothing but totality." Using the genre of aphorism, writing evinces a vastness in representation precisely *because* of its minute scale. The aphorism is like the *multum in parvo*: a poetic phenomenon that, as Susan Stewart notes, mobilizes the optical imaginary of the miniature.[126] Benjamin's careful yet belated aphoristic style performs, as it were, the child's view and the Leibnizian "detail"—both gesturing toward the larger world, but only visible in its abbreviation. The aphorism's ability to represent *multum in parvo* also helps Benjamin's writing live up to the problem posed by childhood: namely, that it is "no longer comprehensible as a whole, it always points the beholder to the larger one."[127] The aphoristic presentation of childhood's small world—not as a fragment (which would only be a portion of the whole and whose remainder one could never recover) but rather as a full totality in itself, to be read as such. Like the monad, the space of childhood expresses, as it were, everything ("das Ganze").

The final effect of the aphoristic approach in *Berlin Childhood* and the hope the author describes in the draft of his foreword places its childhood narratives in a fraught relation with Romanticism. Benjamin's project seems at first to run in parallel with Romantic philosophical poetics. Where the Schlegel brothers famously theorized the aphorism as a fragment qua system, Benjamin's applied theory of *multum in parvo* (the image of the world in its abbreviation) is paradigmatic. As we will see in the remaining sections, the prose representations of childhood in his memoir evidence a consistent focus on the exceptionally acute perception of the material world—childhood cognition employs the imagination but remains in service to the child's metaphysical and epistemological capacities.

Small Worlds of Childhood: Memoir and Fragment

In *Berlin Chronicle* (*Berliner Chronik*), a more traditionally autobiographic manuscript about life in Berlin that Benjamin began to write in 1932, but never submitted for publication, Benjamin speculated that the particular conditions of one's familial upbringing, education, and historical context would establish a "limit to the child's memory" ("Das setzt dem kindlichen Erinnern . . . seine Grenze") of the past that precedes him—and, ultimately, also to later retellings.[128] He takes care, however, to note that such a "limit" is not a reflection of the child's own experience as such.[129] In his later autobiographical work, Benjamin's conception of childhood maintained a commitment to the above-discussed logics of subvisibility and perceptibility: He experiments with representing what lies *beyond* boundaries of memoir, by imagining what is philosophically available to children in experience, and by showing how such childhood cognition can be made available through poetic language. In this penultimate section, I turn now to selected passages from his late work, the unfinished project *Berlin Childhood around 1900*. Here we will see what I would describe as Benjamin's most developed and nuanced thinking of childhood's philosophical poetics. While this late work also contained many of *Berlin Chronicle*'s scenes of childhood, they were substantially revised; and unlike *Berlin Chronicle*, this manuscript and its versioning is, as the title indicates, entirely dedicated to his childhood.

Drawing again on Leibniz's *Monadology* and the metaphorical operation of universal expression, Benjamin's philosophical-poetic strategy can be retraced first with a close reading of the "Loggias," the opening aphorism in multiple manuscript versions of *Berlin Childhood*. Positioned immediately after the foreword in which Benjamin proposes the microscopic and autarkic abilities of writing childhood, "Loggias" appears to position childhood as the starting point for recollection, nostalgia, and a metropolitan romanticism.[130] Benjamin's vignette carefully attends to how the space of the covered balcony of his family's apartment was outfitted with antiquarian objects and the walls were accented with a "Pompeian red" paint, which Nadine Werner aptly argues offers a view of childhood as an "archaeological" remembrance of a moment, as if just before catastrophe.[131] In keeping with the way she reads the various archival versions of *Berlin Childhood*, Werner notes how the seamless temporal and spatial movements made possible in the remembrance of the loggia evince an excavatory process, an unearthing and constellating of objects of the past and their relationships.[132] Although Benjamin himself describes the sight of the courtyard as the most powerful invigorator of childhood remembrance, I want to propose that a slightly different spatial and temporal rhetoric is at work in this six-paragraph vignette—one that is not limited to the mono-directionality of memory (past versus present), but instead one that metaphorizes the loggia's perspective as that of the monad and its multidirectional space and time of reflection. In the first paragraph, Benjamin describes the profound influence of "gazing [from his family's balcony] across the courtyard" at the shaded loggias of his neighbors. Let us a take look now at the first full paragraph:

> For a long time, life deals with the still tender memory of childhood like a mother who lays her newborn on her breast without waking it. Nothing has fortified my own memory so profoundly as gazing into courtyards, one of whose dark loggias, shaded by blinds in the summer, was for me the cradle in which the city laid its new citizen. The caryatids that supported the loggia on the floor above ours may have slipped away from their post for a moment to sing a lullaby beside the cradle—a song containing little of what later awaited me, but nonetheless sounding the theme through which the air of the courtyards has forever remained intoxicating to me. I believe a whiff of this air was still present in the vineyards of Capri where I held my beloved in my arms; and it is precisely this air that sustains the images and allegories which preside over my thinking, just as the caryatids, from the heights of their loggias, preside over the courtyards of Berlin's West End.[133]

To Benjamin, the scene of childhood (and its reflections beyond) depend on a perspectival *mise en abyme*: from these lofty "heights," both the loggia's occupant (the child-subject) and the caryatids above are able to view ever more loggias. Collectively, the balconied buildings form the courtyard, whose counter perspectives reflect far beyond to the ubiquitous balconies that make up all the courtyards of "Berlin's West End." Like Benjamin's earliest observations about the child's world, "Loggias" establishes the crucial interplay of visible and invisible structures with the analogy that the invisible air contained within the visible bounds of the courtyard governs cognition ("image and allegory") just as the caryatids gazed out over the shadowy courtyards of the city. As *visibility*, the poetics of thinking in "Loggias" evokes the construction of a monadic world where the totality of the universe is comprehensible through related but discontinuous, "multiplied" perspectives (§57) and appears in the aggregation of points of view afforded by the child in his balcony, the caryatids above, and all the other balconies in this courtyard and beyond.[134] As invisibility, however, Benjamin frames thinking like "air," as reflection and repletion, that is both in the courtyards of his childhood and, in some way, also everywhere (as far as Capri), both too small to perceive directly, yet present nonetheless. The multiplication of temporalities of childhood sits queerly in the same location as the adult romance and the distant Pompeii. In the loggia, time stands still like "images" and crosses temporalities as "allegories" do.

I want to briefly draw attention here to the ways in which this apparent paradoxical and also palimpsestic construction of thought and perception (embodied by the plurality of lofty points of view) establishes a distinction between childhood and adult perception that is also captured by both metaphorical and literal senses of the German word "übersehen"—or, in English, the double sense of "to overlook" (to look out on or down on, to survey) and "to overlook" (i.e., to fail to see or fail to attend to).[135] "Loggias" presents the idea of perspective and of narrative point of view as the basis for cognition which is governed significantly by both "image and allegories." Thinking, as the balcony view will show, is ruled both by the immediacy of perception (something one can see) and the undisclosed or concealed (that which one might fail to see).

As the passage continues, the loggia of Benjamin's family apartment serves as an overlook and a site of overlooking, as he recalls with great detail how he used to peer down as a child at a tree growing in the courtyard. This pastime afforded precisely by the loggia's height, included both the seeing (gazing down from up high) and not seeing:

> What occupied me most of all in the courtyard was the spot where the tree stood. This spot was set off by paving stones into which a large iron ring was sunk. Metal bars were mounted on it, in such a way as to fence in the bare earth [nackte Erdreich]. Not for nothing, it seemed to me, was it thus enclosed; from time to time, I would brood over what went on within the black pit from which the trunk came.[136]

The child's fascination centers on a play of perceptibility that recalls a Leibnizian commitment to the metaphor of the subvisible: to the child, soil surrounding the tree is itself a small world, "earth." The term Benjamin uses here, "Erdreich," points us not just toward the horticultural but also the cosmological: an earthly bounty and the world-constituting realm of the earth. From the loggia, the child is particularly attentive to the way that this visible ("bare"/"nackte") realm is cordoned off from the rest of the courtyard. And yet, despite the earth's visibility, the child knows there must be yet more. The central focus of the loggia's vantage is a monadological world enclosed within an iron ring: a world which holds still more beyond what the eye can see. This recognition of "what went on" in that obscure realm matches the paradigm of the child's metaphysical guarantee that no space be left unfilled. This most ordinary sight—a tree basin in a courtyard—takes on the divine significance of Leibniz's drop of water, in which the smallest detail secures the subvisible infinitude of creation. And in this sense, the logic of cognition repeats that of the loggias: thinking that is ruled by "both image and allegory."

As a child, Benjamin continues, he could not stop wondering about the goings-on in that tree basin. He remarks how these thoughts eventually extended to other similar tree basins, like those used to anchor horse carriages. To the child, each of these spots around Berlin—with their iron fencing and exposed roots—becomes "a distant province of [his own] courtyard."[137] The knowledge that the loggia produces is both specular and productive: The child's "Grübeleien" (speculations) evoke not only ways of thinking, searching, and investigating, but also the idea of *digging* down, as in the word's root, "grübeln."[138] This one *Erdreich*, which was exposed where a basin had been dug and encircled with a fence, mirrors the child's own digging thoughts ("Grübeleien"), as a kind of thinking that eventually establishes that there are many more of these earthen realms all over the city. And in the same way, each one of them is a similar yet detached outpost of the child's own downward view from the loggia. To paraphrase Sam Weber's reading of the monad as *detail*, the child's vantage from the loggia is both self-contained and autarchic, as it mirrors the universe even from its limited point of view.[139] The child's view is at once piercing when it bores into the open ground (a kind of *grübeln*), while it also reflects its universe: the tree basin, the earthly realm, and a city populated with these little provinces. An entire "system" of "autarchic" details—each basin, and each view, isolated and distinct while still mirroring each of the others at the same time. This child's specular view is depicted as the very formation of the Berlin metropolis.

In Werner's view, Benjamin's child-subject encounters a world for which he is "not yet grown" enough, and thus requires a future adult self to attribute meaning.[140] It can absolutely be said that part of the seeing described in "Loggias" is also the belated adult vision: the nostalgia of long past evenings, his future romantic embraces. However, when the narration attends to *the child's* elevated viewpoint from the loggia, it favors the most ordinary objects. Each time the child's gaze and meditation—qua *grübeln*—returns again and again to the most ordinary things, peering deeply into them. From the seasonal dance of flora climbing the courtyard walls to the noisy roller shades on their way up or down, the child's eye not only catches these details, but awes at each's hidden meaning. Benjamin imagines the biblical scale of the messages left unread by these objects. To the child, the "ominous dispatches" and, indeed, Job-like sense ("Hiobsposten") of the daily movements of a neighbor's "thundering" shutters point beyond the visible events to the transcendent.[141] The child cognizes the world as a sublime expanse, a monadological system of meaning-making that accounts for both the visible (the bare soil, the rise and fall of the roller shades, images) and the invisible ("what went on," "Job-like messages," "allegories") in times of presence and absence. "Loggias" thus creates a careful contrast between what we might describe as the difference of perception in the child's monadological view and the melancholic return in his later years. Just as we saw in his 1924 essay, "Old Forgotten Children's Books," Benjamin argues for a kind of perception that is reserved for the child, one that appears puzzling and palimpsestic from adulthood.[142]

Reading "Loggias" in this way, we can also see how Benjamin destabilizes the reader's expectations that children are merely Romantic. Childhood is not only the backyard or backward view ("Blick in Höfe");[143] it mirrors the whole world across time. And while the narrator moves freely between temporalities and locations—e.g., Pompeii, this tree, that carriage post, his later time in Capri—each place allows childhood to serve as an inflection point that refers the reader's gaze backward *and also forward* across time and space. Benjamin's Leibnizian philosophical poetics spatializes childhood time as the near-divine, infinite, and dialectically microcosmic. The notion of time and change, viewed from Benjamin's childhood balcony, repeats Leibniz's own attempt to differentiate monads from one another. If we turn again to the *Monadology* we see how Leibniz accounted for the fact that the world appears to us to change over time and to be filled with variation despite each monad's capacity to reflect all of creation. In §13 he writes that "this diversity must involve a multitude in the unity or in the simple. For, since all natural change is produced by degrees, something changes and something remains. As a result, there must be a plurality of properties ("affections") and relations in the simple substance, although it has no parts." Like the "whiff of air" present in both the courtyard as in Capri, monadological time is not linear time, but rather a queer multiplicity. This view of childhood imagines a palimpsest of temporality and locality as a "plurality" in the Leibnizian sense of events. Childhood experience does exclude that future melancholy—but it is the monadological commitment to the present that is "pregnant with the future" (§22). This is, however, a future that is already here: Like Muñoz's description of "queer time" as that which "steps out of the linearity of straight time," childhood time encompasses more the just "straight time's 'present.'"[144] Here Benjamin's opening foray seems to imagine an "ecstatic and horizontal temporality" that makes possible "a movement to a greater openness to the world."[145] Like Leibniz's *Monadology*, "Loggias" posits a metaphysics that resists consignment to future responsibility, in the double sense of "straight" linear time and finite space. The philosophical poetics of childhood mirrors the narrator's life as a unity, as a queer plurality, because it, like the monad, has no distinct parts.

"Loggias" is followed by one of the most widely remarked scenes in *Berlin Childhood*: "Imperial Panorama." Thematically centered on the optical and photographic technology of the panorama, this passage has been read by commentators as belonging primarily to Benjamin's project of describing the technological aesthetics of modernity.[146] However, as I have argued earlier about the photographic references in the "Enlargements" series, the relationship between representation (e.g., of the projected images of the panorama technology) and childhood perception evinces a unique monadic signature of childhood experience: the small world's partial reflection of another greater one. In Benjamin's telling, the children were the last loyal viewers of the imperial panorama. While this gimmicky technology had lost its charm for adults, it continued to furnish the child with opportunities to exercise his monadological perception. The child's attention is unconcerned with the tension between what Sianne Ngai describes as the product that "works too little/works too much."[147] Despite the "great attractions" of this "art form,"[148] Benjamin indicates that the technological progress of the day had left the *adult* tourist (i.e., the consumer of photographic "travel" or the "tour" putatively offered by the "Imperial Panorama") with little more than that cheapened "ambivalence" of a technology that was both "newfangled" yet also "outdated"; the panorama thus appears to the reader as a "compromised aesthetic form."[149]

Benjamin, however, draws a distinction between that which attracts the adult versus that which attracts the child. The features of this vignette, which Jennings summarizes as the "conditioning of experience by modern media," appear to apply only to adults, as the *child's* perception homes in on the moment of immediate materiality, of that which is present.[150] And thus, the mechanical operations that are not part of the illusion also find no illusion to disrupt. The child's encounter is with the material details: the seating, the operational sounds, all matter that resists both a submission to the would-be magic of technological labor and therefore also any *dis*enchantment with its particular failures. The child escapes the culture of ubiquitous phantasmagoria. Because the child attends to the minutest of details, the faltering "lighting system" that dimmed the images stands on equal footing with the images themselves. Benjamin recounts how "the bell ... sounded ... before each picture moved off with a jolt"; he notes how this produces a "disturbing effect" (presumably) for the adult viewer but one that the child finds to be "superior."[151] The adult experiences a "tour" whose production has suddenly been made *too* transparent, as the bell marks the machinery's awkward engagement. And thus, to borrow Ngai's phrasing again, together these elements draw attention to the panorama's "aesthetic fraudulence," in which the mechanisms of once cutting-edge theatricality now transform the cost of the seat into a rip-off.[152] The child, however, enjoys this without anxiety. The fact that these images bump along on their tracks as they exit from view does not detract from the seeming infinitude of representation made available to him.

Peering into this circular structure, unbothered by its fallen commodity value, the child sees pictures of "distant worlds" that have the unexpected effect of transmitting his own proximal and familiar space: they "spoke more to the [child's] home than anything unknown."[153] The light that abounded "in fjords and under coconut palms" was the "same light [that] illuminated my desk in the evening when I did my school work."[154] The fact that the illuminated stereoscopic pictures are not only snapshots of faraway locales but *also* indexes of his very own desk lamp can be read as the childhood objects appear as limited, monadic reflections. The way in which the child's small world at home stands in specular relation with the larger world beyond recapitulates Leibniz's own speculation about an individual monad's picture of the infinitude beyond itself. Leibniz writes, "It is true that [the monad's] representation is only confused as to the detail of the whole universe, and can only be distinct for a small portion of things . . . for those that are closest" (§60). The panorama brings the faraway close, such that the child's view is, like the monad's, a nearly divine view (*hórāma*) of all (*pan-*). It is not the perfect and infinite God's-eye view with which Leibniz contrasts the monad, but the limited and fuzzy one: the warm glow cast on the familiar childhood desk reflects—if only partially, confusedly—the rest of the world. In this way, "Imperial Panorama" also repeats the logic of "Loggias" as one of *übersehen* (both seeing and failing to see detail): The monadic view from childhood clearly perceives what is closest—the light over his desk—as an index to what is the beyond that is no longer visible—the "fjords and coconut trees" that appeared fleetingly and only under the "faltering" light of the panorama. In Benjamin's rendering, the child's small world indexes the larger one, not because the child can literally see everything, but because the child's perception is monadic; it is structured like the "superior" divine view of all (*pan-hórāma*).

Benjamin frequently presented the child's transfigurative cognition as itself intervening in and reclaiming ordinary technology: In "Imperial Panorama," the child's perception elevates an aging piece of technology from gimmick to a perspective that sets the vast world into relation with its parts, and this ability to see the poetic relationship, as index, as symbol, is more of a law than an exception. Childhood encounter is unique for its radical present-ness, in contrast to the general belatedness that imbues adult experience. In his experimental montage-like collection of citations and aphorisms, *The Arcades Project*,[155] Benjamin describes this unique ability as follows:

> Task of childhood: to bring the new world into symbolic space. The child, in fact, can do what the grownup absolutely cannot: recognize the new once again. For us, locomotives already have symbolic character because we met them in childhood. Our children, however, will find this in automobiles, of which we ourselves see only the new, elegant, modern, cheeky side. . . . To each truly new configuration of nature—and, at bottom, technology is just such a configuration—there correspond new "images."[156]

I want to emphasize here how Benjamin's focus on the power of childhood perception extends beyond the rehabilitation or disruption of modern technological innovation and obsolescence. This is not merely a reversal shifting from seeing things such as the panorama or the locomotive as outdated or gimmicky to seeing them as "new, elegant, modern" as the adult does. It is the poetic production *of* the new by the child's capacity to see *in* the old technology an overlooked character. In the *Arcades Project* as in "Loggias," childhood perception is organized as *übersehen*: seeing what is also not seen. The child's view is thus one that sees new relationships of simultaneity *across time* as well: the new locomotive of the past is re-presented as new in the present by the child. This specularity of past and present, visible in the monadic "configuration" images, involves this paradigmatic, queer temporality. As in Muñoz, the child's perception has a strong affinity with a Blochian sense of time: The child's joy and experience of the new in what is also the old, makes the idea of the "no-longer-conscious" utopian thought visible, even if belated to adults. Predicated on a queer, nonlinear temporality, the child's vision is thus one of hope, looking into the courtyards from the loggia, into the rickety panorama, and at all manner of old, discarded, and overlooked objects; it is one that recognizes a kind of unrealized potential, like a "queer promise."

Having thus far closely read three vignettes from *Berlin Childhood*, I want to emphasize that the manuscript is filled with other examples. These scenes that attend to the child's experience of ordinary objects are powerful not only because they contain, as it were, the later melancholy of exile that Benjamin wishes to prevent through his immunological-poetic strategy, but because he knows that the child—in this case, himself—can cognize the world in a way that moves beyond the loss of the past in a linear conception of the present. The retrospective grief that initiates the project of *Berlin Childhood* nonetheless yields depictions of the incredible capacity of children as philosophical subjects.

Readers of the scene of reading in "Boys' Books," for example, will find that, from the child's perspective, an encounter with worn library books is not only about forms of mediation, but the significance of material objects themselves. Here, Benjamin's evocative description captures the look and feel of tattered and worn-out grade-school library books from the perspective of the young reader. Where the adult might see nothing but entropy at work in the decrepit condition of these objects, the child "recognizes" natural landscapes at a smaller scale:

> Its pages bore traces of fingers that had turned them. . . . But it was the spine, above all, that had had things to endure—so much so, that the two halves of the cover slid out of place by themselves, and the edge of the volume formed ridges and terraces. Hanging on its pages, however, like Indian summer [*Altweibersommer*] on the branches of the trees, were sometimes fragile threads of a net in which I had once become tangled when learning to read.[157]

Books ceased to be merely objects with loosened spines and worn covers, and instead appear to reveal to the child their geological and seasonal character, imbricating themselves as individual small worlds within the larger world of school. For Benjamin's child observer, the most weathered things present themselves as a signs of a world in which, as Leibniz had speculated, "nature knows no boundary."[158] The child's act of reading is also more than just an entrance into a story world: The text itself takes on a three-dimensional quality as he struggles to navigate an arboreal space. Learning to read is learning to move through the woven or fabricated world of text or *textus* in which the child can become "tangled" or, as it were, himself enmeshed ("mich verstricken hatte"). In the double meaning of "Altweibersommer" the encounter with books is out of line: The child's queer act of reading appears as the crossings and knots of the gossamer (spiders' webs) and as a lingering past its time—an "Indian summer"—like weather happening in the wrong season.

The difference between outside and inside the book feels less obvious to the child who easily inhabits both at the same time, just as a monad contains and reflects. In "Boys' Books," the form of cognition while reading bears a striking resemblance to the paradigmatic monadological reflection. Take, for example, the oft-discussed transposition of the words on the page to the weather outside:

> But sometimes in winter, when I stood by the window in the warm little room, the snowstorm outside told me stories no less mutely. What it told, to be sure, I could never quite grasp, for always something new

[*Neues*] and unremittingly dense [*dicht*] was breaking though the familiar [*dem Altbekannten*]. Hardly had I allied myself, as intimately as possible, to one band of snowflakes, than I realized they had been obliged to yield me up to another, which had suddenly entered their midst. But now the moment had come to follow, the flurry of letters, the stories that had eluded me at the window. The distant lands I encountered in these stories played familiarly among themselves, like the snowflakes.[159]

The child experiences the world both as its visible surface and as its sublime depth—in keeping with the logic established in "Loggias," the child's wintertime vision appears again as the dialectical act of *übersehen*: like the view down onto the unseen "earthen realm" below uncovers a city's trees as a system consisting of autarkic "details," the snowfall appears as both the newness of each flake that is inseparable from both the endlessly poetic and lush impermeability ("unablässig dicht") of the bands of snow. Without the mediation of simile, Benjamin's child moves sequentially from the drifts of snowflakes to the "flurry of letters" on the page, the resistance of the former illuminating the latter.[160] Benjamin's child need not leave his "warm little room" to reflect the infinite space of storytelling. With reading, as Benjamin continues here, "the distance leads no longer out into the world but within, so Baghdad and Babylon, Acre and Alaska, Tromsö and Transvaal were places within" the child reader.[161] Like the "Imperial Panorama" before it, Benjamin's child's inversion of scale creates ever more miniature worlds—the home, the desk, the mind—thus reminding us that the stakes of representing childhood are, like his earliest uses of Leibniz's *Monadology*, as much poetic as metaphysical.

The reflection of tiny worlds, like the immunological image around which Benjamin organized his preface, in which the metaphor of the microscopic efficacy of the vaccine depends on modes of (sub)visibility. This serves as a first indication of the form of knowledge *Berlin Childhood* was to associate with child subjects and the spaces and objects of childhood. Looking at vignettes such as the three-paragraph text, "At the Corner of Steglitzer and Genthiner," we see him unite the twin motifs of scales of activity with what we now recognize as the specific specularity, or reflectivity, that the monad entails. The first paragraph of this descriptive passage not only details the child's playful anamorphic cognition of language and names; it also establishes a multiplicity of reflective worlds. First, the young child's aunt, "Tante Lehmann," who lived in an apartment on Steglitzer Street, slides freely into the figure gifted by the location's near-homonym and etymological forebearer, *Stieglitz* (European goldfinch) in its cage.[162] This charming miscognition enables the child to account for the vast genealogical knowledge his aunt possesses: the impressive ability to name and describe family scattered across both time and the entire Brandenburg and Mecklenburg regions is attributed to the finch's bird's-eye view. The vast expanse beyond the oriel window at the street corner of Steglitzer is made visible by the Stieglitz—not as a map (as we saw with Stifter's children in Chapter 1), but as the busy world of "nests and farms" seen from high above.[163]

"At the Corner of Steglitzer and Genthiner" multiplies its monadological specularity when Benjamin depicts the most prized feature of any visit to Tante Lehmann's: an antique clockwork toy, which contained a "complete working mine." This "large glass cube" was inhabited by "miniature miners, stonecutters, and mine inspectors, with tiny wheelbarrows, hammers, and lanterns."[164] Like the child's enchantment with the goldfinch's overlook of genealogical knowledge, the activity of "workplaces and machines" can best be glimpsed as small worlds. The miniature scene of activity enclosed in glass is itself mirrored in the most salient feature of Tante Lehmann's own birdcage-like dwelling, the jewel box effect of the oriel windows.[165] This glass enclosure of her dwelling looks down onto the city street corner while also encasing its own twittering bourgeois activities within. The child too is refigured as an all-knowing goldfinch, gazing down into the bustling small world of the mine. The interiority of each monadic figure (e.g., his aunt's view like a goldfinch's, her oriel apartment and its bourgeois goings-on, the miniature clockwork mine) is inexorably linked with a reflection turned outward: the farms of the Brandenburg region, the city below, the vast world of industrial workplaces. Knowledge of the world, the child shows us, is a specular process.

This specularity is repeated in instances throughout the final version of *Berlin Childhood*. It runs from his childhood fascination with the topology of "retrieving" the titular "Sock" from its folded "pocket" shape through the way the moonlight reverses the relationship of satellite to planet in "The Moon" and the multiplicity of reflections of colors from outside to inside in the single-paragraph "Colors."[166] In the latter of these, the child "loses himself" in the specularity of the colorful surface reflections in his beloved "soap bubbles."[167] There is a fuzzy indistinguishability between the child's heart or bosom, the stained-glass windows of a summer house, his watercolors, and the many brightly colored wrappers and threads that enclose chocolate confections. The epistemological stakes of the child's revelry in such specular forms of perception are clear: Benjamin concludes the passage by declaring how the "higher sense in me" takes precedence over "the lower."[168] In each of these stories, the child's discoveries repeat the metaphysics of reflection, in which the inside, interior, and the intimate each recapitulates the outside, out there, and the faraway. Again and again, the child's epistemological paradigm is always one of monadic reflection. If, as I have argued in this section, the vignettes of *Berlin Childhood* are an invocation of the small world (universe in the drop of water, the microscopic, the immunological), these examples fulfill our expectation to see this monadic figuration repeated throughout. And indeed, like that Jobian sound of the courtyard-neighbor's shutters, the view into the imperial panorama or the miniature model mine, and even the unfolding of an ordinary sock, everyday objects—the detritus of the adult world—depict for the adult reader the child's experience of the world as multum in parvo. The child delights in the very inexhaustibility (*"Unendlichkeit"*), as there is ever more to see in each scene.[169] Even if the adult Benjamin set out to memorialize a city and his own lost youth, the child protagonist in his narrative sees and knows the world in its own richer present time. The view from childhood insists on a queer temporality of its own: Despite being viewed from adulthood, and often hinting elsewhere as if registering a "plurality of properties," the child-subject not only exists expressly for its own time, he revels in the cognition of the unlimited world as it is, unfettered by the belated project of memoir.

Childhood as Metaphysical Paradigm

By way of conclusion, I would like to offer some thoughts on the distinctive relationship that appears now between the *Monadology* and Benjamin's depictions of childhood from his early writings through to *Berlin Childhood*. Leibniz's monad, I have argued, appears for us here as a small world, as a detail, as finitude which points to the infinite, as a dialectic of visibility and invisibility, and as the present that contains the future in ways that are not, as it were, straight. The rare appearances of the monad beyond the *Origin of German Tragic Drama* appear in his theoretical fragments on knowledge—a reminder that Benjamin saw Leibniz's *Monadology* not as prima facie a description of the substance out of which the world is made, but rather as a vital element later deployed in his philosophical poetics. The monad paradigmatically enables Benjamin to articulate, to recall Scholem here, the "philosophical experience of the world and its reality," namely "metaphysics."[170] In "Convolute N [On the Theory of Knowledge, Theory of Progress]" for example, Benjamin sketches out the "monadological structure" of historical objects as containing, much like Leibniz's "plurality of properties," both its "fore-history" and its "after-history." Benjamin's writings on childhood are likewise depictions of the child-subject encountering historical objects and keenly perceiving their structure. Despite the fact that Benjamin otherwise never directly invokes Leibniz in his writing on childhood, his consistency capturing Leibniz's innovation in each case enables us to interpret the epistemological stakes of childhood across his oeuvre. I have suggested throughout this chapter that the relationship between depictions of childhood and a Benjaminian "metaphysics" relies on a philosophical *paradigm*, and with the remaining pages I will explain how this appears for readers of his work as an a posteriori proposition. Thinking with Giorgio Agamben, my final claim here will be that such a reading of Benjamin's writing works *by way of paradigm* to explain that the particular form of knowledge that childhood makes intelligible is as a philosophical-poetic *ensemble*.[171]

In "What Is a Paradigm?" Agamben surveys a range of conceptions of the paradigm, from Plato to Foucault, and by the final section, he proposes a set of six theses to "define a paradigm."[172] For the purpose of understanding his idea of paradigm as ensemble, I summarize the theses as follows: (1) The paradigm is an analogical "form of knowledge" that (2) preserves the singular nature of an individual phenomenon, without the "dichotomous logic" of particulars versus generals; (3, 4) the paradigm is that which appears "immanent" to a group of cases, but where each case remains both exemplary and singular; (5) the paradigm does not develop linearly from a particular "origin"; instead each individual phenomenon is originary or, in his words, "archaic"; and finally, (6) the paradigm's historicity is situated at the "crossing of diachrony and synchrony." In Agamben's telling, the collective nature of the paradigm makes the affinity of any number of phenomena that "unfold across time" legible and comprehensible, even those whose "kinship ha[s] eluded . . . the historian's gaze." By emphasizing that the emergence of a relationship that is neither linear nor hierarchical, and which is as much a phenomenon in a given present (synchronic) as over time (diachronic), the paradigm frees us as readers of both Benjamin *and* Leibniz to see that a novel form arises immanently among their writings. Without being too provocative, I suggest here the paradigm also captures the resistance of Benjamin's writing to what I have described as the straight time of adulthood, in favor of the capaciously queer temporalities of childhood, whose "kinships" can be seen only when the viewer looks at things out of joint.

Here we can also see how a paradigmatic view of Benjamin's writing on childhood avoids the dichotomous move of dismissing those scenes and poetic gestures as repetitious examples of one general concept such as nostalgia or memory, and instead situates each "case" as part of a larger network of sui generis epistemological attempts. The "kinship" between Benjamin's prose of childhood and Leibniz's characterization of the monad is made legible as a paradigm. Agamben derives his fifth thesis (of the formation of paradigmatic knowledge) in part from Goethe's essay "The Experiment as Mediator" ("Der Versuch als Vermittler"), in which scientific perception and understanding issue from the archaic nature of individual phenomena seen from the point of view that regards them as an ensemble. In this same essay Goethe notes that there is a particular form of knowledge made possible by observing in aggregate the relatedness of given phenomena according to "manifold perspectives"[173]—an epistemological term that feels both Leibnizian and, so I have argued, also Benjaminian. In a subsequent passage, which Agamben also quotes, Goethe reflects on how the belated view of his own series of optical experimentation demonstrates that "such an experience, which consists of many others, is clearly of a higher type. It represents the formula in which countless single examples find their expression."[174] Thus knowledge appears through reflection made possible *across* time, without the need for linear historical cause. Likewise, the paradigm of monadological childhood not only enables us to read Benjamin's later writing (e.g., *Berlin Childhood*) alongside some of his earlier ones (*Origin of German Tragic Drama*, "A Child's Perception of Color"), but also frees us to see his occasional interest in Leibniz's monad and the steady pull that childhood had on him as operating with a similar portion of epistemo-critical value that his *Habilitationsschrift* was to convey.

A paradigmatic reading of childhood also accounts for the view that these literary depictions of children are engaged in a specific kind of epistemological-pedagogical work for the adult writer and his readers. Some readings along the lines of Susan Buck-Morss's assessment of Benjamin have argued that his writings offer adults a crucial opportunity to "rediscover" or reencounter childhood cognition, as their mimetic capacities allow for a belated reengagement of cognitive powers unfettered by bourgeois values.[175] Arguments like this have focused, however, on what I have described in this chapter as a straight futurity that only recognized the utopian character of childhood as something primarily for a *future* adulthood. As a paradigm, however, the monad frees the reader to both recognize the critical pedagogical possibilities of childhood while also disrupting "straight" (linear and causal) connections among the various texts at play, and instead making visible a multitude of cross-temporal philosophical affinities. Untethered from future-oriented meaning, the early appearance of Leibniz in *The Origin of German Tragic Drama* can sit achronologically at ease alongside childhood observations and vivid fragments that have been the object of this chapter's study. The figure of the future adult reader is thus also demoted, as it were—no longer part of a "dichotomous logic" of origin and end. In other words, a paradigmatic reading also horizontally refigures each of Leibniz's theses in the *Monadology* and Benjamin's monadological childhood writings as *one among many* individual contributing phenomena. Following both Goethe and Agamben, such relationships appear to us by way of analogies among phenomena across time, from Benjamin's earliest essays to the *Arcades Project*. As a paradigmatic formation of knowledge, the conception of epistemological kinship is also queerly allegorical.

This paradigm makes an array of affinities legible as a network, revealing, for example, the reflection of the child's appearances in the *Arcades Project* in "Convolute K" (on dreams) and in "Convolute N" (on knowledge), in which monadic reflectivity also echoes the child's love affair with the old imperial panorama in *Berlin Childhood*. In "Convolute N," Benjamin reiterates the child's capacities to queer the binaries of old and new in the revitalization of the once-new, yet now out-of-date product:

> By the interest [childhood] takes in technological phenomena, by the curiosity it displays before any sort of invention or machinery, every childhood binds the accomplishments of technology to the old worlds of symbol. There is nothing in the realm of nature that from the outset [*von Hause aus*] would be exempt from such a bond. Only, it takes form not in the aura of novelty but in the aura of the habitual [*Gewöhnung*].[176]

With this play on the familiar, residential, and the domestic (*"von Hause aus"* and *"Gewöhnung"*), Benjamin anticipates Bachelard's observation about the unique connection that the child has to the material world. The now-time of childhood experience is also the crossing of time (diachrony and synchrony) as the adult encounters objects already invested with "symbolic character" (K1a, 3) held from past engagements with the object *as a child*. At first glance, Nicola Gess's argument that Benjamin's depictions of the child's dialectic of enchantment and disenchantment lay the groundwork for the *Arcades Project* appears convincing.[177] However, Gess frames Benjamin's early work in childhood "as inspiration" for his later work and as such the trope of the child simply produces a "straight" connection, as it were, in the binary logic of inspiration and future result.[178] I think we can now rephrase this relationship with more nuance and more epistemological force: namely, that Benjamin's paradigmatic deployment of the monadological perception of the child (their capacities as a metaphysician) elevates the child-figure beyond *both* the particular chronology of his writing and beyond the rigid limits of adult experience. Rather than seeing his depictions of childhood as the "inspiration" for material-historical critique— that is, the still unformed, not-yet of a future *Arcades Project*—the monad invites us to see the queer influence of the paradigm, which allows us to read each of the child's many appearances as already fully formed phenomena, understood as an ensemble.

Even though, as Buck-Morss suggests, writing and reading about childhood subjectivity triggers an intellectual and political opportunity in adulthood, at the same time, childhood, in Benjamin's thinking, is not a model that can be repeated—adults cannot *become* children any more easily than they can perceive the world as children. This is Benjamin's unequivocal declaration above that "the child, in fact, can do what the grownup absolutely cannot" (K1a, 3). Instead, Benjamin saw childhood as bound up with mimetic capacities; and he consequently saw the kind of reflective thinking involved in and made legible in these textual depictions of childhood as offering adults an intervention in their own cognition. In other words, for Benjamin, any philosophical observations about differences between adult and childhood capacities must be coupled with the representational opportunities made possible by poetics. Agamben's conception of the paradigm as a form of knowledge captures not only the general significance that childhood subjectivity has for Benjamin's thought,[179] but also provides a way to describe the relationship between Leibniz's *Monadology* and childhood perception and cognition beyond that of momentary "inspiration" that Gess uses to describe the source of the *Arcades Project* and with more specificity than Scholem's observation that Benjamin was drawn to the power of childhood's "magical" appeal.

We can now read across Benjamin's corpus to see how the philosophical poetics of childhood appears as a grouping of singular instances that become visible as what Agamben phrases as the "crossing of synchrony and diachrony."[180] What is critical in Benjamin's project is that the philosophical picture of childhood experience does *not* arise in a linear fashion, from an early or exemplary model—Benjamin was precisely *not* just "inspired" by children. And likewise, as I have argued, Leibniz's monad is not identical with the actual content of childhood but stands in an analogical relationship. Furthermore, we cannot reasonably read Benjamin's writing on the "idea" qua monad in *The Origin of German Tragic Drama* as standing in any kind of obviously sequential relation with his depictions of childhood. In other words, while we can certainly describe the affinity among the texts analyzed here as constellatory, we also must grapple with the form of knowledge made possible out of a multiplicity of singular instances that have appeared across time. From the perception of colors and the phenomenology of grown-ups' detritus that fills the child's world, to the poetics of the many small worlds now enlarged, as it were, for adult viewing to the microcosmic activities of his own childhood in Berlin, together these constitute the paradigm forming a "medium of intelligibility" for Benjamin's metaphysics. As a paradigm—a configuration of knowledge that crosses time and space—childhood makes queer lines of thought visible. With Sara Ahmed, we might think of writing and reading childhood in Benjamin like the queer work of "desire lines," which, as she explains, "in landscape architecture the term . . . is used to describe unofficial paths . . . where people deviate from the paths they are supposed to follow. Deviation leaves its own marks on the ground, which can even help generate alternative lines, which cross the ground in unexpected ways."[181] Childhood need not only derive its meaning as the promise of futurity, but instead in the possibility of of writing and of being read otherwise.

Coda
Sigmund Freud, Childhood, and the Return of Futurity

Sigmund Freud occupies a surprising place for my study as someone who both wrote prolifically on childhood and whose theoretical framework has been a veritable mainstay within queer theory, from psychoanalytically inclined discourses to queer and feminist critiques of his work.[1] However, as this coda follows the book's central concern with the ways that narrative and descriptive prose represent child-figures and childhood experience, I conclude by attending to *the writer* Freud, rather than the theorist of, say, infantile sexuality. Like his contemporaries Rilke and Benjamin, Freud employed a keen literary sense in his narrative representations of the scene of childhood. This coda thus sits somewhat obliquely in a line of scholarship within German studies that began as far back as Walter Schönau's work on Freud as a literary writer in the 1960s and extends to more recent work by Graham Frankland, who focused on Freud's extensive knowledge and deployment of literary techniques and genres.[2] As I attend here to the *way* Freud tells the story of being a child, I want to emphasize that, in what follows, I necessarily relinquish a kind of fidelity to—or even theoretical interest in—Freud's own stated project of psychoanalysis, adopting instead a willingness to read Freud against the grain. In the tradition of Luce Irigaray's feminist critique of Freud's "Femininity" (1933), in which she shows how the little girl is theorized as "a disadvantaged little man," and Sara Ahmed's elucidation of the heteronormative underpinnings of Freud's "rereading" of queer desire as the "desire for the 'other sex'" in "The Psychogenesis of a Case of Homosexuality in a Woman" (1920), I take seriously the effect of his techniques of representation—even when the result runs counter to his apparent intent.[3]

Just as I outlined in the book's introduction, here I continue to work in the spirit of Sedgwick's proposal for queer reading as "reparative reading." As such, the coda, like the book's other chapters, does not seek to provide a "strong theory" that will account for all of Freud's corpus. And, in keeping with Sedgwick, I would say that here I accept the risks of reading Freud "adventurously": not as I "should" but rather as I "do."[4] The result finds Freud returning the figure of the child to its conventional place within what Edelman describes as the ubiquitous heteronormative social and symbolic regime. In "Femininity," for example, the scene of childhood for boys and girls is not only a phase to be "pass[ed] through," it is a starting point along a set of "parallel lines" that find their narrative end in adult reproductive sexuality.[5] The story of girlhood, as Irigaray has emphasized, is both one of longing to reproduce ("to get the mother with child" and "to bear her child") and one of shedding her suboptimal boyhood in order to become the feminine "instrument of male pleasure."[6] Yet even when Freud's narration does not jump so quickly to the other end of the line, as we will see, telling stories of childhood still depends on "straight" (i.e., normative) temporalities that follow the logics of progress, development, and deferral to adulthood. And while Freud's psychoanalytic framework resists simple directionality, as his theoretical corpus frequently rests on the language of *Verdichtung* (condensation) and *Verspätung* (belatedness), the literary scene of childhood (particularly as it appears in narratives of memory) still exists in absolute relation to its Other, adulthood, and therefore cannot be thought on its own. I thus offer here one final local theory—but one in which the world of childhood is no longer so small. Freud's childhood worlds must be large enough to accommodate not only the child's experience, their future sexual life, and all the things lost to oblivion; such a world must also account for fantasies of meaning that child-figures provide to grown-ups.

Turning first to a relatively early account, from his 1899 essay "Über Deckerinnerungen" ("Screen Memories"), we see Freud describe childhood experience as exhibiting a "fundamental difference" from that of adulthood.[7] Explaining that the memories adults recall from when they were young children are unusually specific and "concerned with everyday and indifferent events," Freud is particularly struck by the appearance of the child's attention to insignificant details, such that ordinary objects on the table at mealtime or the act of breaking a tree branch while taking a stroll are given pride of place, sticking in memory rather than being forgotten.[8] In keeping with his work on repression, he assigns an uncanny significance to these fragments ("*Bruchstücke*") of childhood experience: They are important enough to be retained in memory, and yet their extreme ordinariness means they must be taken as indicating they actually conceal a displaced traumatic event—the thing worth remembering that has, in fact, already been forgotten.[9] In other words, Freud finds the "childish interest" ("kindliches Interesse") in the material world to be so utterly banal as to be vexing and thus theorizes that the value of childhood memories must lie in what is not visible, but perhaps still causally attributable.[10] And so, on the disease model of origin and progression, these shockingly "indifferent" scenes come to have "great pathogenic importance" ("große pathogene Bedeutung").[11] In this sense, I suggest, we can also see the temporality of childhood (both remembered and forgotten) as forming a complex, but generally still linear, history—a genesis that links the past and future of grown-up neuroses,[12] while also dismissing the value of the child's *own* interests as merely aesthetic and etiological. Meanwhile the narrative or literary qualities that Freud attributes to the scene of childhood in its capacity for signification ("Bedeutung") always imply the futurity of a "reader" (the analyst) who will finally not only rescue the forgotten event, but also vouchsafe real meaning of the child's displaced attention: what the future grown-up has long repressed.[13]

In "Screen Memories," Freud dedicates considerable space to the childhood memory of a single patient (who turns out to be himself). Here he recalls in vivid detail a brief scene of childhood play, picking dandelions on a meadow with his two cousins (a boy and a girl). The idyllic scene concludes abruptly after the two boys end up grabbing the girl's bouquet, leaving her in tears, before being called away to eat.[14] Over the course of a fictionalized dialogue between the patient (Freud) and analyst (also Freud), he concludes, by virtue of a network of "suppressed" fantasies, including "de-flowering" his cousin, that even as a "genuine" memory the scene also conceals desires that date to periods *after* the meadow scene itself is thought to have taken place.[15] In a first register, the extreme ordinariness and gendered normativity of childhood play (i.e., a girl picking dandelions and boys being rough) prefigures the reading that Freud's narrator/analyst will eventually offer: namely, that childhood's innocent play indicates (while also cloaking or screening) the child's future heterosexuality. In a second register, Freud's narrative strategy—which includes screening *himself* as the analysand-character—further multiplies the necessity of the future to literalize the force of the past. Childhood play itself has no real meaning on its own, gaining it only through the belated pathogenic narrative.

The signification of objects within the scene (e.g., the yellow dandelions) only appears over the course of the linear, narrative time of Freud's prose—recounting as temporal progression and as discursivity—that constitutes the text of "Screen Memories" itself. Just as the screen memory is a belated phenomenon that renders the grown-up patient's psychical life more visible with the aid of the analyst, so too is childhood autobiographically and theoretically necessary for the belated production of Freudian psychoanalysis itself. As

Madelon Sprengnether argues, what Freud "discovered in the recesses of his own mind were forbidden, hence repressed wishes, which led him to the articulation of childhood sexuality and ultimately to the construction of the Oedipus complex.... Through his self-analysis and the concepts it produced, Freud performed an act of self-reinvention."[16] In other words, by transforming scenes from his own childhood into a narrative, a new adult is born: Freud, the analyst.

As Kathryn Bond Stockton reminds us, Jacques Derrida's classic précis expresses how the "concepts of *Nachträglichkeit* and *Verspätung* . . . govern the whole of Freud's thought and determine all the other concepts" such that with "belated understanding," Freud already indicates the temporality of childhood experience—in this way, both the "protohomosexual child" and, as I am arguing here, even ordinary "childish interest" are structured as "'afterwardness': a 'deferred action,' whereby events from the past acquire meaning only when read through their future consequences."[17] In Freud's conceptual framework, which involves scenes of writing and reading (and rewriting), the child's attention to the world—at the time of their attention—does not have the temporal extension to suffice on its own.

Freud eventually concludes that "incomplete childhood scenes" like these ultimately only appear "innocent by very reason of their incompleteness."[18] Here, Freud deploys both repression and latency to explain the "innocent" and also "uninteresting" ("gleichgültige") appearance of childhood. He also signals that, without its future-Other (the libidinous adult), the child really is boring! Alternatively, James Kincaid suggests that Freud himself falls into the conceptual trap of "innocence": namely, that "a state of being that [is] pure nothingness, secretly nourishe[s] . . . its opposite. Abhorred vacuums get filled up, and depravity will do as well as anything else."[19] In other words, childhood, for Freud, cannot exist without its depraved—and inevitable—Other.

Around 1916 and 1917, Freud develops an essay on childhood memories that foregrounds children smashing or destroying household goods, taking the same pathogenic stance toward stories of childhood evinced by his writing nearly two decades earlier. His inquiry begins with Johann Wolfgang von Goethe's 1811 autobiography *Aus meinem Leben: Dichtung und Wahrheit* (*From My Life: Poetry and Truth*). Here, Freud narrates his initial puzzlement at the apparent arbitrariness with which Goethe—and for that matter, any adult—is able recall specific scenes from childhood, while most others are lost to "general oblivion" ("dem allgemeinen Vergessen").[20] Once again, Freud remarks, the events that are preserved as memories so often seem to him to be "indifferent, worthless even" ("gleichgültig, ja nichtig") on first inspection.[21] In the absence of the psychoanalytic perspective, he notes, one is inclined to assume that some crucial significance must lay within these recollections—why else should they have managed to "resist amnesia" ("es ... ihnen gelungen war, der Amnesie zu trotzen")?[22] Whether the ordinary scene of childhood is narrated by his patients or by Goethe himself, Freud regards it, by itself, to be "worthless even." Unless provided some other meaning by the analyst, author, or adult, childhood experience on its own continues to be theoretically uninteresting.[23]

Freud, perhaps more than any writer at the turn of the century, is regarded as having illuminated the immense value of the first years of life as Ur-scenes of desire, loss, frustration, and pleasure,[24] but the scene of childhood only ever gains its meaning through the dual processes of belated grown-up recollection and, more importantly, through the secondary adult lens of psychoanalytic interpretation. In this essay, Freud cites a scene at length from *Poetry and Truth* in which the young Goethe joyfully tosses crockery from an upstairs window to watch it crash onto the street below; although "there is no need to dispute a child's enjoyment in smashing things," Freud asserts, childhood pleasure *alone* offers insufficient justification for affording this scene "a lasting place in adult memory" or interrogating its possible posterity in literature.[25] Instead, Freud suggests that the action of tossing objects "out!" ("Hinaus!") brings about a "magical action" ("magische Handlung") and makes the belated "hidden meaning" legible, as the child's activity in its memory operates as "a symbolic action" ("eine symbolische ... Handlung") in which the child wishes to remove a newly arrived interloper (e.g., a baby sibling).[26] I think we can take Freud's literary intervention a step further: It is not merely a single symbolic action but storytelling in the sense of both *plot* and *allegory* that is enacted in childhood play. The child's enjoyment is neither here nor there, and the experience of play itself—smashing and throwing things—only gains its validity in the *future*, if the grown-up remembers it and relates it. The story of childhood then attains further validity discursively, as recounting the event to an analyst (Freud) exposes its allegorical qualities and draws a causal relationship between the signification of the narrated childhood experience and the signified content (e.g., fear, loss). The literary quality of childhood is what tethers it to its future reader whose work of "appreciation" ("erkennen") literalizes it as meaning: "Before their significance could be appreciated, a certain work of interpretation was necessary."[27]

Freud dismisses the present-time of childhood experience itself as merely "variable and inessential points" ("inkonstant und unwesentlich") in favor of the doubled directional link provided by the child's "hurling out" ("das Hinausbefördern")—spatially pointing *out* the window and temporally pointing the therapeutic listener and eventual reader *toward* the future time of adulthood, the time that we might say *really* matters for Freud (the time of interpretation).[28] Of course, frequent readers of Freud are not surprised to find that moments of childhood ecstasy or rage, once transformed by Freud's own *re*telling of the patient's story ("It was therefore as if the patient had said") become origin stories of adult sexual disturbance ("dauernde Störung").[29] For example, a subsequent patient recollection (of childhood mischief and destruction while traveling) concludes with the following analysis: "Evidently, the two-year-old child was restless because he could not bear his parents being in bed together. On the journey it was no doubt impossible to avoid the child being a witness to this. The feelings which were aroused at that time in the jealous little boy left him with an embitterment against women which persisted and permanently interfered with the development of his capacity for love."[30] Here, the story of a child's misbehavior finds its full meaning both in its retrospective connection between the belated appearance as plot and the subsequent allegory of the child's horror, with the object of his horror tactfully, if not also literarily, elided in Freud's storytelling. As a narrator who renarrates his patient's childhood (with the liberties of "as if"), Freud presents the parents' sex life as the connective tissue between the "inessential points" of childhood experience and the future grown man's disinterest in women. In this way, Freud offers his reader the opposite of what Barbara N. Nagel calls the *"anti-literary* character" of "a child is being beaten."[31]

This scene of childhood becomes consequential only in light of the future queerness of the child as an adult. As Sara Ahmed has demonstrated elsewhere in Freud's corpus, by relying on assumptions about the formative desire for the parent of the opposite gender, his interpretations regularly "straighten" even his queer patients; this heterosexual "background" thus always figures the child as *already* promised to the future as a reproductive citizen.[32] With Ahmed we can see that this childhood appears as that which is "behind" the queer adult patient, but where the allegory of the child's experience is one that assumes even the queer child's bitterness is straight.[33] On this reading, childhood recollection is thus an origin story that, in Freud's own literary hand, follows the logic of Edelman's reading of the book of Genesis where "no fucking could ever effect such creation: all sensory experience, all pleasure of the flesh, must be borne away from this fantasy of futurity secured. . . . Paradoxically, the child of the two-parent family thus proves that its parents don't fuck and on its tiny shoulders it carries the burden of maintaining the fantasy of a time to come in which meaning, at last made present to itself, no longer depends on the fantasy of its attainment in time to come."[34] Freud's allegory of the child (who grows up to be queer) thereby serves as a warning: parents' "fucking" risks the very fantasy of reproductive futurity that having a child promised in the first place. Devoid of this promise, the innocent and empty child of psychoanalysis can only be invested with pathogenic value; and the scene of childhood—from Freud snatching yellow dandelions to Goethe's childish thrills—is revealed to be nothing more than the fantasy of future meaning that literary interpretation provides.

Acknowledgments

Although I began thinking about the intersections of representations of nineteenth-century childhood and philosophy in my dissertation, I could not have written this book without the development and enrichment of my thinking that occurred over the years since—having had ample opportunities to read and teach what I was interested in and to allow my other projects on queer figures to cross-pollinate here. *The Small Worlds of Childhood* is therefore very much like the ship of Theseus, having had every plank painstakingly replaced; this essential transformation is very much indebted to many colleagues, friends, mentors, and loved ones who supported me along the way.

I thank the Department of Germanic and Slavic Languages and Literatures at the University of Colorado Boulder for encouraging me to work across disciplines and for providing material support to write this book. I am grateful to Jennifer Ho and CU's Center for the Humanities and Arts for their support of the project, especially as I prepared the manuscript and dossier for publication. As this book belongs to a generation of pandemic projects, I also want to thank Michele Moses and CU's Office of Faculty Affairs, who worked to ensure all faculty (especially parents of small children) were supported as much as possible under otherwise impossible conditions.

I feel particularly grateful for the generosity and solidarity I received over the years from so many of my dear colleagues and friends, close and far, who collectively filled blind spots in my reading with their wonderful suggestions, responded to frantic queries with reasoned advice, championed my work, summered in the library with me, wrote in coffee shops with me, provided essential feedback on drafts, and generally made the unbearable moments bearable: Emmanuel David, Patrick Greaney, Paul Fleming, Hannah Freed-Thall, Alys X.

George, Jason Groves, Dania Hückmann, Ervin Malakaj, Adrienne Merritt, Helmut Muller-Sievers, Barbara N. Nagel, Jillian Porter, Ben Robertson, Florian Sedlmeier, Leif Weatherby, and Beverly Weber.

The Small Worlds of Childhood owes so much to the editorial support I received while producing and finalizing the manuscript. My thanks go to Daniel Hoffman-Schwartz for his insight and support at the eleventh hour. I cannot thank Tom Lay at Fordham University Press enough: His immediate advocacy for this project and his thoughtful advice for its improvement have been essential. I am profoundly grateful to Michael Thomas Taylor, not only for his editorial work, and for his relentless warmth and care, but also for being my trusted interlocutor, both live and in the document's margins, all of which helped me see the project in and beyond its details.

And my most heartfelt gratitude is reserved for Brooke—for bearing with me, for ensuring that I very literally had the time and the space to write, and for believing in me. I could not have done this without you.

Notes

Introduction: Small Worlds, Local Theories

1. The quotation in the epigraph may be found in Eve Kosofsky Sedgwick, "Paranoid and Reparative Reading; or You're So Paranoid, You Probably Think This Introduction Is about You," in *Novel Gazing: Queer Readings in Fiction*, ed. Eve Kosofsky Sedgwick (Durham, NC: Duke University Press, 1997), 25. Sedgwick cites Litvak from a "personal communication," see 40n25.

2. Martin Swales, "Homeliness and Otherness: Reflections on Stifter's Bergkristall," in *The German Bestseller in the Nineteenth Century*, ed. Charlotte Woodford and Benedict Schofield (Rochester, NY: Camden House, 2012): 115–116. As Swales notes, the story's history is intertwined with Christmas: the first published version from 1845 was titled "Der heilige Abend" (Christmas Eve), and the eventual version in *Bunte Steine* ("motley" or "many-colored stones") bore the holiday-themed subtitle and was published in 1852 (though dated 1853) "with an eye on the book market."

3. Adalbert Stifter, *Motley Stones*, trans. Isabel Fargo Cole (New York: New York Review Books Classic, 2021), 127–128; Adalbert Stifter, *Werke und Briefe, Historisch-kritische Gesamtausgabe*, 2:2, ed. Alfred Doppler and Wolfgang Frühwald (Stuttgart: Kohlhammer Verlag, 1982), 183–184. Hereafter referred to as HKG II, 2; Swales, "Homeliness and Otherness," 118.

4. Stifter, *Motley Stones*, 128; Stifter, HKG II:2, 184.

5. Stifter, *Motley Stones*, 128; Stifter, HKG II:2, 185.

6. Stifter, *Motley Stones*, 128; Stifter, HKG II:2, 184–185.

7. Joe Perry, *Christmas in Germany: A Cultural History* (Chapel Hill: University of North Carolina Press, 2010), 36; Ingeborg Weber-Kellermann, *Das Weihnachtsfest: Eine Kultur- und Sozialgeschichte der Weihnachtszeit* (Lucerne: Verlag CJ Bucher, 1978), 98–101.

8. Stifter, *Motley Stones*, 127; Stifter, HKG II:2, 183.
9. Stifter, *Motley Stones*, 127; Stifter, HKG II:2, 183.
10. Stifter, *Motley Stones*, 127–128; Stifter, HKG II:2, 183–184.
11. Stifter, *Motley Stones*, 128–129; Stifter, HKG II:2, 185. "Weil dieses Fest so lange nachhält, weil sein Abglanz so hoch in das Alter hinaufreicht." I note that Cole translates the phrase "so lange nachhält" as "has such a long echo," but that the verb *nachhalten* itself can have a range of senses of extending and enduring: e.g., to last, to make an impression, to persist, etc.
12. Stifter, *Motley Stones*, 127–128; Stifter, HKG II:2, 183–184. Here I would also note the ways in which Stifter's story participates in the realist strategy that Barbara N. Nagel, thinking with Eric Downing, has summarized as a "repetition of the 'real'" but where "this repetition has realizing as well as derealizing effects," as she likens the effect to a reversible image illusion, in which the viewer can alternate between two perceived images, although only actually seeing one at a time. Here it is Stifter the reader, however, rather than the characters in the story, who encounters two contradicting images of Christmas—and split across two modes of encounter: perception versus recollection. See Barbara N. Nagel, *Ambiguous Aggression in German Realism and Beyond: Flirtation, Passive Aggression, Domestic Violence* (New York: Bloomsbury, 2019), 49–50; Eric Downing, *Double Exposure: Repetition and Realism in Nineteenth-Century German Fiction* (Stanford, CA: Stanford University Press, 2000).
13. Hans Blumenberg, *Zu den Sachen und zurück. Aus dem Nachlass*, ed. Manfred Sommer (Frankfurt am Main: Suhrkamp, 2002), 65–66. See also my discussion in Chapter 2; Michael McGillen, "Free Variation from the Archive of Culture: Blumenberg and Husserl on Phenomenological Description," in *Leistungsbeschreibung/ Describing Cultural Achievements: Literarische Strategien bei Hans Blumenberg/Hans Blumenberg's Literary Strategies*, ed. Timothy Attanucci and Ulrich Breuer (Heidelberg: Universitätsverlag Winter, 2020), 73–94; and Daniela K. Helbig, "No More Than Seeing: Hans Blumenberg's Poetics of Spectatorship," *New German Critique* 49, no. 1 (February 2022): 185–213.
14. Swales, "Homeliness and Otherness," 116.
15. Stifter, *Motley Stones*, 161; Stifter, HKG II:2, 228.
16. Stifter, *Motley Stones*, 161–162; Stifter, HKG II:2, 228.
17. Stifter, *Motley Stones*, 161; Stifter, HKG II:2, 228. Irmscher describes their silent watching as allegorically recalling a wordless revelation against the backdrop of natural (i.e., geophysical, meteorological) disaster. Hans Dietrich Irmscher, "Die Verkündigung auf dem Berge: Zur Theodizee in Adalbert Stifters Erzählung 'Bergkristall,'" *Sprachkunst* 30, no. 1 (1999): 5, 7.
18. See, for example, Elisabeth Strowick's discussion of "stagings of visual perception" in *Der Hochwald* (*The High Forest*) and of the ways in which reality is represented as duration and perception in "Rock Crystal." Elisabeth Strowick, "Poetological-Technical Operations: Representation of Motion in Adalbert Stifter," *Configurations* 18 (2010): 273–289; Elisabeth Strowick, "'Dumpfe Dauer': Langeweile

und Atmosphärisches bei Fontane und Stifter," *Germanic Review: Literature, Culture, Theory* 90, no. 3 (2015): 187–203.

19. Hugo Schmidt notes that as an adult who is already far from "the magic of childhood," the mother seems to not understand her daughter or realize that what she is referring to when she speaks of having seen the "Holy Child" is in fact the northern lights. However, he regards Sanna's expression as a "childlike explanation" for a natural phenomenon and argues that the child appears as the point of intersection between the natural and the supernatural, where the unseen becomes visible. Hugo Schmidt, "Eishöhle und Steinhäuschen: Zur Weihnachtssymbolik in Stifters 'Bergkristall,'" *Monatshefte* 56, no. 7 (December 1964): 332–333. See also Claudia Öhlschläger, "Bergkristall," in *Stifter Handbuch: Leben—Werk—Wirkung*, ed. Christian Begemann and Davide Giuriato (Stuttgart: J. B. Metzler, 2017), 85.

20. Cavell articulates a Wittgensteinian sense of "criteria" for knowing what a thing is called. In particular, he argues that for Wittgenstein (in contrast to Austin) the criterion is not whether one already knows a particular piece of information, but rather whether one's world contains (some sense of) that object to begin with. Stanley Cavell, *The Claim of Reason: Wittgenstein, Skepticism, Morality, and Tragedy* (New York: Oxford University Press, 1999), 77–78.

21. Cavell's parenthetical shorthand for the difficulty in expressing the range of concepts that undergird "New York" to a child visiting Times Square is "(To *what* does the child attach the official name <Nyuw York>? The child's world contains no cities.)" *The Claim of Reason*, 77.

22. Irmscher's reading, which places the text within theological discourses, characterizes the children's vision as a divine vision of the present and the mother's response as one steeped in tradition. Irmscher, "Die Verkündigung auf dem Berge," 7.

23. Cavell, *The Claim of Reason*, 52–58, 65–74.

24. Here we might think, for example, of the ways in which Walter Pater imagined childhood as belatedness. Lene Østermark-Johansen, who places Pater in line with Freud, has shown how the former imagines childhood like a wax impression, whose central importance appears as the basis of adult dreams and grown-up creativity in "The Child in the House" (1878) and "Notes on Leonardo da Vinci" (1869). As Kevin Ohi has emphasized, Pater's child-figure, seen from adulthood, exemplifies "aesthetic spectatorship" understood as "dislocation" between poles such as unforgettability and irrecoverability. For Pater, as Ohi interprets him, the adult's view of childhood is the "intuition of loss." Wordsworth likewise shared this worry about the unbridgeable distance from childhood; and, as Linda Austin has shown, poems such as "Ode: Intimations of Immortality" (1807) represent growing up as the ineluctable process of estrangement that separates the extraordinary potential of the self in early life from the prosaic existence of adulthood. Lene Østermark-Johansen, *Walter Pater's European Imagination* (Oxford: Oxford University Press, 2022), 49–50, 60, 69–71; Kevin Ohi, *Innocence and Rapture: The Erotic Child in Pater, Wilde, James, and Nabokov* (New York: Palgrave Macmillan, 2005), 17–19, 53–55, 60. Linda M. Austin, "Children of Childhood:

Nostalgia and the Romantic Legacy," *Studies in Romanticism* 42, no. 1 (March 1, 2003): 83–84.

25. Stifter, *Motley Stones*, 128; Stifter, HKG II:2, 185. As Austin has argued, Wordsworth's influential conception of childhood is one that imagines early life as "movement without memory because the early years are the one time of life when there is not enough of a past to remember." The poet "longed to be free from [memory's] abundance, to relive the time before experience had become the object of reflection. The child devoid of memory could function, partly because of this mental vacuity, as a memorative device." Austin, "Children of Childhood," 85–86.

26. Dana Luciano, *Arranging Grief: Sacred Time and the Body in Nineteenth-Century America* (New York: New York University Press, 2007), 126–127.

27. Lauren Berlant, *The Queen of America Goes to Washington City: Essay on Sex and Citizenship* (Durham, NC: Duke University Press, 1997), 6.

28. Lee Edelman, *No Future: Queer Theory and the Death Drive* (Durham, NC: Duke University Press, 2004). The concept of queerness has a rich and complex set of meanings and theoretical history beyond the sense of homosexuality or non-normative sexualities. Currently, the interdisciplinary framework of queer theory sometimes includes theorization of non-binary gender and transness. However, the overlap of and critical differences between *queer* and *trans** have been the subject of important debates about institutional and interdisciplinary practices in queer theory and transgender studies respectively. Recent work by Cáel M. Keegan provides exemplary insight into these concerns. As my aim here is to avoid arbitrarily collapsing these two conceptual and methodological domains, I will be primarily engaging with the term *queer* to describe a resistance to normative temporalities that would govern childhood's trajectory toward sexual reproductivity and its attending forms of social reproduction in adulthood (via Edelman, Freeman, Love, Stockton, Ahmed, Sedgwick). For discussion on the relationship between *queer* and *trans*, see Cáel M. Keegan, "Against Queer Theory" *Transgender Studies Quarterly* 7, no. 3 (2020): 349–353, and "Transgender Studies, or How to Do Things with Trans*," in *The Cambridge Companion to Queer Studies*, ed. Siobhan B. Somerville (Cambridge UK: Cambridge University Press, 2020): 66–78.

29. Edelman, *No Future*, 2, 12, 19.

30. Edelman, *No Future*, 47. Although Edelman's antirelational thesis has significantly shaped queer theory in the years since its publication—quite often with theorists disagreeing or finding worry in his centering queerness on such radically negative grounds—there is, remarkably, little dispute about his assessment of the representational work of childhood figures. For counter-arguments and criticism of the negativity and anti-relationality of the queer/queerness, see, for example, José Esteban Muñoz, *Cruising Utopia: The Then and There of Queer Futurity* (New York: New York University Press, 2009), Sara Ahmed, *Queer Phenomenology: Orientations, Objects, Others* (Durham, NC: Duke University Press, 2006), 175, 178. Michael D. Snediker, *Queer Optimism: Lyric Personhood and Other Felicitous Persuasions* (Minneapolis: University of Minnesota Press, 2009), 21–25.

31. Sara Ahmed, *The Promise of Happiness* (Durham, NC: Duke University Press, 2010), 183–184.

32. Edelman, *No Future*, 58.

33. Sara Ahmed, "Willful Parts: Problem Characters or the Problem of Character," *New Literary History* 42, no. 2 (Spring 2011): 231–232.

34. Berlant, *The Queen of America Goes to Washington City*, 6.

35. Ahmed, *Queer Phenomenology*, 161.

36. Kathryn Bond Stockton, *The Queer Child, or Growing Sideways in the Twentieth Century* (Durham, NC: Duke University Press, 2009), 4.

37. Heather Love, *Feeling Backward: Loss and the Politics of Queer History* (Cambridge, MA: Harvard University Press, 2007); Ahmed, *Queer Phenomenology*; Elizabeth Freeman, *Time Binds: Queer Temporalities, Queer Histories* (Durham, NC: Duke University Press, 2010).

38. In Stockton's critique, Key's proclamation also reflects a general tendency in the historical treatments of childhood that fail to account for both "queer" and "odd" children but also the "waywardness of [childhood] fictions." In her reading, Freud "queers childhood" in ways that are associated with animality, latency, and trauma. See Stockton, *The Queer Child*, 8, 12, 15. For purposes of my marking a historical shift in representations of childhood with Freud, exemplary essays include "Über Kindeits- und Deckerinnerungen" ("Childhood Memories and Screen Memories") from 1901 and "Infantile Sexualität ("Infantile Sexuality") from 1905. Sigmund Freud, *Gesammelte Werke, chronologisch geordnet*, ed. Anna Freud, vol. 4 (London: Imago, 1941), 51–60, and Sigmund Freud, *Gesammelte Werke, chronologisch geordnet*, ed. Anna Freud, vol. 5 (London: Imago, 1942), 73–107.

39. Davide Giuriato, "Zur Einleitung," in *Kindheit und Literatur: Konzepte—Poetik—Wissen*, ed. Davide Giuriato, Philipp Hubmann, and Mareike Schildmann (Freiburg: Rombach Verlag, 2018), 7–8.

40. Philippe Ariès, *Centuries of Childhood: A Social History of Family Life*, trans. Robert Baldick (New York: Alfred A Knopf, 1962), 34, 403. It should be noted here that while Ariès's rhetoric of "discovery" continues to have significance for childhood studies, especially in literary disciplines, Colin Heywood has surveyed how historians have questioned his assertions, offering alternate characterization of the Middle Ages and early modern period as either long having valued childhood or as a series of "rediscoveries." Colin Heywood, *A History of Childhood: Children and Childhood in the West from Medieval to Modern Times* (Cambridge: Polity Press, 2018), 11–27. Other recent interventions by Michael-Sebastian Honig have significantly expanded the sociological and social historical framework for thinking about childhood as a social construct that enables a range of generational relationships to become legible, through the theoretical lens of childhood as "generationale Ordnung." See also Michael-Sebastian Honig, *Entwurf einer Theorie der Kindheit* (Frankfurt am Main: Suhrkamp Verlag, 1999).

41. Here I employ Dana Luciano's term "chronobiopolitical" in much the way that Elisabeth Freeman does, that is, to describe both the "engroup[ing]" of individuals

"through particular orchestrations of time" and as the "sexual arrangement of the time of life." Luciano, *Arranging Grief*, 9. Freeman, *Time Binds*, 3.

42. Ariès, *Centuries of Childhood*, 119. Edelman, *No Future*. 10–11.

43. James Kincaid, *Child-Loving: The Erotic Child and Victorian Culture* (New York: Routledge, 1992), 62.

44. Kincaid, *Child-Loving*, 10, 64–65; See also Stockton's discussion of Kincaid on the child's "emptiness." Stockton, *The Queer Child*. 12. In another register altogether, Niklas Luhmann's theory of childhood as "black box" replaces centuries of sheer nothingness with fundamental ambivalence and unknowability by describing the actual "world of the child" as perpetually eluding the adult observer. To paraphrase Giuriato, childhood, variously discursively rendered, is but a medium of reflection of adult conceptions of the self. Niklas Luhmann, "Das Kind als Medium der Erziehung," in *Schriften zur Pädagogik*, ed. Dieter Lenzen (Frankfurt am Main: Suhrkamp Verlag, 2004), 166, 180. See also Giuriato, "Zur Einführung," 10–14.

45. Dieter Richter, *Das fremde Kind: Zur Entstehung der Kindheitsbilder des bürgerlichen Zeitalters* (Frankfurt am Main: Fischer, 1987), 26.

46. Reiner Wild, *Die Vernunft der Väter: Zur Psychographie von Bürgerlichkeit und Auklärung in Deutschland* (Stuttgart: Metzler Verlag, 1987), 131–141. See also Ewers's summary in Hans-Heino Ewers, *Kindheit als poetische Daseinsform: Studien zur Entstehung der romantischen Kindheitsutopie im 18. Jahrhundert; Herder, Jean Paul, Novalis und Tieck* (Munich: Wilhelm Fink Verlag, 1989), 10–12.

47. Ewers, *Kindheit als poetische Daseinsform*, 12, 65, 97; Richter, *Das fremde Kind*, 231–235; Rolf J. Goebel, "China as an Embalmed Mummy: Herder's Orientalist Poetics," *South Atlantic Review* 60, no. 1 (January 1995): 116, 123–124. See also the image of the child in Jeffrey Librett's discussion of the co-emergence of Herder's antisemitism and his Orientalist depictions of Chinese, Egyptian, and Jewish cultures. Jeffrey S. Librett, *Orientalism and the Figure of the Jew* (New York: Fordham University Press, 2014), 39–42, 46–47. On a related note, I want to mention Carolyn Steedman's comprehensive work, which has shown the effects that Goethe's child-figure, Mignon, had on a range of discourses across the nineteenth century and beyond. She demonstrates how time and again the child reappears as an idea, as a symbolic figure, and as the personification of "interiority" (e.g., Freud's "unconscious" and other notions of the self that result from the adult's own unrecoverable history), medical, developmental, and historical notions of progress, and other narratives of the past as lost. Carolyn Steedman, *Strange Dislocations: Childhood and the Idea of Human Interiority, 1780–1930* (Cambridge MA: Harvard University Press, 1995).

48. The Enlightenment's notion of childhood as a *tabula rasa* and Romantic ideas, which produced a hierarchized and racialized views of the world's cultures, together prefigure the British and US sentimental discourses that produced what Kyla Schuller describes as a "multiethnic" set science and politics of "impressibility." She argues that in the mid-nineteenth century, the idea that the individual can be "transformed by experience" becomes "a key measure for racially and sexually differentiating the refined, sensitive, and civilized subject who was embedded in

time and capable of progress . . . from the coarse, rigid, and savage elements of the population suspended in the eternal state of flesh and lingering on as unwanted remnants of prehistory." Kyla Schuller, *The Biopolitics of Feeling: Race, Sex, and Science in the Nineteenth Century* (Durham, NC: Duke University Press, 2018), 6–9.

49. Julia Kristeva, "Women's Time," trans. by Alice Jardine and Harry Blake, *Signs* 7, no. 1 (Autumn, 1981): 14–17; Luciano, *Arranging Grief*, 58; Freeman, *Time Binds*, 5–8.

50. Ewers, *Kindheit als poetische Daseinsform*, 121; Freeman, *Time Binds*, 3.

51. Much like Stifter, scholars have noted that Hoffmann had written this story with Christmas in mind, intending it as an "occasional text" to be gifted to the children of a friend, though it eventually made its way to a general (grown-up) readership. The first version was published in 1816 and appeared in the collection, *Kinder-Märchen* (*Children's Fairytales*), and was re-published in 1819 as part of the collection of stories, *Die Serapionsbrüder* (*The Serapion Brethren*), which was directed toward the literary market. In the latter instance, it appeared with an added frame narrative, which made it clear that Hoffmann was intending it as an example of his aesthetic principles of fantasy and the poetic imagination. Hilda Meldrum Brown, *E. T. A. Hoffmann and the Serapiontic Principle: Critique and Creativity* (Rochester, NY: Boydell & Brewer, 2006), 171–172; Alina Boy, "Marie im Wunderland: Animation und Imagination in Hoffmanns Nußknacker und Mausekönig," *E. T. A Hoffmann-Jahrbuch* 24 (2016): 34.

52. Hans-Heino Ewers, *Kinder- und Jugendliteratur der Romantik: Eine Textsammlung* (Stuttgart: Philipp Reclam jun., 1984), 23–25.

53. Hans-Heino Ewers, "Geschichte der deutschen Kinder- und Jugendliteratur: Eine problemgeschichtliche Skizze," https://www.uni-frankfurt.de/64851467/Geschichte-der-KJL.pdf (retrieved May 23, 2024).

54. As Brown notes, Hoffmann deploys his "typically intrusive narrator, who also relates directly to his readership, both adults and children (he even addresses the children, Marie and Fritz, from time to time), and who moves the narrative backwards and forwards between the real and the fantastic worlds." These two worlds, I would suggest, follow the Romantic model, in which the "fantastic world" belongs to childhood (imagination, dreams, creativity, and terror) and the prosaic "real" world is the one governed by adulthood (parents, duties, expectations, and ordinary life). Brown, *E. T. A. Hoffmann and the Serapiontic Principle*, 172–174.

55. E. T. A. Hoffmann, *Poetische Werke in sechs Bänden*, vol. 3 (Berlin: Aufbau, 1963), 252. "Ich wende mich an dich selbst, sehr geneigter Leser oder Zuhörer Fritz—Theodor—Ernst—oder wie du sonst heißen magst, und bitte dich, daß du dir deinen letzten, mit schönen bunten Gaben reich geschmückten Weihnachtstisch recht lebhaft vor Augen bringen mögest, dann wirst du es dir wohl auch denken können, wie die Kinder mit glänzenden Augen ganz verstummt stehenblieben." Translation mine.

56. As scholars have demonstrated, the text's movement between the real bourgeois world and fantasy- and dream-worlds depicts Marie's "feminine

socialization" and "psychosexual development." The story also imagines Marie as the object of Droßelmeier's fantasies of desire. Seifert also notes that the teleological trope of marriage is one among several intertextual affinities between Hoffmann and Tieck. Marion Schmaus, "Nußknacker und Mausekönig: Ein Weihnachtsabend (1816)," in *E. T. A. Hoffmann Handbuch. Leben—Werk—Wirkung*, ed. Christine Lubkoll and Harald Neumeyer (Stuttgart: Metzler Verlag, 2015), 101–102; Carl Pietzker, "'Nussknacker und Mausekönig': Gründungstext der Phantastischen Kinder- und Jugendliteratur," in *E. T. A. Hoffmann: Romane und Erzählungen: Interpretation*, ed. Günter Saße (Stuttgart: Reclam, 2004): 182–198. Gerhard Neumann, "Puppe und Automate: Inszenierte Kindheit in E. T. A. Hoffmanns Sozialisationsmärchen 'Nußknacker und Mausekönig,'" in *Jugend—ein romantisches Konzept?* ed. Günter Oesterle (Würzburg: Königshausen & Neumann, 1997), 135–160. Gisela Vitt-Maucher, *E. T. A. Hoffmanns Märchenschaffen: Kaleidoskop der Verfremdung in seinen sieben Märchen* (Chapel Hill: University of North Carolina Press, 1989). Christoph Seifener, "Zeitwahrnehmung und -darstellung in Ludwig Tiecks *Die Elfen* und den Kindermärchen E. T. A. Hoffmanns," *Seminar: A Journal of Germanic Studies* 60, no. 1 (February 2024): 1, 9, 15.

57. If we consider just commentaries on the poetics of childhood memories in Walter Benjamin and Rainer M. Rilke, the writers featured in parts II and III of this book, an exemplary selection includes Anja Lemke, *Gedächtnisräume des Selbst: Walter Benjamins "Berliner Kindheit um neunzehnhundert"* (Würzburg: Königshausen und Neumann, 2005); Lorna Martens, *The Promise of Memory: Childhood Recollection and Its Objects of Literary Modernism* (Cambridge, MA: Harvard University Press, 2011); Burkhardt Lindner, "Vom 'sentimentalischen' Kinderbild zur Topographie der Kindheit," in *Topographien der Kindheit: Literarische, mediale und interdisziplinäre Perpspektiven auf Orts- und Raumkunstruktionen*, ed. Caroline Roeder (Bielefeld: Transcript Verlag, 2014), 41–58; Nadine Werner, *Archäologie des Erinnerns: Sigmund Freud in Walter Benjamins Berliner Kindheit* (Göttingen: Wallstein Verlag, 2015); Mark Rowlands, *Memory and the Self: Phenomenology, Science, and Autobiography* (New York: Oxford University Press, 2016).

58. Lorna Martens, "Introduction: Writing Childhood Memory," in *The Promise of Memory*, 1–56.

59. Paul Fleming, "The Promises of Childhood: Autobiography in Goethe and Jean Paul," *Goethe Yearbook* 14 (2007): 30.

60. Susan H. Gillespie, "On 'Amorbach,'" *New German Critique* 43, no. 1 [127] (February 2016): 216–219.

61. Hugh Cunningham, *Children and Childhood in Western Society since 1500* (Harlow, Eng.: Pearson, 2005), 58.

62. Kincaid, *Child-Loving*, 284.

63. Joseph Litvak, "Strange Gourmet: Taste, Waste, Proust," in *Novel Gazing: Queer Readings in Fiction*, ed. Eve Kosofsky Sedgwick (Durham, NC: Duke University Press, 1997), 75; Theodor W. Adorno, *Notes to Literature*, vol. 2, trans. Sherry Weber Nicholsen (New York: Columbia University Press, 1992), 315–316;

Theodor W. Adorno, *Gesammelte Schriften*, vol. 2, ed. Rolf Tiedemann (Frankfurt am Main: Suhrkamp Verlag, 1997), 673, cited hereafter as GS 2.

64. Adorno, *Notes to Literature*, 315–316. Adorno, GS 2, 673: "Er hat der Möglichkeit ungeschmälerter Erfahrung aus der Kindheit die Treue gehalten und mit aller Reflexion und Bewußheit des Erwachsenen die Welt so undeformiert wahrgenommen wie am ersten Tag . . ." Litvak also shows that Proust's scenes of childhood bear a more complex relationship with adulthood and adolescence than those in the stories I examine in this book: for Proust childhood is still inseparable from adolescence, which is both "annex[ed]" into childhood and also stands as the "reinforce[ment]" of the opposition between childhood and adulthood. Litvak, "Strange Gourmet," 75, 77.

65. Adorno, *Notes to Literature*, 316. Adorno, GS 2, 673: "prüft die innere und äußerere Realität."

66. Sedgwick, "Paranoid and Reparative Reading," 1.

67. Sedgwick, "Paranoid and Reparative Reading," 3.

68. Kenneth B. Kidd, *Theory for Beginners: Children's Literature as Critical Thought* (New York: Fordham University Press, 2020), 90–91.

69. Although this book's project does not take up Deleuze and Guattari, their characterization of "minor literature" as evincing a deterritorialization nonetheless evokes a kind estrangement or queerness that childhood in Stifter, Rilke, and Benjamin, express. Kidd, *Theory for Beginners*, 80. Gilles Deleuze and Félix Guattari, *Kafka: Toward a Minor Literature*, trans. Dana Polan (Minneapolis: University of Minnesota Press, 1986), 16: "A minor literature doesn't come from a minor language; it is rather that which a minority constructs within a major language. But the first characteristic of minor literature in any case is that in it language is affected with a high coefficient of deterritorialization."

70. Sedgwick, "Paranoid and Reparative Reading," 31. A key part of Sedgwick's argument here is that reparative reading's potential lies precisely in its willingness to be surprised, where the sheer unpredictability of error not only can result in positive affect—as a good surprise—but also assumes that knowledge today will differ tomorrow. In contrast to paranoid reading, which positions all surprises as bad, as indicative of the reader's humiliation from error or oversight or negative in the sense that the discovery is itself one of negativity.

71. Sedgwick locates this surreptitious "image" of the queer child reading at the root of any reparative queer reading. Sedgwick, "Paranoid and Reparative Reading," 2–3. Love, *Feeling Backward*, 6.

72. This book is also indebted to Sara Ahmed's practice of writing "out of line" with her interdisciplinarity, as I move between my "home discipline" of literary studies with my close readings, history of philosophy, and contemporary queer theory. Ahmed, *Queer Phenomenology*, 22.

73. Sedgwick, "Paranoid and Reparative Reading," 23.

74. Here I'm indebted to Rüdiger Campe for the double entendre of "doing theory with a strong German accent," a formulation that encapsulates a generational

approach to "literary theory" at Johns Hopkins University. The phrase captured a practice of reading literature through a largely German philosophical lens, and one that nonetheless moved promiscuously among English, American, and Continental traditions. However, as a German Department, of course, many also spoke or wrote in English "with a German accent."

75. See, for example, Jason Groves, *The Geological Unconscious: German Literature and the Mineral Imaginary* (New York: Fordham University Press, 2020); Timothy Attanucci, *The Restorative Poetics of a Geological Age: Stifter, Viollet-le-Duc, and the Aesthetic Practices of Geohistoricism* (Berlin: De Gruyter, 2020).

76. Michel Foucault, *The Order of Things* (New York: Vintage, 1994), 70.

77. Freeman, *Time Binds*, 8. See also Attanucci, *Restorative Poetics*; Groves, *The Geological Unconscious*; Peter Schnyder, "Die Dynamisierung des Statischen: Geologisches Wissen bei Goethe und Stifter," *Zeitschrift für Germanistik* 19, no. 3 (2009): 540–555.

78. Freeman, *Time Binds*, 8. Here Freeman also points to Love's *Feeling Backward*.

79. Adorno, *Notes to Literature*, 315–316. Adorno, GS 2, 672–673: "unendliche Möglichkeiten von Erfahrung . . . die Realität so genau abzuhören." Adorno is ruminating here on Proust's writerly capacity for observations; the sentiment, as I show in this book, maps just as easily on Rilke and Benjamin.

80. Hans Blumenberg, *The Laughter of the Thracian Woman: A Protohistory of Theory* (New York: Bloomsbury, 2015), viii, 3, 4.

81. Florian Fuchs, "Decoding Aesop: Blumenberg's Fabulistic Turn," *New German Critique* 49, no. 1 (145) (February 2022): 167. See also Andreas Huyssen, "Paris/Childhood: The Fragmented Body in Rilke's *Notebooks of Malte Laurids Brigge*," in *Modernity and the Text: Revisions of German Modernism*, ed. Andreas Huyssen and David Bathrick (New York: Columbia University Press, 1989), 113–141; and Ihor Junyk, "'A Fragment from Another Context': Modernist Classicism and the Urban Uncanny in Rainer Maria Rilke," *Comparative Literature* 62 (June 1, 2010): 262–282.

82. Freeman, *Time Binds*, 4–9; Luciano, *Arranging Grief*, 121–122.

83. Luciano, *Arranging Grief*, 121–122.

84. Stockton, *The Queer Child*, 11.

85. Samuel Weber, *Benjamin's -abilities* (Cambridge, MA: Harvard University Press, 2008), 139.

86. G. W. Leibniz, *Philosophical Essays*, ed. Roger Ariew and Daniel Garber (Indianapolis: Hackett, 1989), 216.

87. Muñoz, *Cruising Utopia*, 25.

88. Gershom Scholem, *On Jews and Judaism in Crisis*, ed. Werner J. Dannhauser (New York: Schocken Books, 1976), 178.

89. Giorgio Agamben, *The Signature of All Things: On Method* (New York: Zone Books, 2009), 31.

90. Edelman, *No Future*, 6.

91. See Edelman, *No Future*, and Kincaid, *Child-Loving*.

1. Adalbert Stifter's Topographical Worlds of Childhood

1. Michel Foucault, *The Order of Things* (New York: Vintage, 1994), 308.

2. Adalbert Stifter, *Werke und Briefe: Historisch-kritische Gesamtausgabe* (Stuttgart: Kohlhammer Verlag, 1997), VIII, 1, 311–312 (hereafter abbreviated as HKG). Written for the short-lived, cultural-political journal *Die Gartenlaube für Österreich: Organ für Familie und Volk, Freiheit und Fortschritt* (The garden arbor for Austria: magazine for family and folk, freedom, and progress).

3. Stifter, HKG VIII, 1, 108.

4. Stifter, HKG VIII, 1, 108. A note on translation: Here and throughout the book, I have chosen to use the gender-neutral pronoun "they" for any instances where the German word *Kind* (child) does not explicitly refer to a boy or girl. The German noun *Kind* is neuter; I have chosen "they" over "it," as the latter lacks the sense of full personhood that I am arguing these authors convey in their philosophical-poetic employment of children as subjects.

5. Stifter, HKG VIII, 1, 108–109: "Baut nicht das Kind neben der Wohnung seines Vaters ein Häuslein von Lehm oder Steinchen oder Hölzlein, und freut sich der Außengestalt des winzigen Dinges, ja baut es nicht ein Hauslein aus Kartenblättern auf dem Tische? . . . Die Kinder bauen sich aus Garben auf dem Felde oder aus Weidenzweigen ein Kämmerlein und hocken hinein und freuen sich oder sie wühlen eine Höhlung in den Heuschober, oder sie kriechen unter Steinüberhänge oder in den Taubenschlag oder gar in die Hundehütte, wenn sie leer ist oder unter ein Brett oder irgendein Wirthschaftsgeräthe, wenn es eine Art Dächelchen bildet. . . . Es ist das Flüchten von dem Weiten in das Enge und Begrenzte." Unless otherwise indicated, all translations of this text are mine.

6. Stifter's depiction is filled with diminutive endings "-lein" and "-chen" that transform the standard grown-up structures (*Kammer, Zimmer, Haus, Dach*) into smaller versions: *Kämmerlein, Zimmerchen, Hauslein, Dächelchen*.

7. Juliane Vogel has argued that the static wooden arbor—like sight of the bare branches in winter—signals an unweaving and disentangling of the wild growth and disorder of the flora that it undergirds. Borrowing from Rosalind Krauss's claim about the grids' "antinarrative" effect, its appearance as an artificial framework for perceiving nature, often signals "mortification." Vogel, "Stifters Gitter: Poetologische Dimensionen einer Grenzfigur," in *Die Dinge und die Zeichen: Dimensionen des Realistischen in der Erzählliteratur des 19. Jahrhunderts*, for Helmut Pfotenhauer, ed. Sabine Schneider and Barbara Hunfeld (Würzburg: Königshausen & Neumann, 2008), 49–51; Rosalind E. Krauss, "Grids," in *The Originality of the Avant-Garde and Other Modernist Myths* (Cambridge, MA: MIT Press, 1984), 15.

8. Stifter, HGK VIII, 1, 109–110.

9. Stifter, HGK VIII, 1, 110.

10. Juliane Vogel suggests that is the (largely unattainable) orderly geometricity of the grid in which both the characters in his narratives and the texts themselves tend

to seek refuge—and that the figure of the grid offers some promise of relief from the overwhelming fullness of realist description of the world. Vogel, "Stifters Gitter," 43.

11. Stifter, HGK VIII, 1, 108.

12. Stifter, HGK VIII, 1, 110–112. Along similar lines, Juliane Vogel reads Stifter's figure of the arbor as a grid that serves to organize the network of branches, undergirding the visible growth of nature by ordering the leaves and branches from the underside or backside, only to become the primary visible grid in winter when that growth dies back. Vogel, "Stifters Gitter," 49–50.

13. Despite the fact that he populates his texts with child-figures, they largely seem to meet virtually every fate except adulthood, ranging from illness and death, to vanishing into the forest, and suicide. Eva Geulen, "Adalbert Stifters Kinder-Kunst: Drei Fallstudien," *Deutsche Vierteljahresschrift für Literaturwissenschaft und Geistesgeschichte* 67, no. 4 (1993): 660; Albrecht Koschorke, "Erziehung zum Freitod: Adalbert Stifters pädagogischer Realismus," in *Die Dinge und die Zeichen*, ed. Schneider and Hunfeld, 326.

14. Foucault, *The Order of Things*, 150.

15. Recent studies by Jason Groves, Tove Holmes, Timothy Attanucci, and Elisabeth Strowick have approached Stifter's realism as variously depicting time as perception and boredom, and geological formation and erosion, as well as broadly operating beyond human time, on the scale of the earth historical. Tove Holmes, "An Archive of the Earth: Stifter's Geologos," *Seminar* 53, no. 3 (September 2018): 281–290; Jason Groves, *The Geological Unconscious: German Literature and the Mineral Imaginary* (New York: Fordham University Press, 2020); Timothy Attanucci, *The Restorative Poetics of a Geological Age: Stifter, Viollet-le-Duc, and the Aesthetic Practices of Geohistoricism* (Berlin: Walter de Gruyter GmbH, 2020); Elisabeth Strowick, "'Dumpfe Dauer': Langeweile und Atmosphärisches bei Fontane und Stifter," *Germanic Review: Literature, Culture, Theory* 90, no. 3 (2015): 187–203.

16. Rita Felski, *Doing Time: Feminist Theory and Postmodern Culture* (New York: New York University Press, 2000), 79.

17. Stifter, HGK VIII, 1, 108–109.

18. Henri Lefebvre, "The Everyday and Everydayness," trans. Christine Levich, *Yale French Studies* 73 (1987): 10.

19. Foucault, *The Order of Things*, 134, 138.

20. Elizabeth Freeman, *Time Binds: Queer Temporalities, Queer Histories* (Durham, NC: Duke University Press, 2010), 5.

21. Eva Geulen, "Tales of a Collector: Adalbert Stifter's Bunte Steine," in *A New History of German Literature*, ed. David Wellbery et al. (Cambridge, MA: Harvard University Press, 2004), 590.

22. Eva Geulen's comprehensive analysis, for example, traces this recurrent figure in Stifter's narratives from its roots in Rousseauean thought and early figures such as Mignon and Kaspar Hauser. Geulen, "Adalbert Stifters Kinder-Kunst."

23. Dieter Borchmeyer, "Ideologie der Familie und ästhetische Gesellschaftskritik in Stifters 'Nachsommer,'" *Zeitschrift für deutsche Philologie* 99 (January 1980): 227–228.

24. As Hans Dietrich Irmscher notes, the division of space can also be thought of as establishing "qualitative" ("qualitative") distinctions in the *types* of space present in Stifter's work. Here, the children's quarters would fall into what he calls a "space of culture" ("Kulterraum"), which stands in contrast to the "space of nature" ("Naturraum")—a distinction that will be addressed in the section titled "'Tourmaline' and Childhood's 'Bad Timing'" in this chapter. Irmscher, *Adalbert Stifter: Wirklichkeitserfahrung und gegenständliche Darstellung* (Munich: Wilhelm Fink Verlag, 1971), 186–187.

25. Adalbert Stifter, *Indian Summer*, trans. Wendell Frye (New York: Peter Lang, 1985), 10. HGK, IV,1: "Mein Vater hatte zwei Kinder, mich, den erstgeborenen Sohn, und eine Tochter, welche zwei Jahre jünger war als ich. Wir hatten in der Wohnung jedes ein Zimmerchen, in welchem wir uns unseren Geschäften, die uns schon in der Kindheit regelmäßig aufgelegt wurden, widmen mußten, und in welchem wir schliefen."

26. Stifter, HGK XIV, 266.

27. Stifter, *Indian Summer*, 11; HKG VI, 2, 12: "Dieser Zug strenger Genauigkeit prägte sich uns ein und ließ uns auf die Befehle der Eltern achten, wenn wir sie auch nicht verstanden. So zum Beispiele durften nicht einmal wir Kinder das Schlafzimmer der Eltern betreten. Eine alte Magd war mit Ordnung und Aufräumung desselben betraut."

28. Beatrice Mall-Grob argues that the family scenes in the first chapter of *Indian Summer* reflect a common nineteenth-century pedagogy of the family, in which the domestic scene is above all one governed by fatherly rule. The entire creation of the house (its organization and the education that takes place there) are within the father's jurisdiction. Beatrice Mall-Grob, *Fiktion des Anfangs: Literarische Kindheitsmodelle bei Jean Paul und Adalbert Stifter* (Stuttgart: Metzler Verlag, 1999), 317–325.

29. Foucault, *The Order of Things*, 41.

30. Stifter, *Indian Summer*, 12; HGK, IV,1: "Die Wände dieses neuen Bilderzimmers wurden mit dunkelrotbraunen Tapeten überzogen, von denen sich die Goldrahmen sehr schön abhoben. Der Fußboden war mit einem mattfarbigen Teppiche belegt, damit er die Farben der Bilder nicht beirre."

31. Stifter, *Indian Summer*, 112.

32. Stifter, *Indian Summer*, 112.

33. Foucault, *The Order of Things*, 70.

34. Foucault, *The Order of Things*, 131.

35. Stifter, *Indian Summer*, 14.

36. Stifter, *Indian Summer*, 14. As Davide Giuriato has suggested, Stifter invests his narratives of childhood with his own nearly Kantian belief in the critical significance of a pedagogy that imposes form; accordingly, Heinrich's upbringing does not start from the Rousseauean concept of childhood (both unknowable and natural). Davide Giuriato, "Kindheit," in *Stifter-Handbuch: Leben—Werk—Wirkung*, ed. Christian Begemann and Davide Giurato (Stuttgart: Metzler Verlag, 2017), 343; Mall-Grob, *Fiktion des Anfangs*, 325.

37. Dana Luciano, *Arranging Grief: Sacred Time and the Body in Nineteenth-Century America* (New York: New York University Press, 2007), 121–122.

38. Luciano, *Arranging Grief*, 122–123.

39. Analogously to my readings of Stifter's vignettes describing the arbor's capacity to serve as a place of refuge, Sarah Hoke has suggested that the very configuration of the bourgeois home reflects a growing interest in the separation of work and private life: "Der starke Drang zu Privatheit und Intimität sowie die Genese eines neuen Familienverständnisses erklären sich zum einen aus einer Separierung der Lebensbereiche Wohnen und Arbeiten, die das Haus bzw. die Wohnung zu einem Refugium werden ließ." Hoke, *Fritz von Uhdes "Kinderstube": Die Darstellung des Kindes in seinem Spiel- und Wohnmilieu* (Göttingen: Universitätsverlag Göttingen, 2011), 126.

40. As Gunter Hertling has argued, the interior spaces of Stifter's narrative universe are as detailed and as critical for his moral-aesthetic program as are his widely discussed landscape depictions. For an overview of Stifter's attention to interior spaces, and *Turmalin* in particular, see Hertling, "'Wer jetzt kein Haus hat, baut sich keines mehr': Zur Zentralsymbolik in Adalbert Stifters 'Turmalin,'" *VASILO* 26, no. 1/2 (1977): 17–34.

41. The practice of physically quartering children away from adults lies at the heart of contemporaneous debates about the proper environment for children to be raised and educated. On one side of the debate stands Rousseau, arguing for radical isolation from the detrimental effects of society; Jean Paul, by contrast, felt that children were essentially "social" beings, and therefore require limited and carefully selected access to society. Hans Heino Ewers, *Kindheit als poetisches Daseinsform: Studien zur Entstehung der romantischen Kindheitsutopie im 18. Jahrhundert: Herder, Jean Paul, Novalis und Tieck* (Munich: Wilhelm Fink Verlag, 1989), 13, 109.

42. Dieter Borchmeyer also shows that the first Drendorf residence in the city in this chapter does not follow the model of the "ganzes Haus": It is used only in part as a living space ("Wohnhaus"), and partly for business ("Geschäftshaus"), and—unlike many such homes at the time—the house servants dined in a separate room, whereas his father's trade assistants ("Handelsdiener") *did* occasionally appear at mealtime. The notion of the domestic community ("häusliche Gemeinschaft") seems instead to be closer to the later structure of a "bürgerliche Kleinfamilie." For more on the relationship to cultural-historical forms of the family in this novel, see Borchmeyer, "Ideologie der Familie," 227–231.

43. Borchmeyer has pointed out that the opposition of outside and inside is repeated from the first and second Drendorf homes, the shift to his studies as a young man with Risach in the "Rose house," and in the other early chapter titles, e.g., "Domesticity" and "The Wanderer." See Borchmeyer, "Ideologie der Familie," 226–227.

44. Borchmeyer, "Ideologie der Familie," 228.

45. Foucault, *The Order of Things*, 132.

46. Foucault, *The Order of Things*, 73.

47. Walter Benjamin, *The Arcades Project*, trans. Howard Eiland and Kevin McLaughlin (Cambridge, MA: Belknap Press of Harvard University, 1999), 220. Walter Benjamin, *Gesammelte Schriften*, ed. Rolf Tiedemann and Hermann Schweppenhäuser, vol. V/1 (Frankfurt am Main: Suhrkamp, 1991), 291–292: "Das Schwierige in der Betrachtung des Wohnens: daß darin einerseits das Uralte— vielleicht Ewige—erkannt werden muß, das Abbild des Aufenthalts des Menschen im Mutterschoße; und daß auf der anderen Seite, diese urgeschichtlichen Motive ungeachtet, im Wohnen in seiner extremsten Form ein Daseinszustand des neunzehnten Jahrhunderts begriffen werden muß. Die Urform allen Wohnens ist das Dasein nicht im Haus sondern im Gehäuse. Dieses trägt den Abdruck seines Bewohners. Wohnung wird im extremsten Falle zum Gehäuse. Das neunzehnte Jahrhundert war wie kein anderes wohnsüchtig. Es begriff die Wohnung als Futteral des Menschen und bettete ihn mit all seinem Zubehör so tief in sie ein, daß man ans Innere eines Zirkelkastens denken könnte, wo das Instrument mit allen Ersatzteilen in tiefe, meistens violette Sammethöhlen gebettet, daliegt. Für was nicht alles das neunzehnte Jahrhundert Gehäuse erfunden hat: für Taschenuhren, Pantoffeln, Eierbecher, Thermometer, Spielkarten—und in Ermanglung von Gehäusen Schoner, Läufer, Decken und Überzüge [14, 4]."

48. Irmscher, *Adalbert Stifter*, 186–187, 217.

49. Foucault, *The Order of Things*, 64.

50. Stifter, *Indian Summer*, 11–12.

51. Stifter, *Indian Summer*, 11.

52. Foucault, *The Order of Things*, 130.

53. Sara Ahmed, *Queer Phenomenology: Orientations, Objects, Others* (Durham, NC: Duke University Press, 2006), 175.

54. Ahmed, *Queer Phenomenology*, 175–176.

55. Ahmed, *Queer Phenomenology*, 175.

56. Mike Goode, *Sentimental Masculinity and the Rise of History, 1790–1890* (Cambridge: Cambridge University Press, 2009), 76–78.

57. Freeman, *Time Binds*, 100.

58. Heather Love, *Feeling Backward: Loss and the Politics of Queer History* (Cambridge, MA: Harvard University Press, 2007), 9.

59. Although my focus is on distinguishing the particular episteme that governs and is associated with the scene of childhood or being-child, recent scholarship has convincingly shown that the arch of geological knowledge in Stifter's novel (i.e., the totality of Heinrich's life story, his *Bildung*) eventually comes to include a "dynamic" view of geology, where earth science is very much a temporalized historical process. See, for example, Peter Schnyder, "Dynamisierung des Statischen: Geologisches Wissen bei Goethe und Stifter," *Zeitschrift für Germanistik* 29, no. 3 (2009): 551–555; Peter Schnyder, "Schrift—Bild—Sammlung—Karte," in *Figuren der Übertragung: Adalbert Stifter und das Wissen seiner Zeit*, ed. Michael Gamper and Michael Wagner (Zurich: Chronos Verlag, 2009), 238; Holmes, "An Archive of the Earth: Stifter's Geologos"; Groves, *Geological Unconscious*.

60. I would not dispute Schnyder's claim that scholarship, which has focused largely on Risach's static view, has neglected the ways in which Heinrich's interest and responses do indeed parallel the dynamic historical processes described by the "junge Wissenschaft," in the emerging discipline of geology. Indeed, he makes a compelling case for reading the protagonist in light of recent shifts toward temporalized (rather than static, taxonomical) theories of the earth, like those of Lyell, Buffon, et al., arguing that the novel's use of narration and autobiography links developments in geology with historicizing practices of contemporaneous "Kulturwissenschaften." Schnyder, "Schrift—Bild—Sammlung—Karte," 237–241.

61. Alejandro Guarín has noted that although Humboldt's own writings can be characterized as deeply invested in the process of description and cataloguing, following practices of eighteenth-century "natural history," his interest in mobilizing research to draw larger conclusions about unseen processes can be seen as the forefront of the shift in epistemological approaches (*episteme*): "In Foucault's words (although he did not refer particularly to Humboldt), as he 'opposed historical knowledge of the visible to *philosophical* knowledge of the invisible, of what is hidden and of the causes.'" Guarín, "Alexander von Humboldt and the Origins of Our Modern Geographical View of the Earth," in *WorldMinds: Geographical Perspectives on 100 Problems*, ed. Donald G. Janelle, Barney Warf, and Kathy Hansen (Berlin: Springer, 2004), 609. Certainly, Stifter as well sought to draw connections between mere observation and recording, on the one hand, and cataclysmic geological processes, on the other. At the point in the novel in which Heinrich is drawn to Humboldt's *Reisen*, however, we see his primary concern is for descriptive and representational functions.

62. Stifter, *Indian Summer*, 22, 25–26. See also Robert Stockhammer's discussion of Heinrich's development as a scientist and mapmaker in *Kartierung der Erde: Macht und Lust in Karten und Literatur* (Munich: Wilhelm Fink Verlag, 2007).

63. Stifter, *Indian Summer*, 27.

64. Foucault, *The Order of Things*, 64, 66.

65. Foucault, *The Order of Things*, 148.

66. Stifter, *Indian Summer*, 190.

67. Foucault, *The Order of the Things*, 64.

68. Schnyder and Robert Stockhammer have both argued that the protagonist is a natural scientist whose map-making impulses eventually develop beyond the Linnéan system, as evidenced by this desire to note the source of each finding and what kind of earth-history might be communicated through it. Schnyder, "Schrift—Bild—Sammlung—Karte," 235–248; Stockhammer, *Kartierung der Erde*.

69. Foucault, *The Order of Things*, 309.

70. Freeman, *Time Binds*, 68–69. Here Freeman is elaborating (from Butler's use of the term) in ways that illuminate how both rhetorical and literary-critical concepts of allegorization enable us to think of queer embodiment and identification.

71. We might also think of this as Stockton's turn to the "horizontal" to describe queer childhood as "growing" or "spreading" "sideways and backwards." See

Kathryn Bond Stockton, *The Queer Child, or Growing Sideways in the Twentieth Century* (Durham, NC: Duke University Press, 2009, 4).

72. Stifter, *Indian Summer*, 454.

73. Eve Kosofsky Sedgwick, *The Coherence of Gothic Conventions* (New York: Arno Press, 1980), xi; Stephen M. Barber and David L. Clark, "Queer Moments: The Performative Temporalities of Eve Kosofsky Sedgwick," in *Regarding Sedgwick: Essays on Queer Culture and Critical Theory*, ed. Barber and Clark (New York: Routledge, 2002), 6.

74. Robert C. Holub. "Adalbert Stifter's 'Brigitta' or the Lesson of Realism," in *A Companion to German Realism, 1848–1900*, ed. Todd Kontje (Rochester, NY: Camden House, 2002), 46. See also Dominik Finkelde, "Tautologien der Ordnung: Zu einer Poetologie des Sammelns bei Adalbert Stifter," *German Quarterly* 80, no. 1 (January 1, 2007): 11.

75. Ahmed, *Queer Phenomenology*, 96.

76. Barber and Clark, "Queer Moments," 6.

77. Adrian Daub, *The Dynastic Imagination: Family and Modernity in Nineteenth-Century Germany* (Chicago: University of Chicago Press, 2021), 60.

78. Earlier scholarship has often translated Stifter's title as *Many-Colored Stones* or *Colorful Stones*. However, I cite the recent and complete translation of the novella collection which opts for *Motley Stones*. Adalbert Stifter, *Motley Stones*, trans. Isabel Fargo Cole (New York: New York Review of Books, 2021).

79. "Rentherr" is an ambiguous epithet that is not translated easily. This portmanteau suggests both a gentleman or landowner ("Herr") who also seemed to be a retiree or pensioner ("Rent-"). Early translations of the story retained the German for this main character. Cole's translation, the most recent, uses "pension man."

80. Stifter, *Motley Stones*, 126; HKG II, 2, 179.

81. Ahmed, *Queer Phenomenology*, 66; Freeman, *Time Binds*, 31.

82. Michel de Certeau, *The Practice of Everyday Life*, trans. Steven Rendall (Berkeley: University of California Press, 1984), 117, 120–121.

83. De Certeau, *The Practice of Everyday Life*, 115.

84. Eva Geulen, "Tales of a Collector," 591.

85. What Benjamin describes as an "addiction to dwelling" neatly encapsulates the tendency of this framing narrative as it comes to its apex with the introduction of the little girl. With each item, the focus narrows within concentric layers of furnishings and decor, revealing the narrative's central figure. This procedure is then repeated over and over again, across the descriptions of the apartment and the things that reside therein, as the apartment ends up being both literally and figuratively inventoried. Here, the holy family (with child, in the mother's arms) is encased in a painting, itself draped in fabric, and is then mirrored by the draped fabric around and over the baby's bassinet, and then again around the woman (or her bed at the very least).

86. Stifter, *Motley Stones*, 95; HKG II, 2, 137–138.

87. De Certeau, *The Practice of Everyday Life*, 117.

88. Freeman, *Time Binds*, 5; Luciano, *Arranging Grief*, 121–123; Julia Kristeva, "Women's Time," trans. Alice Jardine and Harry Blake, *Signs* 7, no. 1 (Autumn 1981): 13–35.

89. Stifter, *Motley Stones*, 95; HKG II, 2, 137–138.

90. Stifter, *Motley Stones*, 96; HKG II, 2, 139.

91. Freeman, *Time Binds*, 23. Eve Mason has described this scene of the wife's worlds as "functionless immobile beauty" in "Stifter's 'Turmalin': A Reconsideration," *Modern Language Review* 72, no. 2 (April 1977): 350.

92. Stifter, *Motley Stones*, 95–96; HKG II, 2, 138.

93. De Certeau, *The Practice of Everyday Life*, 118–119.

94. De Certeau, *The Practice of Everyday Life*, 118–119. With a similar effect to the grandfather's litany in "Granite," an identification compulsion here also creates a "topography"—of household objects. Albrecht Koschorke describes how paratactical narration collapses or "flattens" the landscape in "Granit" and thus transforms the subjective encounter with objects in space into a nonempirical, "cartographic view." Albrecht Koschorke, "Das buchstabierte Panorama: Zu einer Passage in Stifters Erzählung *Granit*," *VASILO* 38, no. 1/2 (1989): 4–6.

95. Stifter, *Motley Stones*, 102; HKG II, 2, 147.

96. Thomas Elsaesser, "Tales of Sound and Fury," in *Home Is Where the Heart Is: Studies in Melodrama and the Woman's Film*, ed. Christine Gledhill (London: British Film Institute, 1987), 43–69, on 61–62. Freeman reads Elsaesser's description of 1940s and '50s filmic mise-en-scène as a way of describing the aesthetics of the domestic "still life" as both "visual order" and a feeling of "temporal plenitude" that is only made possible through the invisible work of the mother. Although both analyses suggest this phenomenon reached its peak in the mid-twentieth century, we can see its modern beginnings as far back as Stifter's novella a century before, perhaps also highlighting the affinities between poetic realist technique and the "dilatory" capacities of film. *Time Binds*, 40.

97. Ahmed, *Queer Phenomenology*, 88, 90.

98. Stifter develops an incredibly elaborate "frame" for this child, a story that then is itself framed by narrative—a *Gehäuse* on every register. Although she is visibly subject to Benjamin's notion of the bourgeois dwelling as an encasement, she is also treated as a precious object, being literally and figuratively embedded in the scene and concentric narrative structure.

99. Freeman, *Time Binds*, 39.

100. De Certeau, *The Practice of Everyday Life*, 118–119.

101. De Certeau, *The Practice of Everyday Life*, 118–119.

102. Stifter, *Motley Stones*, 93–94; HKG II, 2, 135–136.

103. De Certeau, *The Practice of Everyday Life*, 118–119.

104. De Certeau, *The Practice of Everyday Life*, 119–120.

105. De Certeau, *The Practice of Everyday Life*, 119–120.

106. Stifter, *Motley Stones*, 93–94; HKG II, 2, 142; As Eva Geulen notes, Stifter's narratives are also characterized by "the collection of things and their ritualistic recollection," and this scene confirms this. Geulen, "Tales of a Collector," 589.

107. Stifter, *Motley Stones*, 93–94; HKG II, 2, 142.

108. Stifter, *Motley Stones*, 93, 98; HKG II, 2, 136,142.

109. Freeman, *Time Binds*, 27.

110. Freeman, *Time Binds*, 23. See also Ahmed, *Queer Phenomenology*, 90.

111. Freeman, *Time Binds*, 22.

112. Stifter, *Motley Stones*, 122. HKG II, 2, 175.

113. Geulen's thesis turns on the relationship between Stifter's poetics and the depiction of children. In her reading, the girl and her uncanny appearance and behavior exemplify the dangers of identity between word and deed, as well as word and body. Geulen, "Adalbert Stifters Kinder-Kunst," 664.

114. Stifter, *Motley Stones*, 115. HKG II, 2, 164.

115. Freeman, *Time Binds*, 29–30.

116. Freeman, *Time Binds*, 29.

117. Stifter, *Motley Stones*, 114. HKG II, 2, 164.

118. Vogel, "Stifters Gitter," 51; Here, Vogel also cites Rosalind Krauss's *Grids* on the development of the grid or grate as a system of seeing three-dimensional space as geometrically ordered surface.

119. Stifter, *Motley Stones*, 103; HKG II, 2, 148.

120. Stifter, *Motley Stones*, 136; HKG II, 2, 179.

121. Edelman, *No Future*, 10.

122. Freeman, *Time Binds*, 31.

123. Edelman, *No Future*, 4,

124. As Stefan Willer notes, Stifter's stories "Die Narrenburg" (Castle crazy) and "Nachkommenschaften" (Descendants) use narrative framing to reflect premodern conceptions of genealogy, producing the effect of a continual making-present of an ancestral past. Willer, "Familie/Genealogie," in *Stifter-Handbuch*, ed. Christian Begemann and Davide Giurato (Stuttgart: Metzler Verlag, 2017), 332.

125. Stifter, *Motley Stones*, 41. HKG II, 2, 63.

126. Freeman, *Time Binds*, 8; See also Love, *Feeling Backward*. On the trope of inheritance and generation see, for example, Daub, *Dynastic Imagination*; Ulrike Vedder, "Erbe," in *Stifter-Handbuch: Leben—Werk—Wirkung*, ed. Christian Begemann and Davide Giurato (Stuttgart: Metzler Verlag, 2017), 334–338.

127. Stifter, *Motley Stones*, 46; HKG II, 2 89. Here Birgit Ehlbeck has helpfully argued that Stifter's work imagines a specific kind of scientific seeing ("beobachten") that enables a hidden depth in an apparently empty landscape and for which the land surveyor is an exemplary fit. "Zur poetologischen Funktionalisierung des Empirismus am Beispiel von Stifters 'Kalkstein' und 'Witiko,'" in Ehlbeck, *Adalbert Stifter: Dichter und Maler, Denkmalpfleger und Schulmann*, ed. Karl Mösender (Tübingen: Niemeyer Verlag, 1996), 457–460.

128. For example, Attanucci argues that "of the stories collected in *Many-Colored Stones*, Limestone is arguably the most 'geological,'" and that "the narrator, a state-employed land surveyor, . . . reports on the life of the priest as an addendum, so to speak, to his survey of the region. The geological gaze of the land surveyor thus reveals the central analogy between the priest himself and the limestone-based, karst landscape." Attanucci, *Restorative Poetics*, 63, 65.

129. Foucault, *The Order of Things*, 137.

130. Stifter, *Motley Stones*, 46; HGK II, 2, 69.

131. There are some differences between the first and second land surveys—the most critical being the introduction of the surveyor's table. For a complete historical overview of Austrian land survey projects, see Ernst Hofstätter, *Beiträge zur Geschichte der österreichischen Landesaufnahmen: Ein Überblick der topographischen Aufnahmeverfahren, deren Ursprünge, ihrer Entwicklungen und Organisationsformen der vier österreichischen Landesaufnahmen*, 2 vols. (Vienna: Bundesamt für Eich- und Vermessungswesen, 1989); see also Daniel Nell, "Methoden der Genauigkeitsanalyse historischer Karten am Beispiel der Gradkartenblätter 1:25.000 Innsbruck und Lienz der Dritten Österreichischen Landesaufnahme" (PhD thesis, Universität Wien, 2009), 47–49.

132. Foucault, *The Order of Things*, 64–65.

133. Foucault, *The Order of Things*, 148.

134. Foucault, *The Order of Things*, 74.

135. Stifter, *Motley Stones*, 87–88.

136. Lefebvre, "The Everyday and Everydayness," 10.

137. Lefebvre, "The Everyday and Everydayness," 10.

138. Stifter, *Motley Stones*, 60; HGK II, 2, 88–89.

139. Stifter, *Motley Stones*, 62; HGK II, 2 91.

140. As Helena Ragg-Kirkby has argued in drawing on the programmatic tensions between "Maß" (measure) and "Unmaß" (limitlessness) in Stifter's oeuvre, the river's invisible depth mirrors the unseen power of the magnet storm—that which is simple and serene at its surface obscures a vast depth. Ragg-Kirkby, *Adalbert Stifter's Late Prose: The Mania for Moderation* (Rochester, NY: Camden House, 2000), 7–8. In her essay on modes of perception in Realism (esp. space and duration), Elisabeth Strowick argues that Stifter develops a poetics of aggregation in "Rock Crystal" ("Bergkristall"), that produces reality as both optical and aural murkiness ("trübe," "dumpfe") and temporal seriality of "continuing on and on and on" ("fort- und fort- und fortdauern"). In the case of "Limestone," I would amend this thesis to say that the poetics of aggregation do not produce the effect of continuation or progression (i.e., ever more *x*), and instead that aggregation is the endless work of childhood: as doing again, returning, and not making progress. Strowick, "Dumpfe Dauer."

141. Eva Geulen, "Kinderlos," *Internationales Archiv für Sozialgeschichte der deutschen Literatur* (IASL) 40, no. 2 (2015): 424–425.

142. Stifter, *Motley Stones*, 69; HGK II, 2, 101.

143. Stifter, *Motley Stones*, 70; HGK II, 2, 102.
144. Stifter, *Motley Stones*, 70; HGK II, 2, 102.
145. De Certeau, *The Practice of Everyday Life*, 117.
146. Stifter, *Motley Stones*, 70–71; HKG II, 2, 102–103.
147. De Certeau, *The Practice of Everyday Life*, 124.
148. Stifter, *Motley Stones*, 70–71; HKG II, 2, 102–103.
149. Ahmed, *Queer Phenomenology*, 66.
150. Stifter, *Motley Stones*, 72; HKG II, 2, 104.
151. Stifter, *Motley Stones*, 72; HKG II, 2, 105.
152. Stifter, *Motley Stones*, 74; HKG II, 2, 105.
153. Here I'm somewhat paraphrasing Sedgwick's own optimism slightly out of joint: "It happened to my father's father, it happened to my father, it is happening to me, it will happen to my son, and it will happen to my son's son. But isn't it a feature of queer possibility—only a contingent feature, but a real one, and one that in turn strengthens the force of contingency itself—that our generational relations don't always proceed in this lockstep?" Eve Kosofsky Sedgwick, "Paranoid and Reparative Reading; or You're So Paranoid, You Probably Think This Introduction Is about You," in *Novel Gazing: Queer Readings in Fiction*, ed. Eve Kosofsky Sedgwick (Durham, NC: Duke University Press, 1997), 26.
154. Stifter, *Motley Stones*, 78; HKG II, 2, 113–114.
155. Geulen points out that Stifter's scenes of children are often coupled with an observer's gaze. In the case of "Limestone," she notes that the surveyor's roll treads somewhere between the objectively distant to unsettling in its proximity to the pedophilic. Geulen, "Kinderlos," 433–434.
156. Aleida Assmann, "Werden was wir waren: Anmerkungen zur Geschichte der Kindheitsidee," *Antike und Abendland* 24 (1978): 104–105.
157. Stifter, *Motley Stones*, 64; HKG II, 2, 94.
158. Stifter, *Motley Stones*, 64; HKG II, 2, 94.
159. Stifter, *Motley Stones*, 51–52, 56 58–59; HKG II, 2, 76, 86–87
160. Stifter, *Motley Stones*, 59; HKG II, 2, 87
161. Stifter, *Motley* Stones, 92; HKG II, 2, 131.
162. See also Finkelde, "Tautologie der Ordnung," 1–19.
163. Stifter, *Motley Stones*, 83; HKG II, 2, 120.
164. Geulen, "Kinderlos," 425.
165. Stifter, *Motley Stones*, 90; HKG II, 2, 129
166. Stifter, *Motley Stones*, 91–92; HKG II, 2, 131.
167. Stifter, *Motley Stones*, 92; HKG II, 2, 132.
168. De Certeau, *The Practice of Everyday Life*, 123.
169. Stifter, *Motley Stones*, 92; HKG II, 2, 132.
170. Adalbert Stifter, "Mein Leben," in *Werke: Kleine Schriften/Briefe*, ed. Uwe Japp and Hans Joachim Piechotta, vol. 4 (Frankfurt am Main: Insel Verlag, 1978): "Auf diesem Fensterbrett sah ich auch, was draußen vorging, und ich sagte sehr oft: 'Da geht ein Mann nach Schwarzbach, da fährt ein Mann nach Schwarzbach, da

geht ein Hund nach Schwarzbach, da geht eine Gans nach Schwarzbach.' Auf diesem Fensterbrette legte ich auch die Kienspäne ihrer Länge nach hin, verband sie wohl auch durch Querspäne und sagte: 'Ich mache Schwarzbach!'"

171. As Helmut Pfotenhauer has argued, his autobiography unites the literary signatures of his later corpus with an abbreviated view of the self. Helmut Pfotenhauer, "Einfach . . . wie ein Halm": Stifters komplizierte kleine Selbstbiographie, *Deutsche Vierteljahrsschrift für Literaturwissenschaft und Geistesgeschichte* 64 (1990): 134–148. Vogel, "Stifters Gitter," 52–53; Marianne Schuller, "Das Kleine der Literatur: Stifters Autobiographie," in *Mikrologien: Literarische und philosophische Figures des Kleinen*, ed. Marianne Schuller and Gunnar Schmidt (Bielefeld: Transcript Verlag, 2003), 87, 88.

172. Foucault, *The Order of Things*, 64–65.

173. Pfotenhauer, "Einfach . . . wie ein Halm," 144. Vogel, "Stifters Gitter," 52–53.

174. Freeman, *Time Binds*, 8. See also Attanucci, *Restorative Poetics*; Groves, *The Geological Unconscious*; Schnyder, "Die Dynamisierung des Statischen."

175. Freeman, *Time Binds*, 8. Here Freeman also points to Love's *Feeling Backward*.

176. Freeman, *Time Binds*, 8.

2. Rainer Maria Rilke's Lifeworlds of Childhood

1. The critical edition of Rilke's collected works puts the bulk of his prose publications between roughly 1893 and 1900. Rainer Maria Rilke, *Werke: Kommentierte Ausgabe in vier Bänden*, vol. 3, ed. Manfred Engel et al. (Frankfurt am Main: Insel Verlag, 1996), 792–793. Cited hereafter as KA with volume and page number. Unless otherwise cited, all translations in this text are mine.

2. Nonetheless, scholarly interest in the philosophical qualities of Rilke's work has largely focused on his lyrical writing, with phenomenological comparisons ranging from Husserl and Heidegger to Merleau-Ponty. See, for example, Luke Fischer, *The Poet as Phenomenologist: Rilke and the New Poems* (New York: Bloomsbury Academic, 2015); Rochelle Tobias, "Rilke, Phenomenology, and the Sensuality of Thought," *Konturen* 8 (2015): 40–61; Jennifer Anna Gosetti-Ferencei, *The Ecstatic Quotidian: Phenomenological Sightings in Modern Art and Literature* (University Park: Pennsylvania State University Press, 2007); Thomas Pfau, "Absolute Gegebenheit: Image as Aesthetic Urphänomen in Husserl and Rilke," in *Phenomenology to the Letter: Husserl and Literature*, ed. Philippe P. Haensler, Kristina Mendicino, and Rochelle Tobias (Berlin: De Gruyter, 2020), 227–260; and the classic essay by Käte Hamburger, "Die Phänomenologische Struktur der Dichtung Rilkes," in *Rilke in neuer Sicht*, ed. Käte Hamburger (Stuttgart: Kohlhammer, 1971), 83–158.

3. I use "lifeworld" (*Lebenswelt*) in the sense as developed by Husserl, as the everyday world which underlies our knowledge and experience. The term, which originates with nineteenth-century microscopic perspectives, comes to stand in

opposition to scientific systems of knowledge, and in line with the self-evident world that encompasses the objects of scientific inquiry. Husserl's early thinking about the "natural" (nonscientific, ordinary) concepts of the world and our experience of the world as it is continues through his later critiques of the "mathematization" of the world in natural sciences. Blumenberg deploys Husserl's concept in various ways across his corpus. David Woodruff Smith, *Husserl* (New York: Routledge, 2013), 30, 327–328, 466. Christian Bermes, "Die Lebenswelt," in *Husserl Handbuch: Leben—Werk—Wirkung*, ed. Sebastian Luft and Maren Wehle (Stuttgart: Metzler Verlag, 2017), 230–236. Hannes Bajohr, Florian Fuchs, and Joe Paul Kroll, Introduction to *History, Metaphors, Fables: A Hans Blumenberg Reader*, ed. Bajohr, Fuchs, and Kroll (Ithaca, NY: Cornell University Press, 2020), 1–29.

4. Hans Blumenberg, *The Laughter of the Thracian Woman: A Protohistory of Theory* (New York: Bloomsbury, 2015), viii, 3, 4.

5. Blumenberg, *The Laughter of the Thracian Woman*, vii. Blumenberg's central argument here is that with each retelling of this philosophical anecdote, the protophilosopher's role can be seen to represent all manner of theoretical positions: often it is the philosopher's ignorance of or blindness to material matters at hand that are the source of his "stumbling," and it is the marginal figure (a maid or coachman) who points this out. See also, for example, 86–87.

6. Like most of Rilke scholarship, Blumenberg's own interest in Rilke was largely limited to the late lyrical work, such as the *Duino Elegies* and *The Book of Hours*. As Ben Hutchinson has argued, Blumenberg's notions of the "unsayable" and his aesthetics of negation generally are exemplified in an unpublished essay on a notebook of Rilke's in which only the phrase "Ici commence l'indicible" was written. Hutchinson draws productive connections between two groups of texts: Blumenberg's work in *Cave Exits* and *Paradigms for a Metaphorology* on "unsayability," and the unique sense of the impossibility of expression of concepts of beginning, natality, origin; and Rilke's poetic writings (and writing on poetics) on origins and beginnings. Ben Hutchinson, "'Ici commence l'indicible': Hans Blumenbergs Überlegungen zur Unmöglichkeit des Beginnens beim späten Rilke," *Études Germaniques* 249, no. 1 (April 2008): 115–129. Blumenberg, *The Laughter of the Thracian Woman*, 29–45.

7. Blumenberg, *The Laughter of the Thracian Woman*, 5–6.

8. In Rilke's work, as I show in this chapter, children disrupt the accepted wisdom of adulthood which Florian Fuchs distills from Blumenberg's critique of pure theory represented by the Thracian woman's response: "The laughter of these common folk is representative not only of this thicket of things but also of the unrealistic steps philosophy takes, which cause the subsequent stumbling back into reality. Both are included in the bystander's laughter: the amplified call of reality and the signal to interrupt philosophical transcendence." Florian Fuchs, "Decoding Aesop: Blumenberg's Fabulistic Turn," *New German Critique* 49, no. 1 (145) (February 2022): 167. Here, I intend to read somewhat against prevailing scholarly characterization of, for example, Rilke's protagonist Malte, who often

serves as the modern subject par excellence. See, for instance, Andreas Huyssen, "Paris/Childhood: The Fragmented Body in Rilke's *Notebooks of Malte Laurids Brigge*," in *Modernity and the Text: Revisions of German Modernism*, ed. Andreas Huyssen and David Bathrick (New York: Columbia University Press, 1989), 113–141, and more recently Ihor Junyk, "'A Fragment from Another Context': Modernist Classicism and the Urban Uncanny in Rainer Maria Rilke," *Comparative Literature* 62 (June 1, 2010): 262–282.

9. KA 4, 530; Rainer Maria Rilke, *Letters to a Young Poet*, trans. M. D. Norton (New York: W. W. Norton, 2004), 35–36.

10. Lee Edelman, *No Future: Queer Theory and the Death Drive* (Durham, NC: Duke University Press, 2004), 41.

11. Rilke, KA 4, 263. His literary texts stand in contrast to his 1902 essay in praise of Swedish feminist Ellen Key's *The Century of Childhood*, a text which advocates for children's rights and education as part of her vision of the century to come.

12. Edelman, *No Future*, 2–3.

13. Rilke, KA 3, 396: "Was tun unsere Eltern? Sie gehen mit bösen Gesichtern umher, nichts ist ihnen recht, sie schreien und schelten, aber dabei sind sie doch so gleichgültig, wenn die Welt unterginge, sie würden es kaum bemerken. Sie haben etwas, was sie 'Ideale' nennen."

14. Rilke, KA 3, 396: "Sie ziehen den Hut vor einander, und wenn eine Glatze dabei zum Vorschein kommt, so lachen sie."

15. Theodor W. Adorno, *Minima Moralia: Reflections on a Damaged Life* (London: Verso, 2005), §5, 26. Theodor Adorno, *Minima Moralia: Reflexionen aus dem beschädigten Leben* (Frankfurt am Main: Suhrkamp, 1970), 22: "Alles Mitmachen, alle Menschlichkeit von Umgang und Teilhabe ist bloße Maske fürs stillschweigende Akzeptieren des Unmenschlichen." As Brigitte Bradley succinctly puts it: "By their very conduct the adults belie their professed beliefs." Brigitte Bradley, "Rilke's 'Geschichten vom lieben Gott': The Narrator's Stance toward the Bourgeoisie," *Modern Austrian Literature* 15, no. 3/4 (1982): 9.

16. Rilke, KA 3, 396.

17. Rilke, KA 3, 396. In arguing for Rilke's literary critique of bourgeois "shallow religiousness," Brigitte Bradley notes that this short story evinces "a critical stance toward the adults as an all-inclusive group" and, in particular, their "function of shaping the mental attitudes of the upcoming generation." Bradley, "Rilke's 'Geschichten vom lieben Gott': The Narrator's Stance toward the Bourgeoisie," 10, 4.

18. Rilke, KA 3, 396–397.

19. Rilke, KA 3, 851.

20. Rilke, KA 3, 397.

21. Rilke, KA 3, 397: "Hier entstand eine große Verlegenheit. Wie sollte das geschehen? Konnte man denn den lieben Gott in die Hand oder in die Tasche stecken?"

22. Rilke, KA 3, 397: "Ein jedes Ding kann der liebe Gott sein. Man muß ihm nur sagen . . . ein Ding, siehst du, es steht, du kommst in die Stube bei Tag, bei Nacht: es ist immer da, es kann wohl der liebe Gott sein."

23. Similarly, Gosetti-Ferencei has suggested that here Rilke's "narrator insists on the vitality of ordinary things, on the grounds that they can take on other usual uses or meanings." Jennifer Anna Gosetti-Ferencei, "Interstitial Space in Rilke's Short Prose Works," *German Quarterly* 80, no. 3 (2007): 314. See also Walter Seifert, *Das epische Werk Rainer Maria Rilkes* (Bonn: Bouvier, 1969), 89.

24. Rilke, KA 3, 397–398. "Da zeigten sich nun sehr seltsame Dinge: Papierschnitzel, Federmesser, Radiergummi, Federn, Bindfaden, kleine Steine, Schrauben, Pfeifen, Holzspänchen und vieles andere, was sich aus der Ferne gar nicht erkennen läßt, oder wofür der Name mir fehlt. Und alle diese Dinge lagen in den seichten Händen der Kinder, wie erschrocken über die plötzliche Möglichkeit, der liebe Gott zu werden, und welches von ihnen ein bißchen glänzen konnte, glänzte, um dem Hans zu gefallen."

25. Bernard Dieterle, "Erzählungen," in *Rilke Handbuch: Leben—Werk—Wirkung*, ed. Manfred Engel (Stuttgart: Metzler 2004), 260.

26. Rilke, KA 3, 398. All quotes from Rilke's text in this paragraph are from pages 388–399.

27. Fuchs, "Decoding Aesop," 167.

28. Paul Fleming, "On the Edge of Non-contingency: Anecdotes and the Lifeworld," *Telos* 158 (Spring 2012): 30.

29. Husserl's term for this "abschatten" ("adumbrate"). All parenthetical citations (*Ideas*) by paragraph refer to Edmund Husserl, *Ideas for a Pure Phenomenology and Phenomenological Philosophy*, vol 1 (Indianapolis: Hackett, 2014). See also Edmund Husserl, *Husserliana: Gesammelte Werke*, III, 1 (The Hague: Martinus Nijhoff, 1976).

30. Sara Ahmed, *Queer Phenomenology, Orientations, Objects, Others* (Durham, NC: Duke University Press, 2006), 65–66.

31. Kathryn Bond Stockton, *The Queer Child, or Growing Sideways in the Twentieth Century* (Durham, NC: Duke University Press, 2009), 4.

32. Sara Ahmed, "Willful Parts: Problem Characters or the Problem of Character," *New Literary History* 42, no. 2 (April 1, 2011): 231.

33. Ahmed, "Willful Parts," 231.

34. Ahmed, "Willful Parts," 231.

35. John Locke, *Some Thoughts concerning Education* (New York: Dover, 2007), 25; see also the discussion in Ahmed, "Willful Parts," 236–237.

36. Ahmed, "Willful Parts," 231, 245.

37. Blumenberg, *The Laughter of the Thracian Woman*, 128–129; Hans Blumenberg, *Zu den Sachen und zurück; Aus dem Nachlass*, ed. Manfred Sommer (Frankfurt am Main: Suhrkamp, 2002), 349.

38. Dieterle, "Erzählungen," 239.

39. Dieterle, "Erzählungen," 240.

40. R. M. Rilke, *The Notebooks of Malte Laurids Brigge*, trans. Burton Pike (Champaign, IL: Dalkey Archive Press, 2008), 3. Rilke, KA 3, 457. Rilke, KA 4, 430. Rilke scholarship has addressed how his oeuvre is rife with his varying interests in the visible world, and in the particular ways in which painting and sculpture work to

make their subject or content visible, however independent of academic and optical rules, such as perspective. For a concise discussion of the impact of visual arts on Rilke's poetic project, see Antje Büssgen, "Bildende Kunst," in *Rilke Handbuch: Leben—Werk—Wirkung*, ed. Engel (Stuttgart: Metzler, 2004), 131–134.

41. As Michael McGillen and Daniela K. Helbig have variously argued, both Husserl and Blumenberg (in his critique of the former) similarly recognized that a central philosophical-poetic challenge is putting into language that which can be seen. Michael McGillen, "Free Variation from the Archive of Culture: Blumenberg and Husserl on Phenomenological Description," in *Leistungsbeschreibung/ Describing Cultural Achievements: Literarische Strategien bei Hans Blumenberg/ Hans Blumenberg's Literary Strategies*, ed. Timothy Attanucci and Ulrich Breuer (Heidelberg: Universitätsverlag, Winter 2020), 73–94; and Daniela K. Helbig, "No More Than Seeing: Hans Blumenberg's Poetics of Spectatorship," *New German Critique* 49, no. 1 (February 2022): 185–213.

42. Blumenberg, *Zu den Sachen und zurück*, 65–66. Franz Josef Wetz laconically reformulates the problem as "apparently vision is more powerful than language" ("Anscheinend ist Schauen mächtiger als Sagen"). Wetz, "Der Mensch ist das Unmögliche: Blumenbergs Phänomenologische Anthropologie im Nachlass," *Zeitschrift für philosophische Forschung* 62, no. 2 (April 2008): 274–293, on 277. See also McGillen's discussion in "Free Variation from the Archive of Culture," 73–74.

43. Blumenberg, *Zu den Sachen und zurück*, 66.

44. Rilke, KA 3.

45. Rilke, KA 4.

46. McGillen, "Free Variation from the Archive of Culture," 73–94.

47. Rilke, KA 4, 211–212: "wie schlecht man die Dinge sieht, unter denen man lebt . . . gegenständlich als eine große vorhandene Wirklichkeit." See also Thomas Pfau's commentary on this in the context of Rilke's writings on art/image perception as a phenomenology of the image and Husserl's development of the *noematic*. Pfau, "Absolute Gegebenheit," 244.

48. Rilke, KA 3, 14: "ein kaum elfjähriger Knirps."

49. Dieterle emphasizes that the impressionistic tendencies of the text serve to foreground mood above all else. Dieterle, "Erzählungen," 242–243.

50. Büssgen, "Bildende Kunst," 134.

51. Büssgen, "Bildende Kunst," 134. Rainer M. Rilke, *Die Briefe an Karl und Elisabeth von der Heydt 1905–1922*, ed. Ingeborg Schnack and Renate Scharffenberg (Frankfurt am Main: Insel Verlag, 1986) 114.

52. Rilke, KA 3, 14: "Pierre stand indessen am Fenster und schaute in die Gegend hinaus. Sie waren hart vor der Station. Der Zug fuhr langsamer und polterte über die Wechsel. Draußen glitten grüne Grasdämme, weite Flächen und winzige Häuschen vorüber, an deren Türen riesige Sonnenblumen mit ihren gelben Heiligenscheinen als Wächter standen. Die Türen aber waren so klein, daß Pierre dachte, er müßte sich wohl gar auch bücken, um eintreten zu können.—Da verloren sich schon die Häuschen.—Schwarze, rauchige Magazine kamen . . ."

53. As Wolfgang Schivelbusch has described how train passengers in the nineteenth century reported the high-speed experience as "dull" and "boring" in comparison to preindustrial modes of travel (i.e., by carriage), explaining that they had yet to "develop modes of perception appropriate to the new form of transportation. Dullness and boredom resulted from attempts to carry the perceptual apparatus of traditional travel, with its intense appreciation of landscape." Wolfgang Schivelbusch, *The Railway Journey: The Industrialization of Time and Space in the Nineteenth Century* (Berkeley: University of California Press, 2014), 54.

54. David Woodruff Smith, *Husserl*, 2nd ed. (London: Routledge, 2013). Here, I am working in agreement with Woodruff-Smith's assessment that Husserl's ontological doctrine fits within a "systematic philosophical image of consciousness and the world," and need not be seen as wholly separate from his phenomenological philosophy (6); both system branches make their appearance in *Ideas I*, which serves as the significant touchpoint for this chapter.

55. Dorrit Cohn, *Transparent Minds: Narrative Modes for Presenting Consciousness in Fiction* (Princeton, NJ: Princeton University Press, 1978), 7.

56. See, for example, Cohn, *Transparent Minds*, 102–107.

57. Following Cohn's taxonomy, the narrator's own attitude is "consonant" ("cohesive" and "neutral") with respect to the protagonist's own thoughts. Cohn, *Transparent Minds*, 31; "thinking with" on 111.

58. In the essay "Von den Sachen zurück," Blumenberg narrates the scene of philosophical struggle as particularly visible in Husserl's own marginalia ("Ja, gibt es perzeptive Phantasie?!") vis-à-vis his writings on the role of fantasy and in the experience of art (and art-like experience of the world). Blumenberg, *Zu den Sachen und zurück*, 100–109.

59. Blumenberg, *Zu den Sachen und zurück*, 104: "mit dem eigentümlichen Wechselverhältnis von reeller Wahrnehmung und Bildwerdung des Wahrgenommenen charakteristische Merkmale der Erlebnisform 'Landschaft' beschreiben."

60. Edmund Husserl, *Husserliana: Gesammelte Werke*, vol. 23. (The Hague: Martinus Nijhoff, 1980), 144. Cited hereafter as *Hua 23*. For the English, see Edmund Husserl, *Phantasy, Image Consciousness, and Memory, 1898–1925*, trans. John B. Brough (Dordrecht: Springer, 2005), 167.

61. Schivelbusch notes that for travelers "the depth perception of pre-industrial consciousness was, literally, lost: velocity blurs all foreground objects, which means that there no longer is a foreground—exactly the range in which most of the experience of pre-industrial travel was located." Rilke's child protagonist however seizes the opportunity at slow speed and immediately is returned to the immersive visual depth of field. Schivelbusch, *The Railway Journey*, 63.

62. Blumenberg, *Zu den Sachen und zurück*, 104: "Die Grundfrage ist, ob Phantasie die Perzeption einfach nur unterbricht und sich und deren Stelle setzt oder ob das Phantasieren immer ein 'Hineinphantasieren' in den reellen Zusammenhang des Wirklichkeitsbezugs ist."

63. Blumenberg, *Zu den Sachen und zurück*, 105.

64. Blumenberg, *Zu den Sachen und zurück*, 350. See also Helbig, "Hans Blumenberg's Poetics of Spectatorship," 187.

65. Blumenberg's point of departure is the role of error and revision in Husserl's discussion of, among other things, "image-distortion" ("Bilddehnung") in the "Thing" ("Ding") lecture and notes from 1907. Blumenberg, *Zu den Sachen und zurück*, 65–80, citing Husserl, *Hua* 16, 231–232.

66. Blumenberg, *Zu den Sachen und zurück*, 68–69.

67. Rilke, KA 3, 19.

68. Blumenberg, *Zu den Sachen und zurück*, 73–74, Husserl, *Hua* 16, 131.

69. Blumenberg, *Zu den Sachen und zurück*, 74. Husserl, *Hua* 16, 131–133.

70. Blumenberg, *Zu den Sachen und zurück*, 76: "die Null-Grenze entschwundener Gegenstand dieser Erlebnissphäre."

71. Blumenberg, *Zu den Sachen und zurück*, 75–76; Husserl, *Hua* 16, 249.

72. Blumenberg, *Zu den Sachen und zurück*, 112–119.

73. Blumenberg, *Zu den Sachen und zurück*, 119: "Übertragbarkeit von Subjekt zu Subjekt gibt es im strengen Sinne nicht. Immer muß das Medium der Beschreibung eingeschaltet werden, dessen instrumentaler Sinn allein darin besteht, die dem einen gegebene Anschauung bei dem anderen zu induzieren, also wiederum als diejenige Anschauung zu erzeugen, die allererst Zustimmung zur Beschreibung herbeiführt."

74. Alternatively, Jennifer Anna Gosetti-Ferencei has suggested that these stories engage in "personification" of objects and "atmospheric elements" as part of a larger argument she makes about the centrality of what she terms "interstitial space" in Rilke's poetics. She draws on his notions of experience ("Erlebnis") and "Weltinnenraum" as concepts that enable "an intimacy between a self and surrounding world, sometimes mediated through objects." See Gosetti-Ferencei, "Interstitial Space," 309, 320.

75. Edelman, *No Future*, 41–50, 66.

76. Rilke, KA 3, 126–127.

77. Rilke, KA 3, 128.

78. Rilke, KA 3, 128.

79. Rilke, KA 3, 122: "'Gestorben' stand im gleichgültigen, brutalen, feuchtleuchtenden Lettern in dem dicken, grünen Krankenhausbuch. In derselben Zeile war zu lesen: 11. Stock, Zimmer 12, Nummer 78. Horvát, Elisabeth, Förstersstochter, 9 Jahre alt."

80. Rilke, KA 3, 129: "Wir haben das Christkind gesehen—mitten im Wald. Es lag neben einem herrlich leuchtenden Bäumchen und ruhte aus. Und es war schön, das Christkind,—so schön." Note: German uses the neuter pronouns "es" for both nouns here, "child" (as in "Christkind") and "little tree" ("Bäumchen").

81. Gérard Genette, *Narrative Discourse: An Essay in Method*, trans. Jane E. Lewin (Ithaca, NY: Cornell University Press, 1980), 190–193.

82. Rilke, KA 3, 127–128. "Der ganze, weite Wald schien das Christfest mitzufeiern. Die hohen, schwarzen Tannen standen weit im Umkreis wie ehrfurchtsvolle Beter und staunten das just noch so unbedeutende Bäumchen an, wie Menschen ein Wunderkind betrachten. Die fernen Sterne sogar schienen sich über der Stelle zusammenzudrängen, um ja nichts von dem Schauspiel zu verlieren und dem lieben Gott und den Engeln und der guten Mutter der kleinen Elisabeth erzählen zu können, was für ein braves Kind sie wäre."

83. Rilke, KA 3, 127. "Sie warf der Steinmadonna einen neckisch-ehrfurchtsvollen Blick zu, der besagen sollte: Gelt, ich bin brav? Heut hast du mich nicht erwartet."

84. Blumenberg, *Zu den Sachen und zurück*, 102–103. Here I refer to Blumenberg's recounting of one position that Husserl takes vis-à-vis the constitution of reality in the 1920s as *"als ob sie ein 'Bild' wäre. Man fingiere dabei die Wirklichkeit so um, daß sie als ein Bild genommen wird, in dem eben dieselbe Wirklichkeit dargestellte wäre"* (102). See also Thomas Pfau's "Absolute Gegebenheit."

85. Blumenberg, *Zu den Sachen und zurück*, 329. All quotes in this paragraph are from pages 329 and 330.

86. Edelman, *No Future*, 45.

87. Rilke, KA 4, 685.

88. It's worth noting that, as Eva-Maria Simms points out, Rilke generally had a strong aversion to dolls. His lyric writing repeatedly emphasizes the terror that the corpse-like doll inspires. Eva-Maria Simms, "Uncanny Dolls: Images of Death in Rilke and Freud," in *New Literary History* 72, no. 4 (Autumn 1996): 665. However, as Jennifer Gosetti-Ferencei has shown, the relationship between dolls and *children* is more nuanced: the doll is both a "transitional object" in the psychoanalytic sense, as well as a gateway and an interstitial buffer between the child-subject and the larger world. Gosetti-Ferencei, "Interstitial Space," 313–314.

89. Rilke, KA 4, 687: "sie würde fast empören durch ihre schreckliche dicke Vergeßlichkeit, der Haß, der, unbewußt, sicher immer einen Teil unserer Beziehungen zu ihr ausmachte, schlüge nach oben, entlarvt läge sie vor uns da, als der grausige Fremdkörper, an den wir unsere lauterste Wärme verschwendet haben; als die oberflächlich bemalte Wasserleiche, die sich von den Überschwemmungen unserer Zärtlichkeit heben und tragen ließ, bis wir wieder trocken wurden und sie in irgend einem Gestrüpp vergaßen."

90. Rilke, KA 4, 686.

91. Rilke, KA 4, 688: "Wie in einem Probierglas mischten wir in ihr, was uns unkenntlich widerfuhr, und sahen es dort sich färben und aufkochen. Das heißt, auch das *erfanden* wir wieder, sie war so bodenlos ohne Phantasie, daß unsere Einbildung an ihr unerschöpflich wurde ... aber ich kann mir nicht anders vorstellen, als daß es gewisse zu lange Nachmittage gab, in denen unsere doppelten Einfälle ermüdeten und wir plötzlich gegenüber saßen und etwas von ihr erwarteten."

92. Rilke, KA 4, 690. "Aber wir begriffen bald, daß wir sie weder zu einem Ding noch zu einem Menschen machen konnten, und in solchen Momenten wurde sie

uns zu einem Unbekannten, und alles Vertrauliche, womit wir sie erfüllt und überschüttet hatten, wurde uns unbekannt in ihr."

93. Rilke, KA 4, 690. See also Kenneth Gross, Introduction to *On Dolls*, ed. Kenneth Gross (London: Notting Hill Editions, 2018), xi–xx, on xiii. Gross reads the doll as the child's "compass" or "signpost on a journey."

94. Rilke, KA 4, 689.

95. Husserl, *Hua* 33, 151; *Phantasy, Image Consciousness, and Memory*, 180.

96. Husserl, *Hua* 33, 151; *Phantasy, Image Consciousness, and Memory*, 180. See also Blumenberg, *Zu den Sachen und zurück*, 105.

97. Indeed, in Rilke's telling, one that has *less* being on its own than most things!

98. Husserl, *Hua* 33, 151–152; *Phantasy, Image Consciousness, and Memory*, 180.

99. Husserl, *Hua* 33, 152; *Phantasy, Image Consciousness, and Memory*, 181.

100. Rilke, KA 4, 690.

101. Rilke, KA 4, 691.

102. Husserl, *Hua* 33, 153; *Phantasy, Image Consciousness, and Memory*, 181–182.

103. Rilke, KA 4, 691–692.

104. Rilke, KA 4 692.

105. Judith Ryan, "Rilke's Early Narratives," in *A Companion to the Works of Rainer Maria Rilke*, ed. Erika A. Metzger and Michael M. Metzger (Rochester, NY: Camden House, 2001), 67–89, on 68.

106. See the section of this chapter titled "'Seeing more; not more than seeing': What Children See in 'Pierre Dumont,'"and Blumenberg, *Zu den Sachen und zurück*, 105.

107. Stockton, *The Queer Child*, 15.

108. Stockton, *The Queer Child*, 15.

109. Stockton argues that both dolls and dogs are metaphorically enlisted by and for the queer child: "The dog is a living, growing metaphor for the child itself, . . . for the child's own propensities to stray by making the most of its sideways growth. The dog is a vehicle for the child's strangeness. It is the child's companion in queerness. As a recipient of the child's attentions—its often bent devotions—and a living screen for the child's self-projections . . . the dog is a figure for the child beside itself, engaged in a growing quite aside from growing up." Stockton, *The Queer Child*, 90.

110. Gossetti-Ferencei argues that Rilke captures the "vitality" of "native originality" in how objects "might be first be encountered by an awakening consciousness, how it comes to be constituted in experience." However, she sets Husserl aside as ultimately too "technical" to be able to capture a child that is not yet self-reflecting, and self-reflection, she suggests, already places the child on the way to adulthood. I have explicitly argued against this view in the preceding pages. Gosetti-Ferencei, *The Ecstatic Quotidian: Phenomenological Sightings in Modern Art and Literature* (University Park: Pennsylvania State University Press, 2007), 41. See also Fischer, *The Poet as Phenomenologist*.

111. Rilke, KA 4, 110: "xxx. Ich will ein ganz kleines Beispiel andeuten: Abend. Eine kleine Stube. Am Mitteltisch unter der Lampe sitzen zwei Kinder einander gegenüber, ungern über ihre Bücher geneigt. Sie sind beide weit—weit. Die Bücher verdecken ihre Flucht. Dann und wann rufen sie sich an, um sich nicht in dem weiten Wald ihrer Träume zu verlieren. Sie erleben in der engen Stube bunte und phantastische Schicksale. Sie kämpfen und siegen. Kommen heim und heiraten. Lehren ihre Kinder Helden sein. Sterben wohl gar. Ich bin so eigenwillig, das für Handlung zu halten."

112. Like his Romantic forebears, Rilke represents poetic imagination as predicated on the child's autonomy. This corresponds to what Aleida Assmann has described as "die Spontaneität der Phantasie" (the spontaneity of fantasy) that is central to the Romantic ideal of childhood that poets seek to emulate. Rilke, I will argue, transposes this ideal structure into quotidian terms. Aleida Assmann, "Werden was wir waren: Anmerkungen zur Geschichte der Kindheitsidee." *Antike und Abendland* 24 (1978): 120.

113. Husserl, *Hua* 23, 59–60; Husserl, *Phantasy, Image and Memory*, 64–65.

114. Husserl, *Hua* 23, 61–62; Husserl, *Phantasy, Image and Memory*, 66–67.

115. Rilke, KA 4, 110: "Ohne diesen ganzen dunklen Hintergrund, durch welchen sie die Fäden ihrer Fabeln ziehen. Wie anders würden die Kinder im Garten träumen."

116. Sara Ahmed, "Orientations: Toward a Queer Phenomenology," *GLQ: A Journal of Lesbian and Gay Studies* 12, no. 4 (2006): 545.

117. Ahmed, "Orientations: Toward a Queer Phenomenology," 546.

118. Ahmed, "Orientations: Toward a Queer Phenomenology," 546.

119. Rilke repeats this connection between writing and calling in "Über den jungen Dichter" (KA 4, 674). Just as the children call to each other ("rufen sich an"), so too does Rilke refer to the poet's work as a calling ("Beruf") and thus this scene of imagining further emphasizes that childlike vision is akin to the poet's vision.

120. Although Bachelard's *Poetics of Space* touches on a number of issues raised by my reading of Rilke's prose texts, this essay seeks to argue along slightly different lines: Rather than seeing the home as a reflection of the poet's "intimate being," here I consider it as the material condition of the poet's production. See, for example, Bachelard, *Poetics of Space*, trans. Maria Jolas (Boston: Beacon Press, 1994), xxxv, 4, 8, 10, 12, 26, 50, 83, 199.

Rilke, KA 4, 110.

121. Rilke, KA 4, 110.

122. Articulating the relationship between sense-perception and imagination (or representation), Aristotle writes "and, since sight is sense-perception *par excellence*, the name for imagination (*phantasia*) is taken from light [*phaos*], because without light, it is not possible to see" (*De Anima* 428b30). This quasi-causal relationship, moreover, parallels the intellect's creative capacity (430a10). I use these terms in anticipation of Husserl's phenomenological approach, not intending to wade into debates about Aristotle's usages in *De Anima*, *Metaphysics*, or elsewhere. For a

discussion of the relationship between sense-perception and imagination, see Ronald Polansky, *Aristotle's De Anima: A Critical Commentary* (Cambridge: Cambridge Unversity Press, 2007), 431.

123. See the introduction to this volume.

124. Alternatively, Jennifer Gosetti-Ferencei reads the "imaginatively generative space" as that which lies "between" the children and the material "background." Gosetti-Ferencei, "Interstitial Space," 307.

125. Goethe also shared the prevailing view of the late eighteenth and nineteenth centuries that rationalized that vision was the key to artistic skill, and that visual (and geometric) acuity could be developed through training. See Steffen Arndal, "Sehenlernen und Pseudoskopie," *Orbis Litterarum* 62, no. 3 (2007): 213.

126. As Eva Fauconneau-Dufresne has argued, Malte makes a shift away from the drive toward "rechten Sehen" focusing instead on two planes of consciousness—"erlebte Welt" and "Vorstellung." This follows from the anxiety produced by the discrepancy between visual perception and mental activity. Eva Fauconneau-Dufresne, "Wirklichkeitserfahrung und Bewußtseinsentwicklung in Rilkes *Malte Laurids Brigge* und Sartres *La Nausée*," *Arcadia* 17 (1982): 258–273, on 260–261.

127. For a more complete discussion of Rilke's relationship to the *Reformpädogogen*, see Arndal, "Sehenlernen und Pseudoskopie," 213–215.

128. My use of this Husserlian terminology will fall roughly along the lines of Smith's and Føllesdal's interpretation, where intentionality is a "mental act" (i.e., directing one's attention and perception toward an object) that constitutes its object through consciousness, and noematic *Sinn* potentially corresponds to linguistic *Sinn*. For more on debates around the interpretation of Husserl's terms, see Dagfinn Føllesdal, "The Lebenswelt in Husserl," in *Science and the Life-World: Essays on Husserl's Crises of the European Sciences*, ed. David Hyder and Hans-Jörg Rheinberger (Stanford, CA: Stanford University Press, 2010), 27–45; David Woodruff Smith and Ronald McIntyre, *Husserl and Intentionality: A Study of Mind, Meaning, and Language* (Dordrecht: Reidel, 1982).

129. In agreement with Otto Friedrich Bollnow's assessment that Rilke's lyrical work is indeed a "poeticized form of thought" ("dichtende Gestaltung des Gedankens"), Käte Hamburger argues that the interpretation of Rilkean poetry might be expanded through a specifically Husserlian phenomenological perspective. Focusing primarily on the period around the *Neue Gedichte (New Poems)*, she suggests that one can draw "contemporary historical parallels" ("zeitgeschichtliche Parallele") between epistemology and poetry. She uses the concept to emphasize the idea of affinity without "contact" ("Berührung"). Though Hamburger also pays close attention to the act of seeing or looking ("schauen"), she arrives at the "intentionality" of the lyrical-I by way of personification, i.e., the noetic process in "eidetic vision" ("Wesensschau"). By contrast, I am concerned primarily with "transcendent objects" rather than "immanent" and "eidetic" images. Käte Hamburger, *Philosophie der Dichter: Novalis, Schiller, Rilke* (Stuttgart: W.

Kohlhammer, 1966), 179–185, 188–195. Otto Friedrich Bollnow, *Rilke* (Stuttgart: W. Kohlhammer, 1956), 13.

130. Though I refer to the text as "prose" (and as narratives of the ordinary), the task of making stable determinations of genre is not so easy. Scholars have referred to *The Notebooks* as both a "lyrical novel" and as a "prose poem." The "Notes" are similarly *poeticized* or *verdichtet*. At least provisionally, I would say that Rilke's narrative prose language is *also* poetic.

131. Paul Crowther, *The Phenomenology of Aesthetic Consciousness and Phantasy: Working with Husserl* (London: Routledge, 2022), 6–8.

132. Husserl, *Hua* 33, 59; Husserl, *Phantasy, Image Consciousness, and Memory*, 64.

133. Rilke, *The Notebooks of Malte Laurids Brigge*, 18. Rilke, KA 3, 470–471: "So wie ich es in meiner kindlich gearbeiteten Erinnerung wiederfinde, ist es kein Gebäude; es ist ganz aufgeteilt in mir; da ein Raum, dort ein Raum und hier ein Stück Gang, das diese beiden Räume nicht verbindet, sondern für sich, als Fragment, aufbewahrt ist. In dieser Weise ist alles in mir verstreut, —die Zimmer, die Treppen, die mit so großer Umständlichkeit sich niederließen, und andere enge, rundgebaute Stiegen, in deren Dunkel man ging wie das Blut in den Adern; die Turmzimmer, die hoch aufgehängten Balkone, die unerwarteten Altane, auf die man von einer kleinen Tür hinausgedrängt wurde: —alles das ist noch in mir und wird nie aufhören, in mir zu sein. Es ist, als wäre das Bild dieses Hauses aus unendlicher Höhe in mich hineingestürzt und auf meinem Grunde zerschlagen."

134. Husserl, *Hua* 33, 65; *Phantasy, Image Consciousness, and Memory*, 60. This fragmented image, when interpreted as memory, also lends itself to a "psychical" narrative of a generally "incoherent" childhood in Susan Nurmi-Schomers, *Visionen dichterischen Mündigwerdens: Poetologische Perspektiven auf Robert Musil, Rainer Maria Rilke und Walter Benjamin* (Tübingen: Niemeyer Verlag, 2008), 196. Andreas Huyssen, in "Paris/Childhood," argues that the "hallucinatory perception" and "fragmented" body (and language) in Rilke's novel reflect the fragmented modern subject in the metropolitan context (117–120, 125–126, 131–138). For more on Rilke's narrative strategies of constructing subjective identity, see also Lorna Martens, *The Promise of Memory: Childhood Recollection and Its Objects in Literary Modernism* (Cambridge, MA: Harvard University Press, 2011), and Ulrich Fülleborn, "Form und Sinn der Aufzeichnungen des Malte Laurids Brigge," in *Deutsche Romantheorien*, ed. R. Grimm (Frankfurt am Main: De Gruyter, 1968), 251–273.

135. Blumenberg, *Zu den Sachen und zurück*, 105. See also the section of this chapter titled "'Seeing more; not more than seeing': What Children See in 'Pierre Dumont.'"

136. Stanley Cavell, *The Claim of Reason: Wittgenstein, Skepticism, Morality, and Tragedy* (New York: Oxford University Press, 1999), 73–74.

137. Cavell's sense of a child's limited capacity for intuiting the "entirety" of Manhattan also parallels a notion of the *intuitional indefiniteness* of an individual object, whereby "immediate" acquaintance with the object does not necessarily bring about a full accounting for that object's meaning. As Smith and McIntyre

have noted, Husserl himself does not elaborate on the problem of "indefinite intentions," though they note that the act of intention—*as* it happens—determines the object in a final manner, thus "mak[ing] the act's object count as this one and no other." Smith and McIntyre, *Husserl and Intentionality*, 20–21.

138. Although I will address the processing of largely limited sense data of a physical object as a definite side of mental representation, from the perspective of experience of the "Ego-experience," moments of *excess* perception can be said to blur the distinctions between exterior space ("Umwelt") and interior subject-identity. See also Fauconneau-Dufresne, "Wirklichkeitserfahrung und Bewußtseinsentwicklung," 264–266, and Fülleborn, "Form und Sinn," 251–273.

139. Here, I want to disagree with Luke Fischer's quasi-Romantic claims that, for Rilke, childhood is a "time of experiential monism" and "pre-dualistic," and that Rilke envisions an "identity" and "radical sympathy" between children and things (*The Poet as Phenomenologist*, 78–87). Despite the appearance of monistic unity between child-subject and object (i.e., that the image is "in me"), Rilke's depiction of the child's incomplete perspective or infelicitous intention ultimately underscores the ways in which childhood intuition is informed by the gap between the object's manifold appearance and the child-subject's limited perceptions.

140. Rilke, *The Notebooks of Malte Laurids Brigge*, 18–19. Rilke, KA 3, 471: "Dieser hohe, wie ich vermute, gewölbte Raum war stärker als alles; er saugte mit seiner dunkelnden Höhe, mit seinen niemals ganz aufgeklärten Ecken alle Bilder aus einem heraus, ohne einem einen bestimmten Ersatz dafür zu geben. Man saß da wie aufgelöst; völlig ohne Willen, ohne Besinnung, ohne Lust, ohne Abwehr. Man war wie eine leere Stelle. Ich erinnere mich, daß dieser vernichtende Zustand mir zuerst fast Übelkeit verursachte, eine Art Seekrankheit, die ich nur dadurch überwand, daß ich mein Bein ausstreckte, bis ich mit dem Fuß das Knie meines Vaters berührte, der mir gegenübersaß. . . . Und nach einigen Wochen krampfhaften Ertragens hatte ich, mit der fast unbegrenzten Anpassung des Kindes, mich so sehr an das Unheimliche jener Zusammenkünfte gewöhnt, daß es mich keine Anstrengung mehr kostete, zwei Stunden bei Tische zu sitzen; jetzt vergingen sie sogar verhältnismäßig schnell, weil ich mich damit beschäftigte, die Anwesenden zu beobachten."

141. Blumenberg, *Zu den Sachen und zurück*, 105.

142. The image of a vaulted ceiling involves what Albrecht Koschorke calls a "sanctioning compulsion" as it is an image of heaven/sky (*Himmel*) against which one could bump their head. Vaulting has the double task of symbolizing heaven in cathedral architecture (as the immaterial, infinite) while also designating its opposite (as a ceiling, it is by definition a finite and material limit. Albrecht Koschorke, *Die Geschichte des Horizonts: Grenze und Grenzenlosigkeit in literarischen Landschaftsbildern* (Frankfurt am Main: Suhrkamp, 1990), 258–259.

143. Koschorke further stresses that nineteenth-century literature (realism in particular) corresponds to a philosophical investment in domestic space (as either limiting or expansive) as an aesthetics rendered through metaphors of containment. For a comprehensive discussion of the trope of space across nineteenth-century literature, see Koschorke, *Die Geschichte des Horizonts*.

144. Rilke uses "Übelkeit" and not the Latinate "nausea" (i.e., seasickness), which underscores the infinitely transformative possibilities of childhood perception. As the Grimms note, the etymological roots of "übel" include the notion of excess: "das über das maasz, die norm hinausgehende."

145. Husserl articulates the unity of consciousness of transcendent (physical) objects as the perception of sense data (ulh) and mental, or noetic, processes that "bestow sense" or form (morfh) to that sensuous objective "Stoff" (*Ideas*, §85). As Smith and McIntyre note, although Husserl borrows from Aristotle's matter-form dichotomy, he puts the terms to new use here. *Husserl and Intentionality*, 137.

146. Rilke, KA 3, 466: "die Kindheitstage, die noch unaufgeklärt sind." My translation.

147. Rilke, *The Notebooks of Malte Laurids Brigge*, 18. Rilke, KA 3, 471: "Ganz erhalten ist in meinem Herzen, so scheint es mir, nur jener Saal, in dem wir uns zum Mittagessen zu versammeln pflegten, jeden Abend um sieben Uhr. Ich habe diesen Raum niemals bei Tage gesehen, ich erinnere mich nicht einmal, ob er Fenster hatte und wohin sie aussahen; jedesmal, so oft die Familie eintrat, brannten die Kerzen in den schweren Armleuchtern, und man vergaß in einigen Minuten die Tageszeit und alles, was man draußen gesehen hatte."

148. Gosetti-Ferencei includes Rilke's term "Weltinnenraum" in her discussion of "Zwischenraum." She attributes the peculiarity of space in Rilke's lyrical and prose writing to a representation of perception that must be thought of as "challeng[ing] . . . a Cartesian separation between a subject and the object" (303). This form of "poetical consciousness" creates the effect of "felt space between subject and object which annuls their division," namely, "interstitial space" (ibid.). In Rilke's writings on childhood, this effect is particularly visible in the intensity of perception of the external, "sensuous" world (304). See also Hamburger, "Die Phänomenologische Struktur der Dichtung Rilkes."

149. This "bi-stable" image is a drawing that, depending on what the viewer focuses on, appears to be either a duck or rabbit. Joseph Jastrow used it to demonstrate how perception arises from a combination of external stimuli and mental activity. It was later made famous by Wittgenstein's simple line drawing in *Philosophical Investigations*. See Joseph Jastrow, "The Mind's Eye" *Popular Science Monthly* 54 (1899): 312.

150. Føllesdal, "The Lebenswelt in Husserl," 32–33.

151. See Huyssen's psychoanalytic discussion of fragmentation and childhood memories, "Paris/Childhood," 120–121, 134, 137.

152. Rilke, *The Notebooks of Malte Laurids Brigge*, 12, 47. Rilke, KA, 465, 499.

153. Ahmed, *Queer Phenomenology*, 161.

154. Stockton, *The Queer Child*, 11.

155. Hans Blumenberg, "Pensiveness," in *History, Metaphors, Fables: A Hans Blumenberg Reader*, trans. Hannes Bajohr, Florian Fuchs, and Loe Paul Kroll (Ithaca, NY: Cornell University Press, 2020), 529.

156. Blumenberg, "Pensiveness," 529–530.

157. Rilke, KA 4, 530; Rilke *Letters to a Young Poet*, trans. Norton, 36.

158. Blumenberg, *The Laughter of the Thracian Woman*, 46.

159. Situating her argument in the US context, Luciano describes the ways in which nineteenth-century sentimental views of children temporalized them as future-bound ways, as "sacred investments" that connected family temporalities with national ones. Although maternal love was figured as timeless, the child "is launched toward a deep future conceived as inspirational horizon (national progress, global regeneration, eternal bliss)." Dana Luciano, *Arranging Grief: Sacred Time and the Body in Nineteenth-Century America* (New York: New York University Press: 2007), 121–122.

160. Husserl, *Ideas I*, §19, 37–38.

161. Rilke, KA 4, 530; Rilke, *Letters to a Young Poet*, trans. Norton, 5–36.

3. Walter Benjamin's Small Worlds of Childhood

1. Walter Benjamin, *The Arcades Project*, trans. Howard Eiland and Kevin McLaughlin (Cambridge, MA: Belknap Press of Harvard University Press, 1999), 361; Walter Benjamin, *Gesammelte Schriften*, vol. 5, ed. Rolf Tiedemann (Frankfurt: Suhrkamp Verlag, 1982), 456 (J75, 2): "Auch für sie stellt die fouriersche Utopie ein Leitbild." References to Benjamin's texts in German are cited hereafter as GS, and in English as SW when applicable to the edition of *Selected Writings*, edited by Michael W. Jennings, Howard Eiland, and Gary Smith,. 4 vols. (Cambridge, MA: Belknap Press of Harvard University Press, 2004).

2. Benjamin, *The Arcades Project*, 361; GS V, 456: "Es ist das Bild einer Erde, auf der alle Orte zu Wirtschaften geworden sind. Der Doppelsinn des Wortes blüht hierbei auf: alle Orte sind vom Menschen bearbeitet, von ihm nutzbar und schön gemacht; alle aber stehen, wie eine Wirtschaft am Weg, allen offen. . . . Auf ihr wäre die Tat mit dem Traum verschwistert."

3. Sam Dolbear and Hannah Proctor, "'Cracking Open the Natural Teleology': Walter Benjamin, Charles Fourier, and the Figure of the Child," *Pedagogy, Culture & Society* 24, no. 4 (Fall 2016): 496.

4. Kathryn Bond Stockton, *The Queer Child, or Growing Sideways in the Twentieth Century* (Durham, NC: Duke University Press, 2009), 4.

5. Benjamin, *The Arcades Project*, 361; GS V, 456.

6. Gottfried W. Leibniz, *Philosophical Essays*, trans. Andrew Ariew and Daniel Garber (Indianapolis: Hackett, 1989), 222. Cited hereafter as PE.

7. Leibniz, PE, 220.

8. Benjamin, GS I, 228. "Die Idee ist Monade—das heißt in Kürze: jede Idee enthält das Bild der Welt. Ihrer Darstellung ist zur Aufgabe nic *The Origin of German Tragic Drama* hts Geringeres gesetzt, als dieses Bild der Welt in seiner Verkürzung zu zeichnen." "The idea is a monad—in short that means: every idea contains the image of the world. The purpose of the representation of the idea is nothing less than an abbreviated outline of this image of the world." Walter

Benjamin, *The Origin of German Tragic Drama*, trans. John Osborne (New York: Verso, 1998), 48.

9. Benjamin, GS I: 228; Benjamin, *The Origin of German Tragic Drama*, 47.

10. Paula Schwebel has argued persuasively that Benjamin's conception of Leibniz's monad was likely filtered through secondary theological scholarship, such that his understanding reflects the only secondary Leibniz scholar that Benjamin is known to have read: Heinz Heimsoeth. Paula Schwebel, "Intensive Infinity: Walter Benjamin's Reception of Leibniz and Its Sources," *MLN* 127, no. 3 (2012): 589–610.

11. Larry M. Jorgensen, "Leibniz on Perceptual Distinctness, Activity, and Sensation," *Journal of the History of Philosophy* 53, no. 1 (2015): 54.

12. Jorgensen, "Leibniz on Perceptual Distinctness," 55.

13. For Leibniz, memory (e.g., *mémoire*, *réminiscences*) plays a significant role in his theory of consciousness (as the basic ability to hold an object in thought) and in experience (as the accumulation of similar memories). Larry M. Jorgensen, "Leibniz on Memory and Consciousness," *British Journal for the History of Philosophy* 19, no. 5 (2011): 903–904.

14. Here and elsewhere in this chapter I draw on recent scholarship by Chris Swoyer and Larry M. Jorgensen that has articulated a relatively consistent concept of expression that underpins Leibniz's theory of mental representations and the metaphysical principles of monadic reflection. See, for example, Chris Swoyer, "Leibnizian Expression," *Journal of the History of Philosophy* 33, no. 1 (1995): 65–99, and Jorgensen's discussion of Swoyer in "Leibniz on Perceptual Distinctness, Activity, and Sensation," 50–55.

15. This, as we will see, is also where Benjamin departs from Leibniz's totalizing theory. Perceptual distinctness, in Jorgensen's view, "provide[s] the metaphysical basis" in *The Origin of German Tragic Drama Monadology*, whereas Benjamin's writings on childhood are, in my view, explorations in what and how children perceive and cognize the world. Jorgensen, "Leibniz on Perceptual Distinctness, Activity, and Sensation," 55.

16. Leibniz, PE, 220.

17. Here I am employing the term "aphorism" in line with scholars of the Frankfurt School who have characterized this genre of short texts and "miniature" scenes that bear philosophical weight. Richter describes what he calls the modernist Denkbild as "a brief, aphoristic prose text typically ranging in length between a few sentences and couple of pages that both illuminates explodes the conventional distinctions among literature, philosophy, journalistic intervention, and cultural critique" and as "creative appropriations of the baroque emblem and of subsequent eighteenth-century versions of the genre in Herder and others." Gerhard Richter, *Thought-Images: Frankfurt School Writers' Reflections from Damaged Life* (Stanford, CA: Stanford University Press, 2007), 7; See also Michael Jennings, introduction to *One-Way Street* by Walter Benjamin, edited by Michael W. Jennings (Cambridge, MA: Harvard University Press, 2016), 2–4.

18. Schwebel, "Intensive Infinity," 591–592.

19. It is through Leibniz's use of "detail" and "envelope," Samuel Weber argues, that he is able to preserve this dialectical structure (e.g., "unity" and "multiplicity," "separation" and "self-containment" etc.). Samuel Weber, *Benjamin's -abilities* (Cambridge, MA: Harvard University Press, 2008), 245, 303.

20. Schwebel, "Intensive Infinity," 592.

21. Schwebel, "Intensive Infinity," 609.

22. Peter Szondi, "Hope in the Past: On Walter Benjamin," *Critical Inquiry* 4, no. 3 (Spring 1978): 493; Lorna Martens, *The Promise of Memory: Childhood Recollection and Its Objects in Literary Modernism* (Cambridge, MA: Harvard University Press, 2011), 138–140; Nadine Werner, *Archäologie des Erinnerns: Sigmund Freud in Walter Benjamins Berliner Kindheit* (Göttingen: Wallstein Verlag, 2016), 55–77.

23. See Szondi, "Hope in the Past: On Walter Benjamin," 491–506; Richard Wolin, *Walter Benjamin: An Aesthetic of Redemption* (New York: Columbia University Press, 1982), 3; as well as more recent interventions such as Anja Lemke, *Gedächtnisräume des Selbst: Walter Benjamins "Berliner Kindheit um neunzehnhundert"* (Würzburg: Königshausen und Neumann, 2005), and Tara Forrest, *The Politics of Imagination: Benjamin, Kracauer, Kluge* (Bielefeld: Transcript Verlag, 2007).

24. Weber, *Benjamin's -abilities*, 139.

25. Indeed, Benjamin's engagement with the idea of children and childhood extends well past the selected texts I discuss here. Kenneth Kidd offers an excellent discussion of Benjamin's writing on the idea of "children's literature" and as a minor literature in Deleuze and Guattari's sense. He also shows that Benjamin's radio broadcasts "promote critical-theoretical engagement for minors." Kenneth B. Kidd, *Theory for Beginners: Children's Literature as Critical Thought* (New York: Fordham University Press, 2020), 80–83. Gilles Deleuze and Félix Guattari, *Kafka: Toward a Minor Literature*, translated by Dana Polan (Minneapolis: University of Minnesota Press, 1986). See also Jeffrey Mehlman, *Walter Benjamin for Children: An Essay on His Radio Years* (Chicago: University of Chicago Press, 1993).

26. For a comprehensive survey of Benjamin's work on children and childhood, and his recurring interest in theorizing fantasy and perception in general, see Heinz Brüggemann, *Walter Benjamin: Über Spiel, Farbe und Phantasie* (Würzburg: Königshausen und Neumann, 2011).

27. See, for example, on discussions of reproduction and inheritance, Michael Thomas Taylor, "Right Queer: Hegel's Philosophy of Marriage," *Republics of Letters: A Journal for the Study of Knowledge, Politics, and the Arts* 3, no. 2 (November 2013): 15, as well as Albrecht Koschorke et al., *Vor der Familie: Grenzbedingungen einer modernen Institution* (Munich: Wilhelm Fink Verlag, 2010).

28. Lee Edelman, *No Future: Queer Theory and the Death Drive* (Durham, NC: Duke University Press, 2004), 11.

29. See the introduction to this book, as well as Dolbear and Proctor, "Cracking Open the Natural Teleology."

30. See discussion in the introduction to this book.

31. José Esteban Muñoz, *Cruising Utopia: The Then and There of Queer Futurity* (New York: New York University Press, 2009), 25–27.

32. Here, Muñoz's characterization of queer temporality that contains a utopian notion of hope without falling into "straight" conceptions of time is helpful: "A turn to the no-longer-conscious enabled a critical hermeneutics attuned to comprehending the not-yet-here. This temporal calculus performed and utilized the past and the future as armaments to combat the devastating logic of the world of the here and now, a notion of nothing existing outside the sphere of the current moment, a version of reality that naturalizes cultural logics such as capitalism and heteronormativity." Muñoz, *Cruising Utopia*, 12.

33. Writing on classical and Roman rhetorical and philosophical uses of allegory, Theresa M. Kelley paraphrases Heinrich Lausberg's modern definition of allegory as "a larger narrative and figural framework" that consists of individual metaphors, which are the "unnarratized parts." Theresa M. Kelley, "'Fantastic Shapes': From Classical Rhetoric to Romantic Allegory," *Texas Studies in Literature and Language* 33, no. 2 (1991): 235.

34. George Steiner, introduction to *Origin of German Tragic Drama* (New York: Verso, 1998), 22–23; also cited in Schwebel, "Intensive Infinity," 590–591.

35. Heinz Brüggemann has situated Benjamin's writing on the aesthetics of childhood and in the visual arts, roughly from early Romanticism through the modernists such as Klee, arguing that the essays on aesthetics should be understood within Benjaminian theoretical frameworks of the image (*Bild*) and modern sites that act as media of fantasy. See "Fragmente zur Ästhetik / Phantasie und Farbe," in *Benjamin Handbuch: Leben—Wirkung—Werk*, ed. Burkhart Lindner (Stuttgart: Metzler, 2006), 124, as well as Brüggemann, *Walter Benjamin*.

36. Gaston Bachelard, *The Poetics of Space*, trans. Maria Jolas (New York: Penguin, 2014), 27.

37. Gershom Scholem, "Walter Benjamin," in *On Jews and Judaism in Crisis* (New York: Schocken Books, 1976), 175; See also Susan Buck-Morss, *The Dialectics of Seeing: Walter Benjamin and the Arcades Project* (Cambridge, MA: MIT Press, 1989), 262.

38. Scholem, "Walter Benjamin," 178.

39. Benjamin, SW I, 50; GS VI, 110.

40. Benjamin, SW I, 50–51; GS VI, 110: "nicht der schichthafte Überzug der Substanz . . . da sie die Gegenstände nach ihrem farbigen Gehalt anschaut und folglich nicht isoliert, sondern sich die zusammenhängende Anschauung der Phantasiewelt in ihnen sichert." Translation modified from "something superimposed on matter" to "cloaks the surface of phenomena." A note on the noun gender of child (*Kind*) in translation: wherever Benjamin writes about "a child" or "the child" (*ein Kind, das Kind*) in generic or universal terms, I use the nonbinary "they" as the default—rather than masculine—to translate what is a neuter noun in the German. However, when the child subject is definitively in reference to himself as narrator (e.g., in *Berlin Childhood around 1900*), I use the masculine.

41. Leibniz, PE, 215.

42. Translation adapted from SW I, 408. (Here I translate "they do not so much imitate the works of adults as bring together, in the artifact produced in play, materials of widely different kinds" so that it more closely follows the original German: "They do not so much imitate the works of adults as bring these residual materials and waste products together in a disjointed, new relationship with one another"); GS III, 16–17: "Unwiderstehlich fühlen [die Kinder] sich vom Abfall angezogen, der sei es beim Bauen, beim Garten- oder Tischlerarbeit, beim Schneidern oder wo sonst immer entsteht. In diesen Abfallprodukten erkennen sie das Gesicht, das die Dingwelt gerade ihnen, ihnen allein zukehrt. Mit diesen bilden sie die Werke von Erwachsenen nicht sowohl nach als daß sie diese Rest- und Abfallstoffe in eine sprunghafte neue Beziehung zueinander setzen. Kinder bilden sich damit ihre Dingwelt, eine kleine in der großen, selbst."

43. See also Susan Buck-Morss's discussion of this passage and the "revolutionary power" of childhood perception and mimetic faculties in *Dialectics of Seeing*, 262–264.

44. Leibniz, PE, 221 and 222.

45. Leibniz, PE, 222.

46. Leibniz, PE, 222.

47. Thank you to Michael Thomas Taylor for the conversation on this Benjamin text, in particular reminding me of some of the rich connotations and wordplay at work in it.

48. Julia Kristeva, "Women's Time," trans. Alice Jardine and Harry Blake, *Signs* 7, no. 1 (Autumn 1981): 14–17; Dana Luciano, *Arranging Grief: Sacred Time and the Body in Nineteenth-Century America* (New York: New York University Press, 2007), 121–122; Elizabeth Freeman, *Time Binds: Queer Temporalities, Queer Histories* (Durham, NC: Duke University Press, 2010), 5–8.

49. Luciano, *Arranging Grief*, 121–122; Freeman, *Time Binds*, 5–8.

50. Leibniz, PE, 222.

51. Benjamin, SW I, 408. The standard translation employs "spiritual" for the ever-difficult-to-translate "geistig." Benjamin, GS III, 16–17: "Kinder bilden sich damit ihre Dingwelt, eine kleine in der großen, selbst. Ein solches Abfallprodukt ist das Märchen, das gewaltigste vielleicht, das im geistigen Leben der Menschheit sich findet: Abfall im Entstehungs- und Verfallsprozeß der Sage. Mit Märchenstoffen vermag das Kind so souverän und unbefangen zu schalten wie mit Stoffetzen und Bausteinen. In Märchenmotiven baut es seine Welt auf, verbindet es wenigstens ihre Elemente."

52. Remarking on this same scene of children playing with trash when it appears in *One-Way Street*, Michael Jennings regards it as exemplary of Benjamin's interest in "alternate modes of perception" for which "children's perception, as yet untainted by the world of adults, is accorded a privileged place." Jennings, introduction to *One-Way Street*," 16.

53. In distinguishing monadic and divine "knowledge," Leibniz describes how monads, though indeed reflective of the "entire universe," do so in a way that

remains "confused as to the detail of the whole universe" and that in the mode of their knowledge they remain distinct from the divine as "limited and differentiated" in their perceptions. Leibniz, PE, 220–221.

54. Leibniz, PE, 220.

55. See Chapter 2.

56. Walter Benjamin, *Einbahnstraße: Werke und Nachlaß: Kritische Gesamtausgabe*, ed. Detlev Schöttker and Steffen Haug, vol. 8 (Frankfurt a.M.: Suhrkamp Verlag, 2009), 131: "Kind zieht ein Pferdchen hinter sich her" ("Child drags a toy horse along behind himself") and "Sammeln bei Kindern" ("Collecting, in the case of children").

57. For an alternate reading of this dialectics, one that focuses on Benjamin's novel use of the "primitive" aesthetics and the sovereignty of childhood subjectivity, see Nicola Gess, "Gaining Sovereignty: On the Figure of the Child in Walter Benjamin's Writing," *MLN* 125, no. 3 (April 2010): 682–708.

58. Benjamin, GS IV, 937 (Benjamin-Archiv, MS 914).

59. Benjamin GS IV, 937: "Ganz unbedingt muß darüber nachgedacht werden, ob nicht für den unfaßlichen Ernst der kindlichen Anschauung dies ein Ausdruck ist: daß es nichts kennt als Ganze." There is a discrepancy between editions: in the Schöttker edition of *Einbahnstraße* (2009), the text reads as "unfaßlichen Ernst," whereas in volume 4 of the earlier *Gesammelten Schriften* (1991) the phrase is "unfaktischen Ernst." As the Schöttker edition is both more recent and effectively a critical edition, with manuscript edits and notes, I have chosen to interpret this passage as "unfaßlichen Ernst."

60. Leibniz, PE, 221.

61. Benjamin, GS IV, 937: "Hier nur diesen Satz aus Berthold Auerbachs: Schrift und Volk . . . 'In späteren Jahren läßt sich diese kleine Welt' . . . 'nicht mehr so als ganze erfassen, sie deutet dem Beschauer stets auf die größere hin'" [sic]. It appears that he almost included the rest of Auerbach's sentence in his notes. The original manuscript page reads in its entirety: "This small world . . . always points the beholder to the larger one and appears as a fragment." . . . "diese kleine Welt . . . deutet dem Beschauer stets auf die größere hin und erscheint als Bruchstück." Berthold Auerbach, *Schrift und Volk: Grundzüge der volksthümlichen Literatur* (Leipzig: Brockhaus, 1846), 35.

62. Leibniz, PE, 220.

63. Given his well-documented interest in the figure of the collector, it is unsurprising that Benjamin was so struck by Auerbach's words: a multivalent reading of *erfassen* (to comprehend) would include the following: to account for, to gather, to collect. Of course, Auerbach, more so a contemporary of Stifter than Benjamin, easily speaks to the drive to collect and record in the growing enthusiasm for the natural sciences, as we have seen in the figure of the careful scientist recording data in the preface to *Motley Stones*.

64. GS IV, 113–116: "Child Reading" ("Lesendes Kind"), "Tardy Child" ("Zu spät gekommenes Kind"), "Nibbling Child" ("Naschendes Kind"), "Child Riding the Carousel" ("Karussellfahrendes Kind"), "Untidy Child" ("Unordentliches Kind"),

and "Hidden Child "("Verstecktes Kind") in Benjamin, GS IV, 113–116. Translations of these subheadings are mine.

65. Davide Giuriato has argued that the aesthetics of scale in these writings on childhood are to be understood as part of Benjamin's larger poetology of writing and of the self within a constellation of processes such as representing and recalling, drafting, and rewriting. Like many of Benjamin's interpreters, he treats these passages as part of a project on autobiography, autography, and memory, rather than, as I show here, a philosophical and poetic exploration of the experience of childhood subjectivity for itself. Davide Giuriato, *Mikrographien: Zu einer Poetologie des Schreibens in Walter Benjamins Kindheitserinnerungen (1932–1939)* (Munich: Wilhelm Fink Verlag, 2006).

66. Benjamin, SW II, 510; Benjamin, GS II, 371: "die exakteste Technik kann ihren Hervorbringungen einen magischen Wert geben, wie für uns ihn eine gemaltes Bild nie mehr besitzen kann."

67. Benjamin, SW II, 510; Benjamin, GS II, 371: "Die Photographie mit ihren Hilfsmittel: Zeitlupen, Vergrößerungen erschließt sie ihm."

68. Benjamin, SW II, 512; GS II, 371: "Strukturbeschaffenheiten, Zellgewebe, mit denen Technik, Medizin zu rechnen pflegen—all dieses ist der Kamera ursprünglich verwandter als die stimmungsvolle Landschaft oder das seelenvolle Porträt. Zugleich aber eröffnet die Photographie in diesem Material die physiognomischen Aspekte, Bildwelten, welche im Kleinsten wohnen, deutbar und verborgen genug, um in Wachtträumen Unterschlupf gefunden zu haben. . . ."

69. Writing on the relationship between aesthetic production and politics in Benjamin's fragments and essay on photography and film, Tara Forrest concludes: "Benjamin argues that the camera's capacity to extend the spectator's vision beyond the realm of subjective intention means that film is ideally placed to counter the diminution in the capacity for perception and experience that both Benjamin and Simmel associate with modernity." Forrest, *The Politics of Imagination*, 72–73.

70. Freeman argues that photographs of children, particularly as they are displayed in middle-class homes, connect individual family lineages with nationalist discourses of "progress" by "ma[king] simple reproductive sequences look like historical consequence." Freeman, *Time Binds*, 21–22. Marianne Hirsch, *Family Frames: Photography, Narrative, and Postmemory* (Cambridge, MA: Harvard University Press, 1997), 6–7.

71. Kracauer's essay "Photography" ("Die Photographie") first appeared in the *Frankfurter Zeitung* in 1927, the same year that Benjamin's *Einbahnstraße* was published, and four years earlier than Benjamin's "Small History of Photography" ("Kleine Geschichte der Photographie") cited above.

72. The photograph, for Kracauer stand in contrast to "the artwork" wherein "meaning takes on spatial appearance." Siegfried Kracauer and Thomas Y. Levin, "Photography," *Critical Inquiry* 19, no. 3 (1993): 427.

73. Leibniz, PE, 220.

74. Kracauer and Levine, "Photography," 428.

75. I emphasize the technological dimension here to show that in a reading of childhood that is not centered on memory, Benjamin appears to have moved from "portraits" (i.e., an image linked to the particular and the personal as a keepsake or familial artifact). Eric Tribunella argues that Benjamin is primarily reflecting on a kind of quasi-Romantic unfettered "seeing" in his writings on childhood, in which "the imaginative work of the child's gaze" is linked to their ability to encounter imagery in books, producing what Tribunellas calls "nostalgia-free contemplation." Eric Tribunella, "Benjamin, Benson, and the Child's Gaze: Childhood Desire and Pleasure in the David Blaize Books," *Pedagogy, Culture & Society* 24, no. 4 (2016): 507. See also Gess, "Gaining Sovereignty."

76. The standard translation, done by Edmund Jephcott and first published in 1978, also appears in the Bullock and Jennings edition of the *Selected Writings*, vol. 1. Jephcott translates the subheading "Zu spät gekommenes Kind" as "Belated Child." I have chosen to use my own translation here (as "Tardy Child") both for consistency and because it better captures the American English institutional rhetoric of lateness, particularly in grade school, without immediately burdening the aphorism with the philosophical jargon of "belatedness." In the passage that follows, Benjamin himself echoes this subheading in the school's judgment of "tardy" ("zu spät"), which Jephcott's translation also uses.

77. Benjamin, GS IV, 113; Benjamin, SW I, 464: "Die Uhr im Schulhof sieht beschädigt aus durch seine Schuld. Sie steht auf 'Zu spät.'"

78. Benjamin, GS IV, 113; Benjamin, SW I, 464: "Und in den Flur dringt aus den Klassentüren, wo es vorbeistreicht, Murmeln von geheimer Beratung. . . . Oder es schweigt alles still, als erwartete man einen. Unhörbar legt es die Hand an die Klinke. Die Sonne tränkt den Flecken, wo es steht. Da schändet es den grünen Tag und öffnet." As noted in previous chapters, all translations of the pronoun for Kind (child) have been adapted, replacing the universal masculine pronoun "he/him" with the gender-neutral "they/them."

79. Forrest, *The Politics of Imagination*, 73.

80. Benjamin, GS IV, 113–114; Benjamin, SW I, 464: "Es hört die Lehrerstimme wie ein Mühlrad klappern; es steht vor dem Mahlwerk. Die klappernde Stimme behält ihren Takt, aber die Knechte werfen nun alles ab und auf das neue; zehn, zwanzig schwere Säcke fliegen ihm zu, die muß es zur Bank tragen. An seinem Mäntelchen ist jeder Faden weiß bestaubt."

81. Freeman, *Time Binds*, 3–10.

82. Leibniz, PE, 216, §22.

83. Leibniz, PE, 216, §22: "And since every present state of a simple substance is a natural consequence of its preceding state, the present is pregnant with the future."

84. Benjamin, SW I, 464; GS IV, 114: "Es hat die Höhe in der man am besten zu fliegen träumt."

85. Benjamin, SW I, 464; GS IV, 114: "Musik setzt ein, und ruckweis rollt das Kind von seiner Mutter fort. Erst hat es Angst, die Mutter zu verlassen. Dann aber merkt es, wie es selber treu ist."

86. Benjamin's language here is decidedly orientalist. It seems very possible that a nineteenth-century carousel in Berlin, on which this passage would be based, would have something like an "oriental" "jungle" theme which his quasi-realist description depicts in detail. The passage is problematic to the extent that for Benjamin it essentially becomes the organizing motif, as not only trees but also "natives" line the path, and in the East or standing on one side, perhaps ("in dem Orient"), he sees his mother standing. Benjamin, SW I, 464; GS IV, 114. It is a passage that points the reader back to Herder's comparison of "oriental" cultures as being in a state of infancy or youth and Benjamin's own discussion of the childlike as "barbaric." Giuriato, *Mikrographien*, 16–19, 60. See my discussion of Herder's influential white supremacist, Romantic trope in the introduction to this book.

87. Benjamin, SW I, 464; GS IV, 114–115: "[Das Kind] thront als treuer Herrscher über einer Welt, die ihm gehört . . . Danach tritt aus dem Urwald ein Wipfel, wie ihn das Kind schon vor Jahrtausenden, wie es ihn eben erst im Karussell gesehen hat."

88. Benjamin, SW I, 464; GS IV, 115. Emphasis mine.

89. Friedrich Nietzsche, *Gay Science*, ed. Bernard Williams, trans. Josefine Nauckhoff (Cambridge: Cambridge University Press, 2001), 194.

90. Forrest, *The Politics of Imagination*, 72–73.

91. Benjamin, OT, 47. See also Weber, *Benjamin's -abilities*, 245, 303.

92. From his letter to Johann Bernoulli, dated November 18, 1698. Leibniz, PE, 169.

93. Nadine Werner provides an excellent survey of scholarship as well as her own reading of the metaphorical significance of metaphors of archaeology for Benjamin's writing on memory and childhood, in particular in its overlap and interlocutions with Freud. Werner, *Archäologie des Erinnerns*.

94. Michael Jennings has shown how Benjamin's practice of rewriting and reworking material between *One-Way Street* and *Berlin Childhood* is fundamental to Benjamin's "attempts . . . to create texts that aspire to the conditions of legibility of the photograph." Michael W. Jennings, "Double Take: Palimpsestic Writing and Image-Character in Benjamin's Late Prose," *Benjamin-Studien* 2 (2011): 35, 36, 40.

95. As Martens recently noted, the story of Benjamin's *Berlin Childhood* is its own long, complex genesis. The posthumously published "final version" (*Fassung letzter Hand*) is one of at least three versions he developed over a six-year period, until he had to flee in 1940. *The Promise of Memory*, 139–140. See also Giuriato's landmark study, *Mikrographien*, which offers detailed analysis of Benjamin's writerly process and poetology as it appears over the course of the project's development: from his earliest writings on childhood, through the first manuscript, titled *Berlin Chronicle*, to the vast archival material on *Berlin Childhood* itself. Giuriato, *Mikrographien*, 27–84.

96. Giuriato, *Mikrographien*, 93.

97. Werner, *Archäologie des Erinnerns*, 13.

98. Benjamin, GW VII, 383; SW III, 344.

99. Johannes Türk, *Die Immunität der Literatur* (Frankfurt am Main: Fischer Verlag, 2011), 300.

100. In her account of seventeenth-century technologies of seeing and their relationship to an aesthetics of the miniature, Susan Stewart emphasizes the microscope's role in "detecting significance" in a "world" that the human eye had previously been unable to see at all. Susan Stewart, *On Longing: Narratives of the Miniature, the Gigantic, the Souvenir, the Collection* (Durham, NC: Duke University Press, 1993). 40.

101. Stewart, *On Longing*, 41.

102. Christiane Frey, "Observing the Small: On the Borders of the Subvisibilia (from Hooke to Brockes)," *Monatshefte* 105, no. 3 (2013): 377.

103. For Leibniz, the revelation of newly visible worlds by microscopic technologies underscored the infinitude of divine creation, in which no space would be left unfilled. Frey, "Observing the Small," 382.

104. Türk, *Die Immunität der Literatur*, 300.

105. Avi Sharma, *We Lived for the Body: Natural Medicine and Public Health in Imperial Germany* (DeKalb: Northern Illinois University Press, 2014), 124–125.

106. Sharma, *We Lived for the Body*, 124.

107. Türk argues that there is a specific tension at work in metaphors of vaccination that arise from the anxiety around real and imagined threats from treatments that use "infection" as prevention or cure. Following a long history of unpredictable effectiveness, inoculation carried with it the potential for illness. In his epilogue, he briefly notes that Benjamin understands the possibility of "losing the places of childhood" as "structurally analogous" to the twin dangers produced by both disease and "immunological praxis" itself. Türk, *Die Immunität der Literatur*, 300.

108. Benjamin, GS VII, 385: "Das Gefühl der Sehnsucht durfte dabei über den Geist ebensowenig Herr werden wie der Impfstoff über einen gesunden Körper."

109. Weber, *Benjamin's -abilities*, 240–247.

110. Weber, *Benjamin's -abilities*, 240–247.

111. Benjamin, GS I, 350–351; Weber, *Benjamin's -abilities*, 241–242.

112. Weber, *Benjamin's -abilities*, 242.

113. Weber, *Benjamin's -abilities*, 243–244, quoting Leibniz, "§11. But it is also necessary that, besides the principle of change, there should be a *detail* of that which changes, which would constitute, so to speak, the specification and variety of simple substances."

114. Weber, *Benjamin's -abilities*, 245–246.

115. The second half of the nineteenth century saw the creation and production of five human vaccines, including live virus and killed bacteria. These whole cell technologies represent the fundamentals of vaccinology, which would not be significantly supplemented by acellular vaccines until the advent of cell culture in

1949. Susan L. Plotkin and Stanley A. Plotkin, "A Short History of Vaccination," in *Vaccines*, ed. Stanley A. Plotkin, Walter A. Orenstein, and Paul A. Offit, 5th ed. (Philadelphia: Elsevier, 2008), 4.

116. See also Giuriato, *Mikrographien*, 60–70, and Nicholas Pethes, *Mnemographie: Poetiken der Erinnerung und Destruktion nach Walter Benjamin* (Tübingen: Niemeyer Verlag, 1999), 358–366.

117. Benjamin, GS VII, 385; Benjamin, SW III, 344. In the standard translation, Jephcott and Eiland translate the verb "sich in etw. niederschlagen" as the more literal sounding "to precipitate in" which doesn't include the valences of expressing or reflecting.

118. Benjamin, GS VII, 385; Benjamin, SW III, 344: "Dagegen habe ich mich bemüht, der *Bilder* habhaft zu werden, in denen die Erfahrung der Großstadt in einem Kinde der Bürgerklasse sich niederschlägt." The translation of "sich niederschlägt" has been modified from "precipitated" to "finds expression."

119. Leibniz, *Monadology*, §67, §68.

120. Frey argues that for Leibniz the distinction between "visible" and "invisible" is an "arbitrary" artifact of the limits of finite human perception and ultimately of technology. That is, it reinforces the idea of an infinite regress of scale, not a hard and fast line between "visible" and "invisible." Frey, "Observing the Small," 382.

121. Frey, "Observing the Small," 383.

122. Friedrich Schlegel, *Athenaeum Fragments*. Translated by Peter Firchow. Foreword by Rudolphe Gasche (Minneapolis: University of Minnesota Press, 1991), 45, §206. For a discussion of Benjamin's writing on the Romantic fragment see Winfried Menninghaus, "Walter Benjamin's Exposition of the Romantic Theory of Reflection," in *Walter Benjamin and Romanticism*, ed. Beatrice Hanssen and Andrew Benjamin (New York: Continuum, 2002), 42–47.

123. Benjamin, GS IV, 937.

124. Benjamin, OT, 48.

125. Lemke, *Gedächtnisräume des Selbst*, 58: "Im Mittelpunkt stehen die unterschiedlichen Ähnlichkeitsbeziehungen zwischen der semantischen, der graphischen und der phonetischen Ebene im Rahmen einer allgemeinen Semiotik, die nicht auf das sprachliche Zeichen begrenzt ist, sondern die Welt als Ganzes zeichenhaft zu lesen versteht."

126. "Multum in parvo, the miniaturization of language itself, displays the ability of language to 'sum up' the diversity of the sensual, or physical, world of lived experience." Stewart, *On Longing*, 52–53. Stewart cites Carl Zigrosser's concept of the *multum in parvo* in her discussion of the ideological and linguistic ramifications of miniature representations. Zigrosser himself writes, "In its terse and compact Latin diction, it exemplifies exactly what it connotes: much in little.... A multiplicity of detail is concentrated into a unified principle, the particular is transformed into the universal, a largeness of meaning is conveyed with the utmost economy of means." Though his brief essay explores primarily tiny engravings, quatrains, and other pithy texts, he could have added Leibniz's monad to this

paradoxical vision. Carl Zigrosser, *Multum in parvo: An Essay in Poetic Imagination* (New York: G. Braziller, 1965), 11.

127. Leibniz, PE, 221.

128. Benjamin, SW 2:2, 613. Benjamin, GS VI, 489 For a brief overview of the archival evidence for the manuscript history of *Berlin Chronicle* and its relationship to the development of the manuscript for *Berlin Childhood around 1900* see the editors' "Notes" ("Anmerkungen") in Benjamin, GS VI, 798–799.

129. Benjamin, SW 2:2, 613. Benjamin, GS VI, 489.

130. Werner, *Archäologie des Erinnerns*, 327.

131. Werner, *Archäologie des Erinnerns*, 259–260.

132. In her argument that *Berlin Childhood* reflects a specific theory of memory, Werner situates the poetic techniques of "archaeology," visible within the vignettes themselves, alongside the larger form of the text as an iterative collection—i.e., Benjamin's process of "archaeological memory" and the critical practice of encountering the author's often differing surviving typescripts. Werner, *Archäologie des Erinnerns*, 298–299.

133. Benjamin, SW III, 345; Benjamin, GS VII, 386: "Wie eine Mutter, die das Neugeborene an ihre Brust legt ohne es zu wecken, verfährt das Leben lange Zeit mit der noch zarten Erinnerung an die Kindheit. Nichts kräftigte die meine inniger als der Blick in Höfe, von deren dunklen Loggien eine, die im Sommer von Markisen beschattet wurde, für mich die Wiege war, in die die Stadt den neuen Bürger legte. Die Karyatiden, die die Loggia des nächsten Stockwerks trugen, mochten ihren Platz für einen Augenblick verlassen haben, um an dieser Wiege ein Lied zu singen, das wenig von dem enthielt, was mich für später erwartete, dafür jedoch den Spruch, durch den die Luft der Höfe mir auf immer berauschend blieb. Ich glaube, daß ein Beisatz dieser Luft noch um die Weinberge von Capri war, in denen ich die Geliebte umschlungen hielt; und es ist eben diese Luft, in der die Bilder und Allegorien stehen, die über meinem Denken herrschen wie die Karyatiden auf der Loggienhöhe über die Höfe des Berliner Westens."

134. Leibniz, PE, 220.

135. Michael Jennings has characterized the covered balcony in this passage as camera-like, thus reading it as part of a larger, ongoing concern of Benjamin for the politics of mediation. He connects the physical box, or loge, of the loggia with Benjamin's interests in spectatorship, the camera obscura, and photographic motifs. As I have already argued, however, not only can we understand his deployment of photographic processes, such as enlargement, as germane to the monadic logic childhood, but Benjamin also seems to have also attempted to incorporate other microscopic models to explain the task of writing childhood. Michael W. Jennings, "The Mausoleum of Youth: Between Experience and Nihilism in Benjamin's *Berlin Childhood*," *Paragraph* 32, no. 3 (November 2009): 313–330.

136. Benjamin, SW III, 345; Benjamin, GS VII, 386: "Im Hofe beschäftigte mich die Stelle, wo der Baum stand, am häufigsten. Sie war im Pflaster ausgespart, in das ein breiter Eisenring versenkt war. Stäbe durchzogen ihn so, daß sie das nackte

Erdreich vergitterten. Es schien mir nicht umsonst so eingefaßt; manchmal sann ich dem nach, was in der schwarzen Kute, aus der der Stamm kam, vorging."

137. Benjamin, SW III, 345 and Benjamin, GS VII, 386.

138. On memory and allegories of representation as excavation, see also Sigrid Weigel, *Entstellte Ähnlichkeit: Walter Benjamins theoretische Schreibweise* (Frankfurt am Main: Fischer Verlag, 1997), 29–31.

139. Weber, *Benjamin's -abilities*, 245–246.

140. Werner, *Archäologie des Erinnerns*, 329.

141. Benjamin, GS VII, 386; SW III, 345.

142. Jennings also uses the term "palimpsestic" in his essay to describe his theory of Benjamin's writing practice as one moves from "an explicitly ekphrastic text" to one which uses "the metaphorics of photography." Here he reads Benjamin childhood-centered texts as deployed in the service of adulthood: namely, "as training manual[s]" for "reading textual images as if they were photographs." "Double Take," 43.

143. Benjamin, GS VII, 386; SW III, 345.

144. Muñoz, *Cruising Utopia*, 25.

145. Muñoz, *Cruising Utopia*, 25.

146. See for example, Buck-Morss, *Dialectics of Seeing*; Jennings, "The Mausoleum of Youth"; Wolin, *Walter Benjamin*; and Giuriato, *Mikrographien*.

147. Sianne Ngai, *Theory of the Gimmick: Aesthetic Judgment and Capitalist Form* (Cambridge, MA: Belknap Press of Harvard University Press, 2020), 209.

148. Benjamin, SW III, 346 and 347.

149. Ngai describes the "capitalist gimmick" as producing an entire "genre of ambivalence" that yields a "perpetual slippage" between feelings such as "marvel" and "distrust" as well "admir[ation]" and "disdain." She also explains that a peculiar feature of the perception of the gimmick is its unavoidable and implicit linkage with cheapness. *Theory of the Gimmick*, 54, 72.

150. Jennings, "The Mausoleum of Youth," 317.

151. Benjamin, SW III, 347; GW VII, 387: "Mir schien ein kleiner, eigentlich störender Effekt ihr überlegen. Das war ein Klingeln, welches wenige Sekunden, ehe das Bild ruckweise abzog, um erst eine Lücke und dann das nächste freizugeben, anschlug."

152. Ngai, *Theory of the Gimmick*, 73.

153. Benjamin, GW VII, 388–389; Benjamin, SW III, 347. "Die fernen Welten waren denen nicht immer fremd. Es kam vor, daß die Sehnsucht, die sie erweckten, nicht in das Unbekannte, sondern nach Hause rief."

154. Benjamin, GW VII, 388–389; Benjamin, SW III, 347. "Regnete es, . . . trat [ich] ins Innere und fand in Fjorden und unter Kokospalmen dasselbe Licht, das abends bei den Schularbeiten mein Pult erhellte. Es sei denn, ein Defekt in der Beleuchtung bewirkte plötzlich, daß die Landschaft sich entfärbte."

155. Benjamin, *Arcades Project*, xi.

156. Here, I have partially modified the Eiland and McLaughlin translation of "das Neue wiedererkennen" ("recognize the new once again") by substituting Buck-Morss's more interpretive "discover the new anew." Benjamin, *Arcades Project*, 390; Buck-Morss, *Dialectics of Seeing*, 274. Benjamin, GS V, 493 (K1a, 3): "Aufgabe der Kindheit: die neue Welt in den Symbolraum einzubringen. Das Kind kann ja, was der Erwachsene durchaus nicht vermag, das Neue wiedererkennen. Uns haben, weil wir sie in der Kindheit vorfanden, die Lokomotiven schon Symbolcharakter. Unsern Kindern aber die Automobile, denen wir selber nur die neue, elegante, moderne, kesse Seite abgewinnen. . . . Jeder wahrhaft neuen Naturgestalt—und im Grunde ist auch die Technik eine solche, entsprechen neue 'Bilder.' Jede Kindheit entdeckt diese neuen Bilder um sie dem Bilderschatz der Menschheit einzuverleiben."

157. Benjamin, SW III, 356; Benjamin, GS V, 396. "In seinen Blättern haftete die Spur von Fingern, die sie umgeschlagen hatten. . . . Vor allem aber hatte sich der Rücken viel bieten lassen müssen; daher kam es, daß beide Deckelhälften sich von selbst verschoben und der Schnitt des Bandes Treppchen und Terrassen bildete. An seinen Blättern aber hingen, wie Altweibersommer am Geäst der Bäume, bisweilen schwache Fäden eines Netzes, in das ich einst beim Lesenlernen mich verstrickt hatte."

158. From Leibniz's letter to Bernoulli, dated November 18, 1698. Leibniz, *PE*, 169.

159. Benjamin, GW VII, 396; Benjamin, SW III, 356. "Manchmal jedoch, im Winter, wenn ich in der warmen Stube am Fenster stand, erzählte das Schneegestöber draußen mir so lautlos. Was es erzählte, hatte ich zwar nie genau erfassen können, denn zu dicht und unablässig drängte zwischen dem Altbekannten Neues sich heran. Kaum hatte ich mich einer Flockenschar inniger angeschlossen, erkannte ich, daß sie mich einer anderen hatte überlassen müssen, die plötzlich in sie eingedrungen war. Nun aber war der Augenblick gekommen, im Gestöber der Lettern den Geschichten nachzugehen, die sich am Fenster mir entzogen hatten. Die fernen Länder, welche mir in ihnen begegneten, spielten vertraulich wie die Flocken umeinander." See Anja Lemke, "'Im Gestöber der Lettern': Mediale Übersetzungsprozesse der Erinnerung in Walter Benjamins 'Berliner Kinderheit im Neunzehnhundert,'" in *Medien und Aesthetik: Festschrift für Burkhardt Lindner*, ed. H. Hillgärtner and Thomas Küpper (Bielefeld: Transcript Verlag, 2003), 42–43. See also Brueggemann, *Walter Benjamin*, 291–296.

160. See also Weigel's discussion of language, perception, and the relationship between representation and materiality of language in *Entstellte Ähnlichkeit*, 49–51.

161. Benjamin, GW VII, 396–7; Benjamin, SW III, 356.

162. Benjamin, SW III, 358; GW VII, 399: "Denn damals hieß sie mir noch nicht nach Steglitz. Der Vogel Stieglitz schenkte ihr den Namen."

163. Benjamin, SW III, 358; GW VII, 399.

164. Benjamin, SW III, 359; GW VII, 399.

165. Benjamin, SW III, 358–359; GW VII, 399, 400.

166. Benjamin, SW III, 374 and 382; GW VII, 417, 426–427.

167. Benjamin, SW III, 380; GW VII, 424: "Es ging mir wie beim Tuschen, wo die Dinge mir ihren Schoß auftaten, sobald ich sie in einer feuchten Wolke überkam. Ähnliches begab sich mit Seifenblasen. Ich reiste in ihnen durch die Stube und mischte mich ins Farbenspiel der Kuppel bis sie zersprang."

168. Benjamin, SW III, 380; GW VII, 424: "Denn ehe ich den Lockungen des Naschwerks erlegen war, hatte der höhere Sinn mit einem Schlage den niederen in mir überflügelt und mich entrückt."

169. Benjamin, SW III, 347; GW VII, 388.

170. Scholem, "Walter Benjamin," 178.

171. Giorgio Agamben, *The Signature of All Things: On Method*, trans. Luca di Santo and Kevin Attell (New York: Zone Books, 2009), 18.

172. Agamben, *The Signature of all Things*, 31. All additional quotes in this paragraph are from this page.

173. Johann Wolfgang von Goethe, *Gedenkausgabe der Werke, Briefe und Gespräche*, ed. Ernst Beutler, vol. 16 (Zurich: Artemis Verlag, 1949), 852.

174. Goethe, *Gedenkausgabe*, 852: "Eine solche Erfahrung, die aus mehreren andern besteht, ist offenbar von einer höhern Art. Sie stellt die Formel vor, unter welcher unzählige einzelne Rechnungsexempel ausgedrückt werden. Auf solche Erfahrungen der höhern Art loszuarbeiten, halt ich für höchste Pflicht des Naturforschers, und dahin weist uns das Exempel der vorzüglichsten Männer, die in diesem Fache gearbeitet haben." English quoted in Agamben, *The Signature of all Things*, 30.

175. Buck-Morss, *Dialectics of Seeing*, 265.

176. Benjamin, *The Arcades Project*, 461; GS V, 576 (N2, 1a): "Jede Kindheit bindet in ihrem Interesse für die technischen Phänomene, ihre Neugier für alle Art von Erfindungen und Maschinerien die technischen Errungenschaften an die alten Symbolwelten. Es gibt nichts im Bereiche der Natur, das solcher Bindung von Hause aus entzogen wäre. Nur bildet sie sich nicht in der Aura der Neuheit sondern in der der Gewöhnung."

177. Gess, "Gaining Sovereignty," 682–708.

178. Gess, "Gaining Sovereignty," 683.

179. Agamben, *The Signature of All Things*, 31.

180. Agamben, *The Signature of All Things*, 31–32.

181. Sara Ahmed, "Orientations toward a Queer Phenomenology," *GLQ: A Journal of Lesbian and Gay Studies* 12, no. 4 (2006): 570.

Coda: Sigmund Freud, Childhood, and the Return of Futurity

1. An incomplete list of queer theorists whose work deploys fragments or selections from Freud might include Judith Butler, Lee Edelman, Jack Halberstam; likewise, an exemplary list of his critics might include Sara Ahmed, Teresa de Lauretis, and Luce Irigaray. And, of course, any such "lists" are in no way mutually exclusive.

2. Walter Schönau, *Sigmund Freuds Prosa: Literarische Elemente seines Stils* (Giessen: Psychosozial-Verlag, 2006); Graham Frankland, *Freud's Literary Culture* (Cambridge: Cambridge University Press, 2000).

3. Luce Irigaray, *The Speculum of the Other Woman* (Ithaca, NY: Cornell University Press, 1992), 26; Sara Ahmed, *Queer Phenomenology: Orientations, Objects, Others* (Durham, NC: Duke University Press, 2006), 72–79; see also Teresa de Lauretis, *The Practice of Love: Lesbian Sexuality and Perverse Desire* (Bloomington: Indiana University Press, 1994). My thanks to Barbara N. Nagel for reminding me of Irigaray's incisive reading of the section, "The Little Girl Is (Only) a Little Boy" in Irigaray's book.

4. Eve Kosofsky Sedgwick, "Paranoid and Reparative Reading; or You're So Paranoid, You Probably Think This Introduction Is about You," in *Novel Gazing: Queer Readings in Fiction*, ed. Eve Kosofsky Sedgwick (Durham, NC: Duke University Press, 1997), 2–3.

5. Sigmund Freud, *The Standard Edition of the Complete Psychological Works of Sigmund Freud*, trans. James Strachey, vol. 22 (London: Hogarth Press, 1964), 117. Hereafter cited as SE 22; Sigmund Freud, *Gesammelte Werke, chronologisch geordnet*, ed. Anna Freud, vol. 15 (London: Imago, 1940), 124–125. Hereafter cites as GW 15.

6. Irigaray, *The Speculum of the Other Woman*, 29–30, and 35; Freud, SE 22, 118–120; Freud, GW 15, 126–128.

7. Sigmund Freud, *The Standard Edition of the Complete Psychological Works of Sigmund Freud*, trans. James Strachey, vol. 5 (London: Hogarth Press, 1950), 303. Hereafter cited as SE 5. Sigmund Freud, *Gesammelte Werke, chronologisch geordnet*, ed. Anna Freud, vol. 1 (London: Imago, 1952), 530. Hereafter cited as GW 1.

8. Freud, SE 5, 305–306; GW 1, 534–535: "daß bei manchen Personen die frühesten Kindheitserinnerungen alltägliche und gleichgültige Eindrücke zum Inhalt haben . . . und die doch mit allen Details—man möchte sagen: überscharf— gemerkt worden sind. . ."

9. Freud, SE 5, 303, 306–307; GW 1, 530, 535–536. Lorna Martens summarizes the context of Freud's writing on childhood memories succinctly: "Freud's memory theory was based in the concept of repression, and Freud first postulated repression in *Studies on Hysteria* to account for the after-effects of 'forgotten' trauma." Lorna Martens, *The Promise of Memory: Childhood Recollection and Its Objects in Literary Modernism* (Cambridge, MA: Harvard University Press, 2011), 37.

10. Freud, SE 5, 311; GW 1, 540.

11. Freud, SE 5, 303; GW 1, 530.

12. As Madelon Sprengnether writes, in "Screen Memories" Freud "makes the startling claim that memories from childhood vividly recalled in adult life bear no specific relationship to what happened in the past. Rather, they are composite formations—elements of childhood experience as represented through the distorting lens of adult wishes, fantasies, and desires." Madelon Sprengnether, "Freud as Memoirist: A Reading of 'Screen Memories,'" *American Imago* 69, no. 2

(Summer 2012): 215. This is pattern is well established across Freud's major works. For example, in *Die Traumdeutung* (*The Interpretation of Dreams*), the reappearance of childhood in adult dreams—the persistence of childhood imagery—is explanatory for the adult's contemporary condition. See, for example, Harvie Ferguson, *The Lure of Dreams: Sigmund Freud and the Construction of Modernity* (London: Routledge, 1996), 73–75.

13. Freud, SE 5, 303; GW 1, 530. For discussion of Freud as literary critic and literary writer, see Frankland, *Freud's Literary Culture*, and for Freud's literary influences on representing childhood memories see Martens, *The Promise of Childhood*, and Nadine Werner, *Archäologie des Erinnerns: Sigmund Freud in Walter Benjamins Berliner Kindheit* (Göttingen: Wallstein Verlag, 2015).

14. Freud, SE 5, 311; GW 1, 540–541.

15. Freud, SE 5, 318–319; GW 1, 549.

16. Sprengnether, "Freud as Memoirist," 217–218.

17. The analogy I am drawing between Freud's descriptions of everyday childhood attention and Stockton's figure of the queer child has its limits, however. She further argues that the queer child ultimately does not belong to such an easy temporality of futurity, and ultimately finds that the latency of belated gayness means that "[protogay children] never 'are' what they latently 'were.'" She thus reads the child's "protogayness" in line with Derrida's notion of *différance* (both "originary" and also "crossed out"). Kathryn Bond Stockton, *The Queer Child, or Growing Sideways in the Twentieth Century* (Durham, NC: Duke University Press, 2009), 14. Jacques Derrida, "Freud and the Scene of Writing," trans. Jeffrey Mehlman, *Yale French Studies* 48 (1972): 81. Jacques Derrida, "Différance," in *Deconstruction in Context: Literature and Philosophy*, ed. Mark C. Taylor (Chicago: University of Chicago Press, 1986), 413.

18. Freud, SE 5, 320; GW 1, 551: "wenn wir nämlich die unvollständige und durch diese Unvollständigkeit harmlose Infantilszene mit unter den Begriff der Deckerinnerung fallen lassen."

19. James Kincaid, *Child-Loving: The Erotic Child and Victorian Culture* (New York: Routledge, 1992), 78.

20. Freud, *Standard Edition*, vol. 17 (London: Hogarth Press, 1955), 148. Hereafter cited as SE 17; *Gesammelte Werke*, vol. 12 (London: Imago, 1947), 17. Hereafter cited as GW 12.

21. Freud, SE 17, 148; GW 12, 17.

22. Freud SE 17, 148; GW 12, 17.

23. By contrast, as Vanessa Smith has shown in her reading of Victorian scenes of children destroying toys that Melanie Klein's theories revalue "psychic development toward early childhood and its objects" as her "observations of children playing involved an increasingly intricate conceptualization of the object as both symbol and mediator of internal states of feeling," thus giving far more credence to the affect and interiority of child subjects. Vanessa Smith, "Toy Stories," *Novel* 50, no. 1 (2017): 40.

24. Martens, *The Promise of Childhood*, 4.

25. Freud, SE 17, 152; GW 12, 21–22: "Wir brauchen das Vergnügen des Kindes beim Zerschellen der Gegenstände nicht zu bestreiten; . . . Aber wir glauben nicht, daß es die Lust am Klirren und Brechen war, welche solchen Kinderstreichen einen dauernden Platz in der Erinnerung des Erwachsenen sichern konnte."

26. Freud, SE 17, 152; GW 12, 22.

27. Freud, SE 17, 148; GW 12, 17: "Um sie in ihrer Bedeutsamkeit zu erkennen, bedurfte es einer gewissen Deutungsarbeit . . ."

28. Freud, SE 17, 153; GW 12, 23.

29. Freud, SE 17, 153–154; GW 12, 23–24: "Es war also so, als ob der Patient gesagt hätte."

30. Freud, SE 17, 153–154; GW 12, 23: "Wir verstehen, daß das zweijährige Kind darum unruhig war, weil es das Beisammensein von Vater und Mutter im Bette nicht leiden wollte. Auf der Reise war es wohl nicht anders möglich, als das Kind zum Zeugen dieser Gemeinschaft werden zu lassen. Von den Gefühlen, die sich damals in dem kleinen Eifersüchtigen regten, ist ihm die Erbitterung gegen das Weib verblieben, und diese hat eine dauernde Störung seiner Liebesentwicklung zur Folge gehabt."

31. Barbara N. Nagel, *Ambiguous Aggression in German Realism and Beyond: Flirtation, Passive Aggression, Domestic Violence* (New York: Bloomsbury, 2019), 88. Freud GW 12, 199: "Auf alle diese Fragen kam keine aufklärende Auskunft, immer nur die eine scheue Antwort: Ich weiß nichts mehr darüber; ein Kind wird geschlagen."

32. Ahmed, *Queer Phenomenology*, 71–79.

33. Ahmed, *Queer Phenomenology*, 71–72.

34. Lee Edelman, *No Future: Queer Theory and the Death Drive* (Durham, NC: Duke University Press, 2004), 41. With this passage Edelman irreverently suggests an equivalent alliance between literalism and fantasy in the biblical "a family is created" and Freud's "a child is being beaten."

Works Cited

Adorno, Theodor. *Gesammelte Schriften*. Edited by Rolf Tiedemann. Frankfurt am Main: Suhrkamp Verlag, 1997.
Adorno, Theodor. *Minima Moralia: Reflexionen aus dem beschädigten Leben*. Frankfurt am Main: Suhrkamp Verlag, 1970.
Adorno, Theodor. *Minima Moralia: Reflections on a Damaged Life*. London: Verso, 2005.
Adorno, Theodor. *Notes to Literature*. Vol. 2. Translated by Sherry Weber Nicholsen. New York: Columbia University Press, 1992.
Agamben, Giorgio. *The Signature of All Things: On Method*. Translated by Luca di Santo and Kevin Attell. New York: Zone Books, 2009.
Ahmed, Sara. "Orientations: Toward a Queer Phenomenology." *GLQ: A Journal of Lesbian and Gay Studies* 12, no. 4 (2006): 543–574.
Ahmed, Sara. *The Promise of Happiness*. Durham, NC: Duke University Press, 2010.
Ahmed, Sara. *Queer Phenomenology: Orientations, Objects, Others*. Durham, NC: Duke University Press, 2006.
Ahmed, Sara. "Willful Parts: Problem Characters or the Problem of Character." *New Literary History* 42, no. 2 (Spring 2011): 231–253.
Ariès, Philippe. *Centuries of Childhood: A Social History of Family Life*. Translated by Robert Baldick. New York: Alfred A Knopf, 1962.
Arndal, Steffen. "Sehenlernen und Pseudoskopie." *Orbis Litterarum* 62, no. 3 (2007): 210–229.
Assmann, Aleida. "Werden was wir waren: Anmerkungen zur Geschichte der Kindheitsidee." *Antike und Abendland* 24 (1978): 98–124.
Attanucci, Timothy. *The Restorative Poetics of a Geological Age: Stifter, Viollet-le-Duc, and the Aesthetic Practices of Geohistoricism*. Berlin: De Gruyter, 2020.
Auerbach, Berthold. *Schrift und Volk: Grundzüge der volksthümlichen Literatur*. Leipzig: Brockhaus, 1846.

Austin, Linda M. "Children of Childhood: Nostalgia and the Romantic Legacy." *Studies in Romanticism* 42, no. 1 (March 1, 2003): 75–98.
Bachelard, Gaston. *The Poetics of Space*. Translated by Maria Jolas. Boston: Beacon Press, 1994.
Bajohr, Hannes, Florian Fuchs, and Joe Paul Kroll. Introduction to *History, Metaphors, Fables: A Hans Blumenberg Reader*, edited by Bajohr, Fuchs, and Kroll, 1–29. Ithaca, NY: Cornell University Press, 2020.
Barber, Stephen M., and David L. Clark. "Queer Moments: The Performative Temporalities of Eve Kosofsky Sedgwick." In *Regarding Sedgwick: Essays on Queer Culture and Critical Theory*, edited by Barber and Clark, 1–53. New York: Routledge, 2002.
Benjamin, Walter. *The Arcades Project*. Translated by Howard Eiland and Kevin McLaughlin. Cambridge, MA: Belknap Press of Harvard University Press, 1999.
Benjamin, Walter. *Einbahnstraße: Werke und Nachlaß: Kritische Gesamtausgabe*. Edited by Detlev Schöttker and Steffen Haug. Vol. 8. Frankfurt a.M.: Suhrkamp Verlag, 2009.
Benjamin, Walter. *Gesammelte Schriften*. Edited by Rolf Tiedemann and Hermann Schweppenhäuser. Vol. I–VII. Frankfurt am Main: Suhrkamp Verlag, 1991.
Benjamin, Walter. *The Origin of German Tragic Drama*. Translated by John Osborne. London: Verso, 1998.
Benjamin, Walter. *Selected Writings*. Edited by Michael W. Jennings, Howard Eiland, and Gary Smith. Vol. 1–5. Cambridge, MA: Belknap Press of Harvard University Press, 2005.
Berlant, Lauren. *The Queen of America Goes to Washington City: Essay on Sex and Citizenship*. Durham, NC: Duke University Press, 1997.
Bermes, Christian. "Die Lebenswelt." In *Husserl Handbuch: Leben—Werk—Wirkung*, edited by Sebastian Luft and Maren Wehle, 230–236. Stuttgart: Metzler Verlag, 2017.
Blumenberg, Hans. *The Laughter of the Thracian Woman: A Protohistory of Theory*. New York: Bloomsbury, 2015.
Blumenberg, Hans. "Pensiveness." In *History, Metaphors, Fables: A Hans Blumenberg Reader*, translated by Hannes Bajohr, Florian Fuchs, and Joe Paul Kroll, 525–530. Ithaca, NY: Cornell University Press, 2020.
Blumenberg, Hans. *Zu den Sachen und zurück; Aus dem Nachlass*. Edited by Manfred Sommer. Frankfurt am Main: Suhrkamp Verlag, 2002.
Bollnow, Otto Friedrich. *Rilke*. Stuttgart: W. Kohlhammer, 1956.
Borchmeyer, Dieter. "Ideologie der Familie und ästhetische Gesellschaftskritik in Stifters 'Nachsommer.'" *Zeitschrift für deutsche Philologie* 99 (January 1980): 226–254.
Boy, Alina. "Marie im Wunderland: Animation und Imagination in Hoffmanns Nußknacker und Mausekönig." *E. T. A Hoffmann-Jarhbuch* 24 (2016): 34–48.
Bradley, Brigitte L. "Rilke's 'Geschichten vom lieben Gott': The Narrator's Stance toward the Bourgeoisie." *Modern Austrian Literature* 15, no. 3/4 (1982): 1–23.

Brown, Hilda Meldrum. *E. T. A. Hoffmann and the Serapiontic Principle: Critique and Creativity.* Rochester, NY: Boydell & Brewer, 2006.
Brüggemann, Heinz. "Fragmente zur Aesthetik / Phantasie und Farbe." In *Benjamin Handbuch: Leben—Wirkung—Werk*, ed. Burkhart Lindner, 124–133. Stuttgart: Metzler Verlag, 2006.
Brüggemann, Heinz. *Walter Benjamin: Über Spiel, Farbe und Phantasie.* Würzburg: Königshausen und Neumann, 2011.
Buck-Morss, Susan. *The Dialectics of Seeing: Walter Benjamin and the Arcades Project.* Cambridge, MA: MIT Press, 1989.
Büssgen, Antje. "Bildende Kunst." In *Rilke Handbuch: Leben—Werk—Wirkung*, edited by Manfred Engel, 130–150. Stuttgart: Metzler Verlag, 2004.
Campbell, Karen J. "Toward a Truer Mimesis: Stifter's Turmalin." *German Quarterly* 57, no. 4 (Autumn 1984): 576–589.
Cavell, Stanley. *The Claim of Reason: Wittgenstein, Skepticism, Morality, and Tragedy.* New York: Oxford University Press, 1999.
Cohn, Dorrit. *Transparent Minds: Narrative Modes for Presenting Consciousness in Fiction.* Princeton, NJ: Princeton University Press, 1978.
Crowther, Paul. *The Phenomenology of Aesthetic Consciousness and Phantasy: Working with Husserl.* London: Routledge, 2022.
Cunningham, Hugh. *Children and Childhood in Western Society since 1500.* Harlow, Eng.: Pearson, 2005.
Daub, Adrian. *The Dynastic Imagination: Family and Modernity in Nineteenth-Century Germany.* Chicago: University of Chicago Press, 2021.
De Certeau, Michel. *The Practice of Everyday Life*, Translated by Steven Rendall. Berkeley: University of California Press, 1984.
De Lauretis, Teresa. *The Practice of Love: Lesbian Sexuality and Perverse Desire.* Bloomington: Indiana University Press, 1994.
Deleuze, Gilles, and Félix Guattari. *Kafka: Toward a Minor Literature.* Translated by Dana Polan. Minneapolis: University of Minnesota Press, 1986.
Derrida, Jacques. *"Différance."* In *Deconstruction in Context: Literature and Philosophy*, edited by Mark C. Taylor, 396–420. Chicago: University of Chicago Press, 1986.
Derrida, Jacques. "Freud and the Scene of Writing." Translated by Jeffrey Mehlman. *Yale French Studies* 48 (1972): 74–117.
Dieterle, Bernard. "Erzählungen." In *Rilke Handbuch: Leben—Werk—Wirkung*, edited by Manfred Engel, 239–263. Stuttgart: Metzler Verlag, 2004.
Dolbear, Sam, and Hannah Proctor. "'Cracking Open the Natural Teleology': Walter Benjamin, Charles Fourier, and the Figure of the Child." *Pedagogy, Culture & Society* 24, no. 4 (2016): 495–503.
Downing, Eric. *Double Exposure: Repetition and Realism in Nineteenth-Century German Fiction.* Stanford, CA: Stanford University Press, 2000.
Edelman, Lee. *No Future: Queer Theory and the Death Drive.* Durham, NC: Duke University Press, 2004.

Ehlbeck, Birgit. "Zur poetologischen Funktionalisierung des Empirismus am Beispiel von Stifters 'Kalkstein' und 'Witiko.'" In *Adalbert Stifter: Dichter und Maler, Denkmalpfleger und Schulmann*, edited by Karl Mösender, 457–460. Tubingen: Niemeyer Verlag, 1996.

Elsaesser, Thomas. "Tales of Sound and Fury." In *Home Is Where the Heart Is: Studies in Melodrama and the Woman's Film*, edited by Christine Gledhill, 43–69. London: British Film Institute, 1987.

Ewers, Hans-Heino. "Geschichte der deutschen Kinder- und Jugendliteratur: Eine problemgeschichtliche Skizze." https://www.uni-frankfurt.de/64851467/Geschichte-der-KJL.pdf (retrieved May 23, 2024).

Ewers, Hans-Heino. *Kinder- und Jugendliteratur der Romantik: Eine Textsammlung*. Stuttgart: Philipp Reclam jun., 1984.

Ewers, Hans-Heino. *Kindheit als poetische Daseinsform: Studien zur Entstehung der romantischen Kindheitsutopie im 18. Jahrhundert: Herder, Jean Paul, Novalis und Tieck*. Munich: Wilhelm Fink Verlag, 1989.

Fauconneau-Dufresne, Eva. "Wirklichkeitserfahrung und Bewußtseinsentwicklung in Rilkes Malte Laurids Brigge und Sartres La Nausée." *Arcadia* 17 (1982): 258–273.

Felski, Rita. *Doing Time: Feminist Theory and Postmodern Culture*. New York: New York University Press, 2000.

Ferguson, Harvie. *The Lure of Dreams: Sigmund Freud and the Construction of Modernity*. London: Routledge, 1996.

Finkelde, Dominik. "Tautologien der Ordnung: Zu einer Poetologie des Sammelns bei Adalbert Stifter." *German Quarterly* 80, no. 1 (January 1, 2007): 1–19.

Fischer, Luke. *The Poet as Phenomenologist: Rilke and the New Poems*. New York: Bloomsbury Academic, 2015.

Fleming, Paul. "On the Edge of Non-contingency: Anecdotes and the Lifeworld." *Telos* 158 (Spring 2012): 21–35.

Fleming, Paul. "The Promises of Childhood: Autobiography in Goethe and Jean Paul." *Goethe Yearbook* 14 (2007): 27–38.

Føllesdal, Dagfinn. "The Lebenswelt in Husserl." In *Science and the Life-World: Essays on Husserl's Crises of the European Sciences*, edited by David Hyder and Hans-Jörg Rheinberger, 27–45. Stanford, CA: Stanford University Press, 2010.

Forrest, Tara. *The Politics of Imagination: Benjamin, Kracauer, Kluge*. Bielefeld: Transcript Verlag, 2007.

Foucault, Michel. *The Order of Things*. New York: Vintage, 1994.

Frankland, Graham. *Freud's Literary Culture*. Cambridge: Cambridge University Press, 2000.

Freeman, Elizabeth. *Time Binds: Queer Temporalities, Queer Histories*. Durham, NC: Duke University Press, 2010.

Freud, Sigmund. *Gesammelte Werke, chronologisch geordnet*. 17 volumes. Edited by Anna Freud. London: Imago, 1940–1952.

Freud, Sigmund. *The Standard Edition of the Complete Psychological Works of Sigmund Freud.* Translated by James Strachey. 24 volumes. London: Hogarth Press, 1953–1974.
Frey, Christiane. "The Art of Observing the Small: On the Borders of the Subvisibilia (from Hooke to Brockes)." *Monatshefte* 105, no. 3 (2013): 376–388.
Fuchs, Florian. "Decoding Aesop: Blumenberg's Fabulistic Turn." *New German Critique* 49, no. 1 (145) (2022): 163–183.
Fülleborn, Ulrich. "Form und Sinn der Aufzeichnungen des Malte Laurids Brigge." In *Deutsche Romantheorien*, edited by R. Grimm, 251–273. Frankfurt am Main: De Gruyter, 1968.
Genette, Gérard. *Narrative Discourse: An Essay in Method.* Edited and translated by Jane E. Lewin. Ithaca, NY: Cornell University Press, 1980.
Gess, Nicola. "Gaining Sovereignty: On the Figure of the Child in Walter Benjamin's Writing." *MLN* 125, no. 3 (2010): 682–708.
Geulen, Eva. "Adalbert Stifters Kinder-Kunst Drei Fallstudien." *Deutsche Vierteljahresschrift für Literaturwissenschaft und Geistesgeschichte* 67, no. 4 (1993): 647–668.
Geulen, Eva. "Kinderlos." *Internationales Archiv fur Sozialgeschichte der deutschen Literatur* (IASL) 40, no. 2 (2015): 424–425.
Geulen, Eva. "Tales of a Collector: Adalbert Stifter's Bunte Steine." In *A New History of German Literature*, edited by David Wellbery et al., 587–591. Cambridge, MA: Harvard University Press, 2004.
Gillespie, Susan H. "On 'Amorbach.'" *New German Critique* 43, no. 1 [127] (February 2016): 215–226.
Giuriato, Davide. "Kindheit." In *Stifter-Handbuch: Leben—Werk—Wirkung*, edited by Christian Begemann and Davide Giuriato, 342–345. Stuttgart: Metzler Verlag, 2017.
Giuriato, Davide. *Mikrographien: Zu einer Poetologie des Schreibens in Walter Benjamins Kindheitserinnerungen (1932–1939).* Munich: Wilhelm Fink Verlag, 2006.
Giuriato, Davide."Zur Einleitung." In *Kindheit und Literatur: Konzepte—Poetik—Wissen*, edited by Davide Giuriato, Philipp Hubmann, and Mareike Schildmann, 7–24. Freiburg: Rombach Verlag, 2018.
Goebel, Rolf J. "China as an Embalmed Mummy: Herder's Orientalist Poetics." *South Atlantic Review* 60, no. 1 (January 1995): 111–119.
Goethe, Johann Wolfgang von. *Aus meinem Leben: Dichtung und Wahrheit.* Zurich: Artemis-Verlag, 1948.
Goethe, Johann Wolfgang von. *Gedenkausgabe der Werke, Briefe und Gespräche.* Edited by Ernst Beutler, vol. 16. Zurich: Artemis Verlag, 1949.
Goode, Mike, *Sentimental Masculinity and the Rise of History, 1790–1890.* Cambridge: Cambridge University Press, 2009.
Gosetti-Ferencei, Jennifer Anna. *The Ecstatic Quotidian: Phenomenological Sightings in Modern Art and Literature.* University Park: Pennsylvania State University Press, 2007.

Gosetti-Ferencei, Jennifer Anna. "Interstitial Space in Rilke's Short Prose Works." *German Quarterly* 80, no. 3 (2007): 302–324.
Gross, Kenneth. Introduction to *On Dolls*, edited by Kenneth Gross, xi–xx. London: Notting Hill Editions, 2018.
Groves, Jason. *The Geological Unconscious: German Literature and the Mineral Imaginary*. New York: Fordham University Press, 2020.
Guarín, Alejandro. "Alexander von Humboldt and the Origins of Our Modern Geographical View of the Earth." In *WorldMinds: Geographical Perspectives on 100 Problems*, edited by Donald G. Janelle, Barney Warf, and Kathy Hansen, 607–612. Berlin: Springer, 2004.
Hamburger, Käte. "Die Phänomenologische Struktur der Dichtung Rilkes." In *Rilke in neuer Sicht*, edited by Käte Hamburger, 83–158. Stuttgart: Kohlhammer, 1971.
Hamburger, Käte. *Philosophie der Dichter: Novalis, Schiller, Rilke*. Stuttgart: W. Kohlhammer, 1966.
Helbig, Daniela K. "No More Than Seeing: Hans Blumenberg's Poetics of Spectatorship." *New German Critique* 49, no. 1 (2022): 185–213.
Hertling, Gunter. "'Wer jetzt kein Haus hat, baut sich keines mehr': Zur Zentralsymbolik in Adalbert Stifters 'Turmalin.'" *VASILO* 26, no. 1/2 (1977): 17–34.
Heywood, Colin. *A History of Childhood: Children and Childhood in the West from Medieval to Modern Times*. Cambridge: Polity Press, 2018.
Hirsch, Marianne. *Family Frames: Photography, Narrative, and Postmemory*. Cambridge, MA: Harvard University Press, 1997.
Hoffmann, E. T. A. *Poetische Werke in sechs Bänden*. Vol. 3. Berlin: Aufbau, 1963.
Hofstätter, Ernst. *Beiträge zur Geschichte der österreichischen Landesaufnahmen: Ein Überblick der topographischen Aufnahmeverfahren, deren Ursprünge, ihrer Entwicklungen und Organisationsformen der vier österreichischen Landesaufnahmen*. 2 vols. Vienna: Bundesamt für Eich- und Vermessungswesen, 1989.
Hoke, Sarah. *Fritz von Uhdes "Kinderstube": Die Darstellung des Kindes in seinem Spiel- und Wohnmilieu*. Göttingen: Universitätsverlag Göttingen, 2011.
Holmes, Tove. "An Archive of the Earth: Stifter's Geologos." *Seminar* 53, no. 3 (September 2018): 281–290.
Holub, Robert C. "Adalbert Stifter's 'Brigitta' or the Lesson of Realism." In *A Companion to German Realism, 1848–1900*, edited by Todd Kontje, 29–52. Rochester, NY: Camden House, 2002.
Honig, Michael-Sebastian. *Entwurf einer Theorie der Kindheit*. Frankfurt am Main: Suhrkamp Verlag, 1999.
Husserl, Edmund. *Husserliana: Gesammelte Werke*. Vol. 23. The Hague: Martinus Nijhoff Publishers, 1980.
Husserl, Edmund. *Husserliana: Gesammelte Werke*. Vol. 3, 1. The Hague: Martinus Nijhoff Publishers, 1976.

Husserl, Edmund. *Ideas for a Pure Phenomenology and Phenomenological Philosophy*. Vol. 1. Indianapolis: Hackett, 2014.
Husserl, Edmund. *Phantasy, Image Consciousness, and Memory, 1898–1925*. Edited and translated by John B. Brough. Dordrecht: Springer, 2005.
Hutchinson, Ben. "'Ici commence l'indicible': Hans Blumenbergs Überlegungen zur Unmöglichkeit des Beginnens beim späten Rilke." *Études Germaniques* 249, no. 1 (2008): 115–129.
Huyssen, Andreas. "Paris/Childhood: The Fragmented Body in Rilke's *Notebooks of Malte Laurids Brigge*." In *Modernity and the Text: Revisions of German Modernism*, edited by Andreas Huyssen and David Bathrick, 113–141. New York: Columbia University Press, 1989.
Irigaray, Luce. *The Speculum of the Other Woman*. Ithaca, NY: Cornell University Press, 1992.
Irmscher, Hans Dietrich. *Adalbert Stifter: Wirklichkeitserfahrung und gegenständliche Darstellung*. Munich: Wilhelm Fink Verlag, 1971.
Irmscher, Hans Dietrich. "Die Verkündigung auf dem Berge: Zur Theodizee in Adalbert Stifters Erzählung 'Bergkristall.'" *Sprachkunst* 30, no. 1 (1999): 1–9.
Jastrow, Joseph. "The Mind's Eye" *Popular Science Monthly* 54 (1899): 299–312.
Jennings, Michael W. "Double Take: Palimpsestic Writing and Image-Character in Benjamin's Late Prose." *Benjamin-Studien* 2 (2011): 33–44.
Jennings, Michael W. Introduction to *One-Way Street*, by Walter Benjamin, edited by Michael W. Jennings, 1–20. Cambridge, MA: Harvard University Press, 2016.
Jennings, Michael W. "The Mausoleum of Youth: Between Experience and Nihilsm in Benjamin's Berlin Childhood." *Paragraph* 32, no. 3 (2009): 313–330.
Jorgensen, Larry M. "Leibniz on Memory and Consciousness." *British Journal for the History of Philosophy* 19, no. 5 (2011): 887–916.
Jorgensen, Larry M. "Leibniz on Perceptual Distinctness, Activity, and Sensation." *Journal of the History of Philosophy* 53, no. 1 (2015): 49–77.
Junyk, Ihor. "'A Fragment from Another Context': Modernist Classicism and the Urban Uncanny in Rainer Maria Rilke." *Comparative Literature* 62 (2010): 262–282.
Keegan, Cáel M. "Against Queer Theory." *Transgender Studies Quarterly* 7, no. 3 (2020): 349–353.
Keegan, Cáel M. "Transgender Studies, or How to Do Things with Trans*." In *The Cambridge Companion to Queer Studies*, edited by Siobhan B. Somerville, 66–78. Cambridge: Cambridge University Press, 2020.
Kelley, Theresa M. "'Fantastic Shapes': From Classical Rhetoric to Romantic Allegory." *Texas Studies in Literature and Language* 33, no. 2 (1991): 225–260.
Kidd, Kenneth B. *Theory for Beginners: Children's Literature as Critical Thought*. New York: Fordham University Press, 2020.
Kincaid, James. *Child-Loving: The Erotic Child and Victorian Culture*. New York: Routledge, 1992.

Koschorke, Albrecht. "Das buchstabierte Panorama: Zu einer Passage in Stifters Erzählung *Granit*." *VASILO* 38, no. 1/2 (1989): 3–13.
Koschorke, Albrecht. *Die Geschichte des Horizonts: Grenze und Grenzlosigkeit in literarischen Landschaftsbildern*. Frankfurt am Main: Suhrkamp, 1990.
Koschorke, Albrecht. "Erziehung zum Freitod: Adalbert Stifters pädagogischer Realismus." In *Die Dinge und die Zeichen: Dimensionen des Realistischen in der Erzählliteratur des 19. Jahrhunderts*, for Helmut Pfotenhauer, edited by Sabine Schneider and Barbara Hunfeld, 319–332. Würzburg: Königshausen & Neumann, 2008.
Koschorke, Albrecht, et al. *Vor der Familie: Grenzbedingungen einer modernen Institution*. Munich: Wilhelm Fink Verlag, 2010.
Kracauer, Siegfried, and Thomas Y. Levin. "Photography." *Critical Inquiry* 19, no. 3 (1993): 421–436.
Krauss, Rosalind E. "Grids." In *The Originality of the Avant-Garde and Other Modernist Myths*, ed. Rosalind E. Kraus, 9–22. Cambridge, MA: MIT Press, 1984.
Kristeva, Julia. "Women's Time." Translated by Alice Jardine and Harry Blake. *Signs* 7, no. 1 (Autumn 1981): 13–35.
Lefebvre, Henri. "The Everyday and Everydayness." Translated by Christine Levich. *Yale French Studies* 73 (1987): 7–11.
Leibniz, G. W. *Philosophical Essays*. Edited by Roger Ariew and Daniel Garber. Indianapolis: Hackett, 1989.
Lemke, Anja. *Gedächtnisräume des Selbst: Walter Benjamins "Berliner Kindheit um neunzehnhundert."* Würzberg: Königshausen und Neumann, 2005.
Lemke, Anja. "'Im Gestöber der Lettern': Mediale Übersetzungsprozesse der Erinnerung in Walter Benjamins 'Berliner Kinderheit im Neunzehnhundert.'" In *Medien und Aesthetik. Festschrift für Burkhardt Lindner*, edited by H. Hillgärtner and Thomas Küpper, 34–50. Bielefeld: Transcript Verlag, 2003.
Librett, Jeffrey S. *Orientalism and the Figure of the Jew*. New York: Fordham University Press, 2014.
Lindner, Burkhardt. "Vom 'sentimentalischen' Kinderbild zur Topographie der Kindheit." In *Topographien der Kindheit: Literarische, mediale und interdisziplinäre Perpspektiven auf Orts- und Raumkonstruktionen*, edited by Caroline Roeder, 41–58. Bielefeld: Transcript Verlag, 2014.
Litvak, Joseph. "Strange Gourmet: Taste, Waste, Proust." In *Novel Gazing: Queer Readings in Fiction*, edited by Eve Kosofsky Sedgwick, 74–93. Durham, NC: Duke University Press, 1997.
Locke, John. *Some Thoughts concerning Education*. New York: Dover, 2007.
Love, Heather. *Feeling Backward: Loss and the Politics of Queer History*. Cambridge, MA: Harvard University Press, 2007.
Luciano, Dana. *Arranging Grief: Sacred Time and the Body in Nineteenth-Century America*. New York: New York University Press, 2007.

Luhmann, Niklas. "Das Kind als Medium der Erziehung." In *Schriften zur Pädagogik*, edited by Dieter Lenzen, 159–186. Frankfurt am Main: Suhrkamp Verlag, 2004.

Mall-Grob, Beatrice. *Fiktion des Anfangs: Literarische Kindheitsmodelle bei Jean Paul und Adalbert Stifter*. Stuttgart: Metzler Verlag, 1999.

Martens, Lorna. *The Promise of Memory: Childhood Recollection and Its Objects in Literary Modernism*. Cambridge, MA: Harvard University Press, 2011.

Mason, Eve. "Stifter's 'Turmalin': A Reconsideration." *Modern Language Review* 72, no. 2 (April 1977): 348–358.

McGillen, Michael. "Free Variation from the Archive of Culture: Blumenberg and Husserl on Phenomenological Description." In *Leistungsbeschreibung/ Describing Cultural Achievements: Literarische Strategien bei Hans Blumenberg/ Hans Blumenberg's Literary Strategies*, edited by Timothy Attanucci and Ulrich Breuer, 73–94. Heidelberg: Universitätsverlag, 2020.

Mehlman, Jeffrey. *Walter Benjamin for Children: An Essay on His Radio Years*. Chicago: University of Chicago Press, 1993.

Menninghaus, Winfried. "Walter Benjamin's Exposition of the Romantic Theory of Reflection." In *Walter Benjamin and Romanticism*, edited by Beatrice Hanssen and Andrew Benjamin, 19–50. New York: Continuum, 2002.

Muñoz, José Esteban. *Cruising Utopia: The Then and There of Queer Futurity*. New York: New York University Press, 2009.

Nagel, Barbara N. *Ambiguous Aggression in German Realism and Beyond: Flirtation, Passive Aggression, Domestic Violence*. New York: Bloomsbury, 2019.

Nell, Daniel. "Methoden der Genauigkeitsanalyse historischer Karten am Beispiel der Gradkartenblätter 1:25.000 Innsbruck und Lienz der Dritten Österreichischen Landesaufnahme." PhD thesis, Universität Wien, 2009.

Neumann, Gerhard. "Puppe und Automate: Inszenierte Kindheit in E. T. A. Hoffmanns Sozialisationsmärchen 'Nußknacker und Mausekönig.'" In *Jugend— ein romantisches Konzept?* Edited by Günter Oesterle, 135–160. Würzburg Königshausen & Neumann, 1997.

Ngai, Sianne. *Theory of the Gimmick: Aesthetic Judgment and Capitalist Form*. Cambridge, MA: Belknap Press of Harvard University Press, 2020.

Nietzsche, Friedrich. *Gay Science*. Edited by Bernard Williams. Translated by Josefine Nauckhoff. Cambridge: Cambridge University Press, 2001.

Nurmi-Schomers, Susan. *Visionen dichterischen Mündigwerdens: Poetologische Perspektiven auf Robert Musil, Rainer Maria Rilke, und Walter Benjamin*. Tübingen: Niemeyer Verlag, 2008.

Ohi, Kevin. *Innocence and Rapture: The Erotic Child in Pater, Wilde, James, and Nabokov*. New York: Palgrave Macmillan, 2005.

Öhlschläger, Claudia. "Bergkristall." In *Stifter Handbuch. Leben—Werk—Wirkung*, edited by Christian Begemann and Davide Giuriato, 83–87. Stuttgart: J. B. Metzler, 2017.

Østermark-Johansen, Lene. *Walter Pater's European Imagination*. Oxford: Oxford University Press, 2022.

Perry, Joe. *Christmas in Germany: A Cultural History*. Chapel Hill: University of North Carolina Press, 2010.

Pethes, Nicholas. *Mnemographie: Poetiken der Erinnerung und Destruktion nach Walter Benjamin*. Tübingen: Niemeyer Verlag, 1999.

Pfau, Thomas. "Absolute Gegebenheit: Image as Aesthetic Urphänomen in Husserl and Rilke." In *Phenomenology to the Letter: Husserl and Literature*, edited by Philippe P. Haensler, Kristina Mendicino, and Rochelle Tobias, 222–260. Berlin: De Gruyter, 2020.

Pfotenhauer, Helmut. "Einfach . . . wie ein Halm": Stifters komplizierte kleine Selbstbiographie. *Deutsche Vierteljahrsschrift für Literaturwissenschaft und Geistesgeschichte* 64 (1990): 134–148.

Pietzker, Carl. "'Nussknacker und Mausekönig': Gründungstext der Phantastischen Kinder- und Jugendliteratur." In *E. T. A. Hoffmann: Romane und Erzählungen: Interpretation*, edited by Günter Saße, 182–198. Stuttgart: Reclam, 2004.

Plotkin, Susan L., and Stanley A. Plotkin. "A Short History of Vaccination." In *Vaccines*, edited by Stanley A. Plotkin, Walter A. Orenstein, and Paul A. Offit. 5th ed. Philadelphia: Elsevier, 2008.

Polansky, Ronald. *Aristotle's De Anima: A Critical Commentary*. Cambridge: Cambridge Unversity Press, 2007.

Ragg-Kirkby, Helena. *Adalbert Stifter's Late Prose: The Mania for Moderation*. Rochester, NY: Camden House, 2000.

Richter, Dieter. *Das fremde Kind: Zur Entstehung der Kindheitsbilder des bürgerlichen Zeitalters*. Frankfurt am Main: Fischer, 1987.

Richter, Gerhard. *Thought-Images : Frankfurt School Writers' Reflections from Damaged Life*. Stanford: Stanford University Press, 2007.

Rilke, Rainer Maria. *Die Briefe an Karl und Elisabeth von der Heydt 1905–1922*. Edited by Ingeborg Schnack and Renate Scharffenberg. Frankfurt am Main: Insel Verlag, 1986.

Rilke, Rainer Maria. *Letters to a Young Poet*. Edited and translated by M. D. Norton. New York: W. W. Norton, 2004.

Rilke, Rainer Maria. *The Notebooks of Malte Laurids Brigge*. Champaign, IL: Dalkey Archive Press, 2008.

Rilke, Rainer Maria. *Werke: Kommentierte Ausgabe in vier Bänden*. Edited by Manfred Engel, Ulrich Fülleborn, Horst Nalewski, and August Stahl. 4 vols. Frankfurt am Main: Insel Verlag, 1996.

Rowlands, Mark. *Memory and the Self: Phenomenology, Science, and Autobiography*. New York: Oxford University Press, 2016.

Ryan, Judith. "Rilke's Early Narratives." In *A Companion to the Works of Rainer Maria Rilke*, edited by Erika A. Metzger and Michael Metzger, 67–89. Rochester, NY: Camden House, 2001.

Schivelbusch, Wolfgang. *The Railway Journey: The Industrialization of Time and Space in the Nineteenth Century.* Berkeley: University of California Press, 2014.

Schlegel, Friedrich. *Athenaeum Fragments.* Translated by Peter Firchow. Foreword by Rodophe Gasche. Minneapolis: University of Minnesota Press, 1991.

Schmaus, Marion. "Nußknacker und Mausekönig. Ein Weihnachtsabend (1816)." In *E.T.A. Hoffmann Handbuch. Leben—Werk—Wirkung.* Edited by Christine Lubkoll and Harald Neumeyer. 100–103. Stuttgart: Metzler Verlag, 2015.

Schmidt, Hugo. "Eishöhle und Steinhäuschen: Zur Weihnachtssymbolik in Stifters 'Bergkristall.'" *Monatshefte* 56, no. 7 (December 1964): 321–335.

Schnyder, Peter. "Dynamisierugn des Statischen: Geologisches Wissen bei Goethe und Stifter." *Zeitschrift für Germanistik* 29, no. 3 (2009): 540–555.

Schnyder, Peter. "Schrift—Bild—Sammlung—Karte." In *Figuren der Übertragung: Adalbert Stifter und das Wissen seiner Zeit*, edited by Michael Gamper and Michael Wagner, 235–248. Zurich: Chronos Verlag, 2009.

Scholem, Gershom. *On Jews and Judaism in Crisis.* Edited by Werner J. Dannhauser. New York: Schocken Books, 1976.

Schönau, Walter. *Sigmund Freuds Prosa: Literarische Elemente seines Stils.* Giessen: Psychosozial-Verlag, 2006.

Schuller, Kyla. *The Biopolitics of Feeling: Race, Sex, and Science in the Nineteenth Century.* Durham, NC: Duke University Press, 2018.

Schuller, Marianne. "Das Kleine der Literatur: Stifters Autobiographie." In *Mikrologien: Literarische und philosophische Figures des Kleinen*, edited by Marianne Schuller and Gunnar Schmidt, 77–89. Bielefeld: Transcript Verlag, 2003.

Schwebel, Paula. "Intensive Infinity: Walter Benjamin's Reception of Leibniz and Its Sources." *MLN* 127, no. 3 (2012): 589–610.

Sedgwick, Eve Kosofsky. *The Coherence of Gothic Conventions.* New York: Arno Press, 1980.

Sedgwick, Eve Kosofsky. "Paranoid and Reparative Reading; or You're So Paranoid, You Probably Think This Introduction Is about You." In *Novel Gazing: Queer Readings in Fiction*, edited by Eve Kosofsky Sedgwick, 1–40. Durham, NC: Duke University Press, 1997.

Seifener, Christoph. "Zeitwahrnehmung und -darstellung in Ludwig Tiecks *Die Elfen* und den Kindermärchen E. T. A. Hoffmanns." *Seminar: A Journal of Germanic Studies* 60, no. 1 (February 2024): 1–20.

Seifert, Walter. *Das epische Werk Rainer Maria Rilkes.* Bonn: Bouvier, 1969.

Sharma, Avi. *We Lived for the Body: Natural Medicine and Public Health in Imperial Germany.* DeKalb: Northern Illinois University Press, 2014.

Simms, Eva-Maria. "Uncanny Dolls: Images of Death in Rilke and Freud." *New Literary History* 72, no. 4 (1996): 663–677.

Smith, David Woodruff. *Husserl.* New York: Routledge, 2013.

Smith, David Woodruff, and Ronald McIntyre. *Husserl and Intentionality: A Study of Mind, Meaning, and Language.* Dordrecht: Reidel, 1982.

Smith, Vanessa. "Toy Stories." *Novel* 50, no. 1 (2017): 35–55.

Snediker, Michael D. *Queer Optimism: Lyric Personhood and Other Felicitous Persuasions*. Minneapolis: University of Minnesota Press, 2009.
Sprengnether, Madelon. "Freud as Memoirist: A Reading of 'Screen Memories.'" *American Imago* 69, no. 2 (Summer 2012): 215–239.
Steedman, Carolyn. *Strange Dislocations: Childhood and the Idea of Human Interiority, 1780–1930*. Cambridge MA: Harvard University Press, 1995.
Stewart, Susan. *On Longing: Narratives of the Miniature, the Gigantic, the Souvenir, the Collection*. Durham, NC: Duke University Press, 1993.
Stifter, Adalbert. *Indian Summer*. Translated by Wendell Frye. New York: Peter Lang, 1985.
Stifter, Adalbert. *Motley Stones*. Translated by Isabel Fargo Cole. New York: New York Review of Books, 2021.
Stifter, Adalbert. *Werke: Kleine Schriften/Briefe*. Edited by Uwe Japp and Hans Joachim Piechotta. Vol. 4. Frankfurt am Main: Insel Verlag, 1978.
Stifter, Adalbert. *Werke und Briefe: Historisch-kritische Gesamtausgabe*. Edited by Alfred Doppler, Wolfgang Frühwald, and Hartmut Laufhütte. Stuttgart: Kohlhammer Verlag, 1978–2017.
Stockhammer, Robert. *Kartierung der Erde: Macht und Lust in Karten und Literatur*. Munich: Wilhelm Fink Verlag, 2007.
Stockton, Kathryn Bond. *The Queer Child, or Growing Sideways in the Twentieth Century*. Durham, NC: Duke University Press, 2009.
Strowick, Elisabeth. "'Dumpfe Dauer': Langeweile und Atmosphärisches bei Fontane und Stifter." *Germanic Review: Literature, Culture, Theory* 90, no. 3 (2015): 187–203.
Strowick, Elisabeth. "Poetological-Technical Operations: Representation of Motion in Adalbert Stifter." *Configurations* 18 (2010): 273–289.
Swales, Martin. "Homeliness and Otherness: Reflections on Stifter's Bergkristall." In *The German Bestseller in the Nineteenth Century*, edited by Charlotte Woodford and Benedict Schofield, 115–126. Rochester, NY: Camden House, 2012.
Swoyer, Chris. "Leibnizian Expression." *Journal of the History of Philosophy* 33, no. 1 (1995): 65–99.
Szondi, Peter. "Hope in the Past: On Walter Benjamin." *Critical Inquiry* 4, no. 3 (1978): 491–506.
Taylor, Michael Thomas. "Right Queer: Hegel's Philosophy of Marriage." *Republics of Letters: A Journal for the Study of Knowledge, Politics, and the Arts* 3, no. 2 (2013): 1–21.
Tobias, Rochelle. "Rilke, Phenomenology, and the Sensuality of Thought." *Konturen* 8 (2015): 40–61.
Tribunella, Eric L. "Benjamin, Benson, and the Child's Gaze: Childhood Desire and Pleasure in the David Blaize Books." *Pedagogy, Culture & Society* 24, no. 4 (2016): 505–515.
Türk, Johannes. *Die Immunität der Literatur*. Frankfurt a. M.: S. Fischer Verlag, 2011.

Vedder, Ulrike. "Erbe." In *Stifter-Handbuch: Leben—Werk –Wirkung*, edited by Christian Begemann and Davide Giurato, 334–338. Stuttgart: Metzler Verlag, 2017.

Vitt-Maucher, Gisela. *E. T. A. Hoffmanns Märchenschaffen: Kaleidoskop der Verfremdung in seinen Sieben Märchen*. Chapel Hill: University of North Carolina Press, 1989.

Vogel, Juliane. "Stifters Gitter: Poetologische Dimensionen einer Grenzfigur." In *Die Dinge und die Zeichen: Dimensionen des Realistischen in der Erzählliteratur des 19. Jahrhunderts*, edited by Helmut Pfotenhauer, Sabine Schneider, and Barbara Hunfeld, 49–51. Würzburg: Königshausen & Neumann, 2008.

Weber, Samuel. *Benjamin's -abilities*. Cambridge, MA: Harvard University Press, 2008.

Weber-Kellermann, Ingeborg. *Das Weihnachtsfest: Eine Kultur- und Sozialgeschichte der Weihnachtszeit*. Lucerne: Verlag CJ Bucher, 1978.

Weigel, Sigrid. *Entstellte Ähnlichkeit: Walter Benjamins theoretische Schreibweise*. Frankfurt am Main: Fischer Verlag, 1997

Werner, Nadine. *Archäologie des Erinnerns: Sigmund Freud in Walter Benjamins Berliner Kindheit*. Göttingen: Wallstein Verlag, 2015.

Wetz, Franz Joseph. "Der Mensch ist das Unmögliche: Blumenbergs Phänomenologische Anthropologie im Nachlass." *Zeitschrift für philosophische Forschung* 63, no. 2 (April 2008): 274–292.

Wild, Reiner. *Die Vernunft der Väter: Zur Psychographie von Bürgerlichkeit und Auklärung in Deutschland*. Stuttgart: Metzler Verlag, 1987.

Willer, Stefan. "Familie/Genealogie." In *Stifter-Handbuch*, edited by Christian Begemann and Davide Giurato, 330–334. Stuttgart: Metzler Verlag, 2017.

Wolin, Richard. *Walter Benjamin: An Aesthetic of Redemption*. New York: Columbia University Press, 1982.

Zigrosser, Carl. *Multum in parvo: An Essay in Poetic Imagination*. New York: Braziller, 1965.

Index

"abgeschattet" (adumbrated), 90
accent, queer, 43
Adorno, Theodor W., 13–14
adulthood, 26, 151n24, 171n8; childhood as not-yet of, 10–14; Christmas in, 2, 5–6; dolls and, 76; Freud and, 140, 144; futurity in, 31; growing up into, 96; heterosexual, 7; photography and, 196n142; progressive logic of, 56; social reproduction in, 152n28; as theater of social niceties, 60
adult memory, 84, 143
adult regimes, 57
adumbrated. *See* "abgeschattet"
Aesop, 68, 70
aesthesis. See sense perception
aesthetics, bourgeois, 31
Agamben, Giorgio, 15, 20, 133, 134, 136
Ahmed, Sara, 7–8, 10, 20, 33, 41, 92, 157n72; on "desire lines," 136; on family pictures, 43; Freud and, 139, 144; "happy baby" and, 63; Husserl and, 15, 81, 82; on queerness, 37, 39
allegorization, 36
allegory, 143–44, 187n33; baroque, 117–18; image and, 122–24
animality, 153n38
animals, 34
antiquarianism, 33–34
apartment, 121, 123, 165n85
aphorism, 98, 107–8, 110–12, 115–21
aphoristic expression, 101
arbor, metaphor of, 26
The Arcades Project (*Das Passagen-Werk*) (Benjamin), 95, 128, 135

archaeology, 195n132
Ariès, Philippe, 10–11, 12, 153n40
Assmann, Aleida, 52, 179n112
atemporal models, 34
Attanucci, Timothy, 160n15, 168n128
"At the Corner of Steglitzer and Genthiner" (Benjamin), 130
Auerbach, Berthold, 108
Die Aufzeichnungen des Malte Laurids Brigge (Rilke). *See The Notebooks of Malte Laurids Brigge*
"Augenmensch." *See* eye-person
aurora borealis. *See* northern lights
Aus meinem Leben (*From My Life*) (Goethe), 142
Austin, Linda, 151n24, 152n25
Austrian Empire, 46
autobiography, 9

Bachelard, Gaston, 82, 102, 179n120
backward, 15, 36, 43–47, 51–52, 125
backward epistemology, 56
backwards, 164n71
baroque allegory, 117–18
"became-nothing," 54
Benjamin, Walter, 3, 8, 10, 14–16, 31–33, 39, 95–101, 139; *The Arcades Project*, 95, 128, 135; "At the Corner of Steglitzer and Genthiner," 130; baroque allegory and, 117–18; *Berlin Childhood around 1900*, 99, 115–21, 126, 128, 130–32; *Berlin Chronicle*, 121–32; "Boys' Books," 129; "A Child's View of Color," 103; "Convolute N [On the Theory of Knowledge, Theory of Progress]," 132;

217

Benjamin, Walter *(continued)*
  cosmology of, 106; intuition and, 102–7;
  Leibniz and, 19–20, 101, 103, 108, 114;
  "Old Forgotten Children's Books," 103,
  108, 119, 125; *One-Way Street*, 107–9, 114,
  120; "On the Portraits of Children in
  'One-Way Street,'" 107–15; *The Origin of
  the German Tragic Drama*, 20, 96, 114,
  117, 132
"Bergkristall" (Stifter). See "Rock Crystal"
Berlant, Lauren, 7, 16
Berlin Childhood around 1900 (*Berliner Kindheit um 1900*) (Benjamin), 99, 115–21, 126,
  128, 130–32
Berlin Chronicle (*Berliner Chronik*) (Benjamin), 121–32
Bildungsroman, 9, 28
Blumenberg, Hans, 3, 15, 18, 58–70, 79, 92–94,
  171n6; Husserl and, 64; "Reflection," 74
Bollnow, Otto Friedrich, 180n129
books, 34, 129
Borchmeyer, Dieter, 162n42
bourgeois, 8, 10, 60, 92, 107, 130; aesthetics, 31;
  domesticity, 17, 29; realism, 16; "shallow
  religiousness," 172n17
"Boys' Books" (Benjamin), 129
Bradley, Brigitte, 172n17
brevity, in writing, 120
Brüggemann, Heinz, 187n35
Buck-Morss, Susan, 135
Bunte Steine (Stifter). See *Motley Stones*
Büssgen, Antje, 64

Campe, Rüdiger, 157n74
carousel, 112–14, 192n86
cartographic view, of childhood, 45–55
Catholic theology, 52
Cavell, Stanley, 5–6, 86, 87, 151n20
Centuries of Childhood (Ariès), 11
certainty, 26, 32, 56, 87
character, consistency and, 63
"Chiffre des Noch-nicht-Menschen" (figure of
  the not-yet-human), 12
Childhood in Amorbach (Adorno). See *Kindheit in Amorbach*
childhood memory, 85
childlike old man. See *Senex-Puer*
children's literature, 15, 186n25
child-subject, 63, 83, 87, 89–91, 106, 112, 124;
  cognitive ambidexterity of, 74; dolls and,
  76; fantasy of, 73; material objects and,
  98; narration and, 67
"A Child's View of Color" (Benjamin), 103
Christianity, 59

"Das Christkind" (The Christ Child) (Rilke),
  72–73, 75
Christmas, 1–3, 4–5, 6, 72, 149n2, 155n51
A Christmas Carol (Dickens), 75
chronobiopolitics, 19, 93, 153n41
chronology, 114
chrononormativity, 20–21, 27, 40
classical rationality, 31
classical thought, 26
cognition, childhood, 103, 112, 121
Cohn, Dorit, 67
collaboration, 60
collection, 34
color, 25, 102–3, 131, 136
commodity-time, 56
conceptual graspability, 6
conceptual knowledge, 65
conceptual thinking, 3
consciousness: figural, 67; unity of, 183n145
consistency, character and, 63
contemplation, 25, 67, 69, 191n75
"Convolute N [On the Theory of Knowledge,
  Theory of Progress]" (Benjamin), 132
cosmology, 106

Daub, Adrian, 37
death, 54
de Certeau, Michel, 17, 39–42, 50, 53–54
deferral, logic of, 7
Deleuze, Gilles, 15, 157n69
Derrida, Jacques, 142
Descartes, Rene, 8
description, 10, 41–42, 70–71, 80–81, 96,
  164n60; literary, 18, 59; memory and, 13;
  phenomenological, 65; of seeing, 3; of
  space, 39; spatial, 35; as spectatorship, 65
desire lines, 136–37
detail, 32; attention to, 6; of Leibniz, 117–18,
  120, 186n19; material, 98, 126; modernism
  and, 16; monad as, 124
diachrony, 135, 136
Dichtung und Wahrheit (Goethe). See *Poetry
  and Truth*
Dickens, Charles, 75
Dieterle, Bernard, 64
discontinuity, 85
divine knowledge, 106, 188n53
dogs, 178n109
dolls, 75–78, 79, 178n109
"Dolls" (Rilke), 75–76
domestic community, 162n42
domesticity, 7, 24, 28, 30–32; bourgeois, 17, 29;
  movability and, 42; tableau of, 41; timelessness of, 34, 36

INDEX

domestic sphere, 39
double perceptual apprehension, of objects, 78–79
Downing, Eric, 150n12
dream, 74
duck-rabbit image, 90–91
dwelling, 17, 24, 32–33, 39, 82, 131, 165n85
dynamic spaces, 41, 54

Edelman, Lee, 20, 27, 44, 59, 100, 140, 144, 152n30; child-figures and, 58, 72; *No Future*, 7; queer theory and, 16; social reproduction and, 11
ego-experience, 84, 182n138
Einbahnstraße (Benjamin). See *One-Way Street*
Elsaesser, Thomas, 40, 166n96
English Romanticism, 6. See also Romanticism
enlargements, 107–16
Enlightenment, 10, 31, 100, 154n48
episteme, 17, 27, 42, 163n59
epistemological kinship, 133, 135
epistemology, 7, 100, 116; backward, 56; certainty and, 26; illumination and, 29; traditional, 6; visibility and, 29
error, 12, 157n70, 176n65
espace. See "space"
the "everyday," 27, 48, 98
everyday life, 9, 11, 24, 26, 99
everyday objects, 39, 60–61
everyday space, 87
Ewers, Hans Heino, 30
experimental prose, 3
"The Experiment as Mediator" ("Der Versuch als Vermittler") (Goethe), 133–34
expression, principle of, 96
eye-person ("Augenmensch"), 69

failure, 43, 44, 53
fairy tales, 12
familial spaces, 25
family life, 110
family pictures, 43
family timing, 43
family trees, 43
fantasy, 58, 80, 83–84; of child-subject, 73; of futurity, 7, 100; Husserl and, 81; phenomenology and, 85
Fauconneau-Dufresne, Eva, 180n126
felicity, 86
Felski, Rita, 26
"Femininity" (Freud), 139–40
figural consciousness/mind, 67

figure of the not-yet-human. See "Chiffre des Noch-nicht-Menschen"
flat, 38–40, 50
Fleming, Paul, 13, 62
focalization, on the child, 73
Føllesdal, Dagfinn, 90
Forrest, Tara, 114, 190n69
forts, 17, 23–27, 32, 52–53, 55–56
Foucault, Michel, 23, 35, 37, 46, 55, 133; bourgeois domesticity and, 29; classical epistemes and, 17, 27, 42; knowledge and, 26; Linnean taxonomy and, 33; *Port Royal Logic*, 35
Fourier, Charles, 95, 96
fragments, 20, 58, 81, 82, 95, 102
Franciscan Land Survey (Franziszeische Landesaufnahme), 47
Frankfurt School, 185n17
Frankland, Graham, 139
Freeman, Elizabeth, 10, 16, 27, 40, 42–43, 153n41; allegorization and, 36; chrononormativity and, 20, 112; progressive logic and, 56; queer affect and, 17, 55
Freud, Sigmund, 10, 13, 16, 20, 142–43, 151n24; adulthood and, 140, 144; Ahmed and, 139, 144; "Femininity," 139–40; psychoanalysis and, 140–41; "The Psychogenesis of a Case of Homosexuality in a Woman," 139; "Screen Memories," 140–41
From My Life (Goethe). See *Aus meinem Leben*
frontier, childhood as, 54
Fuchs, Florian, 171n8
futurity, 8–9, 14, 41, 59, 93, 112, 137; in adulthood, 31; fantasy of, 7, 100; paradigm and, 72; refusing, 27; reproductive, 45

"Die Gartenlaube" (The garden arbor) (Stifter), 23, 25, 55
genealogical knowledge, 131
generation, 17
Genesis, book of, 144
Genette, Gérard, 73
"Gentle Law" (Stifter), 48
geography, 44
geology, 34, 164n60
Gess, Nicola, 135, 136
Geulen, Eva, 39, 43, 50, 53, 160n22, 167n113, 169n155
gift-giving, 1, 5
Gillespie, Susan, 14
Giuriato, Davide, 161n36, 190n65
God, nearness to, 62

Goethe, Johann Wolfgang von, 13, 133–34, 142–43, 145, 180n125
Goode, Mike, 33
Gosetti-Ferencei, Jennifer Anna, 176n74, 180n124
grid, 26, 55, 159n10, 160n12
Groves, Jason, 160n15
growing sideways, 164n71
growing up, 8–9, 96
Guarín, Alejandro, 164n61
Guattari, Felix, 15, 157n69

Habsburg Empire, 47
Hamburger, Käte, 84, 180n129
"happy baby," 63
Hertling, Gunter, 162n40
heteronormativity, 3, 59, 139
heterosexual adulthood, 7
heterosexual objects, 41
heterosexual reproduction, 43, 75
Heywood, Colin, 153n40
history, 44
Hoffmann, E. T. A., 13, 17, 155n51
Hoke, Sarah, 162n39
Holmes, Tove, 160n15
"Holy Child," 5
home, 2
homosexuality, 42, 152n28. See also queer
Hooke, Robert, 116
house, 24, 28–32
"How the Thimble Came to Be God" (Rilke), 59, 71
von Humboldt, Alexander, 34
Husserl, Edmund, 8, 18, 62, 66–67, 69–70, 77, 90, 93; Ahmed and, 15, 81, 82; Blumenberg and, 64; discontinuity and, 85; double perceptual appearance and, 76; on everyday space, 87; fantasy and, 81; Hamburger and, 84; *Ideas for a Pure Phenomenology and Phenomenological Philosophy*, 94; intentionality and, 83; phantasy image and, 78; phenomenological description and, 65; phenomenology and, 64; transcendent objects and, 83; unity of consciousness and, 183n145
Hutchinson, Ben, 171n6

ideal spectators, 70
Ideas for a Pure Phenomenology and Phenomenological Philosophy (Husserl), 94
identification, 34
illumination, 29
image, 42, 75, 109, 128; allegory and, 122–24; duck-rabbit, 90–91; of family trees, 43; of Habsburg Empire, 47; landscape perception as, 67–68; "modernist Denkbild," 98; "phantasy image," 78; of queer adulthood, 56; utopian, 96; of "windowless" dining room, 91
imagination, 19, 24, 83, 92, 103; fragment and, 82; perception and, 67, 86, 98; poetic, 89; pure, 91; sense-perception and, 179n122; signification and, 77; subjectivity and, 76; transcendental view of, 100
immunization, 117, 118
"Imperial Panorama," 127
Indian Summer (Stifter), 17, 28–37, 46, 48
individual perception, 70–71
infelicity, 84
inner Child, 59
inoculation, 118, 193n107
intentionality, 83
intergenerational formation, 37
intuition, 102–7
intuitional indefiniteness, 181n137
invisibility, 19, 46, 61, 123
Irigaray, Luce, 139–40
Irmscher, Hans Dietrich, 161n24
irrationalism, 11

Jastrow, Joseph, 90, 91, 183n149
Jennings, Michael, 115, 126, 188n52, 195n135
Johns Hopkins University, 157n74
Jorgensen, Larry M., 97, 185n14

"Kalkstein" (Stifter). See "Limestone"
Kandinsky, Wassily, 102
Kappus, Franz Xavier, 58
Keegan, Cáel M., 152n28
Kelley, Theresa M., 187n33
Key, Ellen, 10, 153n38
Kidd, Kenneth B., 15, 186n25
Kincaid, James, 11, 142
Kindheit in Amorbach (*Childhood in Amorbach*) (Adorno), 13
kinship, 9, 38; epistemological, 133, 135
Klee, Paul, 102, 187n35
Klein, Melanie, 200n23
knowledge, 9, 157n70; classical forms of, 32, 34; conceptual, 65; divine, 106, 188n53; Foucault and, 26; gaps in, 44; genealogical, 131; invisibility of childhood, 61; microstructure of, 117–18; obsession with, 37; rational, 65; scientific categorization and, 29; space as system of, 31; as spatial practice, 39; taxonomic, 47; temporality and, 35, 46; through spatial limitation, 25
Koschorke, Albrecht, 182nn142–43

INDEX 221

Kracauer, Siegfried, 110
Krauss, Rosalind, 159n7
Kristeva, Julia, 12, 30

landscape, 46–50, 66, 68; paintings, 65; spectatorship, 67
land survey, 45–47
Lausberg, Heinrich, 187n33
Lefebvre, Henri, 27, 48
Lehmann, Tante, 130
Leibniz, G. W., 15–16, 110, 119, 123–24, 129; Benjamin and, 19–20, 101, 103, 108, 114; detail and, 117–18, 120, 186n19; memory and, 185n13; monad and, 96–97, 104, 106, 114, 127; *Monadology*, 19, 106–7, 111, 120–21, 125, 130, 132, 136; perception and, 106
Lemke, Anja, 120
lesbians, 42
Letters to a Young Poet (Rilke), 93
lieu. See "place"
lifeworld, 18, 57–59, 62, 65, 68–69, 80, 90
light, 61
"Limestone" ("Kalkstein") (Stifter), 45–55, 169n155
Linnaeus, 26, 27, 33, 34
Linnean taxonomy, 33, 36
literary description, 18
Litvak, Joseph, 1, 14
lived experience, 112
local historical meaning, 4
"Loggias," 121–23, 126–28
logic of deferral, 7
Love, Heather, 10, 34
Luciano, Dana, 7, 18–19, 30, 93, 153n41, 184n159
Luhmann, Niklas, 154n44
lyrical prose, 57

the Madonna, 72
Mall-Grob, Beatrice, 29, 161n28
manifold perspectives, 134
maps/mapping, 46–47, 49–50, 51
Martens, Lorna, 199n9
material detail, 98, 126
materiality, 62
maternal sensibility, 39
McGillen, Michael, 65
Mein Leben (Stifter). See *My Life*
memory, 14, 99, 185n13, 195n132; adult, 84; childhood, 85; description and, 13; poetics of, 13
metaphor, 104–5, 109, 119; of arbor, 26; Stockton and, 79
metaphysical paradigm, childhood as, 132–37
metaphysics, 20, 102, 132

microcosm, 2, 19, 105, 107, 116
microscope, 116, 119
microworld, 95
Middle Ages, 52
miniature/miniaturization, 101, 115–21
misperception, 84
modernism, 9
"modernist Denkbild" (thought-image), 98, 185n17
modernity, 31, 126
monad: as detail, 124; Leibniz and, 96–97, 104, 106, 114, 127; as philosophical thought, 19, 97; principle of expression and, 96
monadological time, 19
Monadology (Leibniz), 19, 96–107, 111, 120–21, 125, 130, 132, 136
monotony, 48
motion, 113
Motley Stones (*Bunte Steine*) (Stifter), 17, 38, 45
movability, 42
Muñoz, José Esteban, 19, 100, 125, 128, 187n32
My Life (*Mein Leben*) (Stifter), 55

Der Nachsommer (Stifter). See *Indian Summer*
Nagel, Barbara N., 144, 150n12
narrated monologue, 67
narration, 10, 54; boundaries of, 19, 93; child-subject and, 67; fantasy in, 81; grid and, 55; of movement through space, 41; observation and, 36; paratactical, 166n94; phenomenological capacity of, 64; psycho-narration, 67; third-person, 107
narrative figments, 64
narratological techniques, 67, 70, 73
nature, beauty of, 25
Nazi regime, 115
Ngai, Sianne, 126–27
Nietzsche, Friedrich, 114
noema, noematic, 90–91, 174n47
No Future (Edelman), 7
"no-longer-conscious," 100, 107, 128, 187n32
nonlinear time, 100
nonprogressive time, of sensation, 19, 93
northern lights (aurora borealis), 4–5
nostalgia, 3, 5–6, 23, 110, 117
The Notebooks of Malte Laurids Brigge (Rilke), 18, 57, 80, 83–84, 92, 113
Notes on Literature (Adorno), 14
"Notes on the Melody of Things" ("Notizen zur Melodie der Dinge") (Rilke), 80–81, 92
novellas, 9
Nußknacker und Mausekönig (*Nutcracker and Mouse King*) (Hoffmann), 13

"Old Forgotten Children's Books" (Benjamin), 103, 108, 119, 125
One-Way Street (*Einbahnstraße*) (Benjamin), 107–9, 114, 120
"On Landscape" (Rilke), 65
"On the Portraits of Children in 'One-Way Street'" ("Zu den Kinderporträts der 'Einbahnstraße'") (Benjamin), 107–15
ordinary culture, 42
ordinary experience, 2–3, 6–7, 10, 18, 20–21, 62–64, 99
Orientalism, 12
origin, 13, 20, 133–34, 141
The Origin of German Tragic Drama (Benjamin), 20, 96, 114, 117, 132
Østermark-Johansen, Lene, 151n24

paintings, 29, 64, 173n40; color and, 102; landscape, 65
panorama, 126–28, 132, 135
paradigm, 20, 99, 101, 124; futurity and, 72; metaphysical, 132–37; philosophical, 19; spatial, 115
paratactical narration, 166n94
Das Passagen-Werk (Benjamin). See *The Arcades Project*
Pater, Walter, 6, 151n24
penmanship, 51
pensée avec, 67
pensiveness, 92–93
perceptibility, 121
perception, 2, 58, 82, 88, 123; of color, 136; hybrid characterization of, 86; imagination and, 67, 86, 98; individual, 70–71; landscape, 67–68; Leibniz and, 106; misperception, 84; of motion, 113; sense, 83, 179n122; temporality of, 4; visual, 3
perceptual distinctness, 97
Pfotenhauer, Helmut, 170n171
phantasia. *See* imagination
phantasmagoria, 126
"phantasy image," 78
phenomenological description, 65
phenomenology, 7, 79–81, 94; of everyday world, 62; fantasy and, 85; of Husserl, 64; of individual perception, 70; of narrated "things," 69
philosophical paradigm, 19
philosophical storytelling, 57
philosophy, 65; history of, 8; literary representation is, 3; of material life, 98; poetics and, 71, 80, 97; "straight theory" of, 15
photographic enlargement, 114–16
photographic reproduction, 109
photography, 77, 108–10, 126, 196n142

picture, 34–37
"Pierre Dumont" (Rilke), 63–71, 73, 75, 86
"place" (*lieu*), 39–40
planned obsolescence, 56
plastic, children as, 63
Plato, 42, 133
play, 74, 103–4
pleasure, 143
plot, 143
poetic imagination, 89
Poetics of Space (Bachelard), 179n120
Poetry and Truth (*Dichtung und Wahrheit*) (Goethe), 13, 143
poiesis, 107
Port Royal Logic (Foucault), 35
portraits, 41–43, 108–10
potentiality, 14
Pritzel, Lotte, 75
progressive logic, 56
prose, 8, 10, 58–59, 65; experimental, 3; of Freud, 20; lyrical, 57; of Proust, 14
Proust, Marcel, 13, 14, 84
psychoanalysis, 140, 141, 143, 145
"The Psychogenesis of a Case of Homosexuality in a Woman" (Freud), 139
psycho-narration, 67
puberty, 31
pure imagination, 91

queer accent, 43
queer affect, 17, 55
queer desire, 139
queer erotics, 33
queerness, 37, 152n28
queer offspring, 42
queer reading, 140
queer temporality, 19, 26, 36, 112, 128, 187n32
queer theory, 7, 15, 139, 152n30, 198n1
queer time, 125

Ragg-Kirkby, Helena, 168n140
rational knowledge, 65
reading, 129, 140
realism, 1, 9, 16, 182n143
reality, 74
reflection, childhood, 71–75
"Reflection" ("Reflexion") (Blumenberg), 74
reparative reading, 140
representation, 108
reproduction: heterosexual, 43, 75; photographic, 109; sexual, 7, 152n28; social, 3, 11, 152n28
reproductive futurity, 45
resemblance, 29
Richter, Dieter, 12, 98, 185n17

INDEX

Rilke, Rainer Maria, 3, 8–10, 14–16, 19, 58–62, 100, 106, 139, 171n6; childhood reflection and, 71–75; "Das Christkind," 72–73, 75; "Dolls," 75–76; "How the Thimble Came to Be God," 59, 71; *Letters to a Young Poet*, 93; narrative figments of, 64; *The Notebooks of Malte Laurids Brigge*, 18, 57, 80, 83–84, 92, 113; "Notes on the Melody of Things," 80–81, 92; "On Landscape," 65; "Pierre Dumont," 63–71, 73, 75, 86
"Rock Crystal" ("Bergkristall") (Stifter), 1–3, 4–7
Romanticism, 4, 31, 110, 119–20, 154n48, 187n35; English, 6; fairy tales, 12; ideals of childhood, 12
Rousseau, Jean-Jacques, 11, 23, 162n41
Ruskin, John, 83, 102
Ryan, Judith, 79

sameness, 37
scale, 101, 108–9, 114–16, 119
Schivelbusch, Wolfgang, 175n53, 175n61
Schlegel, Friedrich, 119, 120
Schmidt, Hugo, 151n19
Schnyder, Peter, 36, 164n60, 164n68
Scholem, Gershom, 20, 102, 132, 136
Schönau, Walter, 139
Schuller, Kyla, 154n48
Schwebel, Paula, 98, 185n10
science, 118
scientific categorization, 29
"Screen Memories" ("Über Deckerinnerungen") (Freud), 140–41
sculpture, 64, 77, 173n40
Sedgwick, Eve Kosofsky, 1, 15, 16, 37, 140, 157n70
"seeing more," 70–71
self-reflexivity, 80
self-representation, 88
Senex-Puer (childlike old man), 52–53
sensation: nonprogressive time of, 19, 93; of silence, 6
sense data, 86, 90, 91, 182n138, 183n145
sense-making, 58
sense perception (*aesthesis*), 83, 179n122
sensibility, of objects, 69
sensory experience, 33, 67
sensory impressions, 90
sexuality, 30
sexual reproduction, 7, 152n28
short stories, 9
signification, 77
silence, 111; of dolls, 77; sensation of, 6
Simms, Eva-Maria, 177n88

"simple seeing," 70, 72, 75
smallpox, 117
Smith, Vanessa, 200n23
social history, 11
social reproduction, 3, 11, 152n28
space: of culture, 32; description of, 39; dynamic, 41, 54; everyday, 87; familial, 25; as system of knowledge, 31
"space" (*espace*), 39
spatial conventions, 43
spatial description, 35
spatial paradigm, 115
spectatorial gaze, 52
spectators, ideal, 70
spectatorship: description as, 65; landscape, 67
Sprengnether, Madelon, 142
stability, 39
Steedman, Carolyn, 154n47
Stewart, Susan, 116, 120, 193n100
Stifter, Adalbert, 8, 10, 14–16, 18, 21, 24–27, 100; "Die Gartenlaube," 23, 25, 55; "Gentle Law," 48; *Indian Summer*, 17, 28–37, 46, 48; "Limestone," 45–55, 169n155; *Motley Stones*, 17, 38, 45; *My Life*, 55; revolving worlds of childhood, 55–56; "Rock Crystal," 1–3, 4–7; "Tourmaline," 38–40, 43–44, 46, 51
Stockhammer, Robert, 36, 79, 153n38, 164n68
Stockton, Kathryn Bond, 16, 19, 62, 92, 96, 142; on dolls and dogs, 178n109; metaphor and, 79; on vertical movement of growing up, 8
storytelling, 9, 105; dynamic spaces and, 41, 54; philosophical, 57; queer experiments in, 16–21; two modes of, 39
"straight theory," of philosophy, 15
strangeness, 17, 18, 21, 39, 58, 65, 79
Strowick, Elisabeth, 6, 160n15
structure preservation, 97
subjective intention, 114
subjectivity, 58, 76, 102, 135
subvisibility, 121, 130
supericonicity, 7, 8
Swales, Martin, 1
Swoyer, Chris, 185n14
Symposium (Plato), 42
synchrony, 135, 136

tableau, 37, 39–42
tabula rasa, childhood as, 154n48
tabular organization, 26
tabular representation, 36, 47, 55
taxonomic knowledge, 47
taxonomy, Linnean, 33, 36

"teleologies of the living," 27
temporal anteriority, 30
temporality, 38–39, 56, 99, 104, 109, 114; knowledge and, 35, 46; of perception, 4; queer, 187n32
Thales anecdote, 18, 58, 93, 171n5. *See* Thracian Woman
theory, 58; blindness of, 61; queer theory, 7, 15, 139, 152n30, 198n1; "straight theory" of philosophy, 15
third-person narration, 107
thought-image. *See* "modernist Denkbild"
Thracian Woman, 18, 58, 62, 93, 171n8. *See* Thales anecdote
time: commodity-time, 56; monadological, 19; nonlinear, 100; nonprogressive, 19, 93; queer, 125
timelessness, of domesticity, 34, 36
Tiny Tim (fictional character), 72
topographical knowledge, 35
topography, 46–49
"Tourmaline" ("Turmalin") (Stifter), 38–40, 43–44, 46, 51
toys, 75–79
traditional epistemology, 6
train passengers, 175n53
trains, 65–68
"A Tramp Abroad" (Twain), 74
transcendent objects, 83
travel, 126, 175n53
trees, 1–2, 72–73, 113, 123–24
Tribunella, Eric, 191n75
"Turmalin" (Stifter). *See* "Tourmaline"
Twain, Mark, 74

"Über Deckerinnerungen" (Freud). *See* "Screen Memories"
UE. *See* universal expression thesis
uncertainty, 29, 88
universal expression thesis (UE), 97, 105
utopia, 12–14, 19, 95–96, 100, 134

vaccines/vaccination, 116–18, 117 193n107, 193n115
"Der Versuch als Vermittler" (Goethe). *See* "The Experiment as Mediator"
visibility, 44, 49; epistemology and, 29; invisibility, 19, 46, 61, 123; subvisibility, 121, 130
visual organization, 27
visual perception, 3
Vogel, Juliane, 159n7, 159n10, 160n12

water, 124
Weber, Samuel, 98–99, 117–18, 124
Werner, Nadine, 121
"what a thing is called," 5–6
"What Is a Paradigm?" (Agamben), 133
"Wie der Fingerhut kam dazu, der liebe Gott zu sein" (Rilke). *See* "How the Thimble Came to Be God"
Wild, Reiner, 12
Wittgenstein, Ludwig, 151n20
Wordsworth, William, 6, 152n25
world-building, 95–96
world of culture, 32

"Zu den Kinderporträts der 'Einbahnstraße'" (Benjamin). *See* "On the Portraits of Children in 'One-Way Street'"

Lauren Shizuko Stone is Assistant Professor of German at the University of Colorado at Boulder. She is co-editor (with Daniel Hoffman-Schwartz and Barbara Natalie Nagel) of *Flirtations: Rhetoric and Aesthetics This Side of Seduction* (Fordham, 2015)

www.ingramcontent.com/pod-product-compliance
Lightning Source LLC
Chambersburg PA
CBHW020406080526
44584CB00014B/1197